T0178608

India Studies in Business and Economics

The Indian economy is considered to be one of the fastest growing economies of the world with India amongst the most important G-20 economies. Ever since the Indian economy made its presence felt on the global platform, the research community is now even more interested in studying and analyzing what India has to offer. This series aims to bring forth the latest studies and research about India from the areas of economics, business, and management science.The titles featured in this series will present rigorous empirical research, often accompanied by policy recommendations, evoke and evaluate various aspects of the economy and the business and management landscape in India, with a special focus on India's relationship with the world in terms of business and trade.

More information about this series at
http://www.springer.com/series/11234

Aditi Ramdorai • Cornelius Herstatt

Frugal Innovation in Healthcare

How Targeting Low-Income Markets Leads
to Disruptive Innovation

 Springer

Aditi Ramdorai
Hamburg University of Technology
Hamburg
Germany

Cornelius Herstatt
Hamburg University of Technology
Hamburg
Germany

ISSN 2198-0012   ISSN 2198-0020 (electronic)
India Studies in Business and Economics
ISBN 978-3-319-36796-5   ISBN 978-3-319-16336-9   (eBook)
DOI 10.1007/978-3-319-16336-9

Springer Cham Heidelberg New York Dordrecht London

Printed on acid-free paper

Springer International Publishing AG Switzerland is part of Springer Science+Business Media (www.springer.com)

Preface

This book is based on Aditi Ramdorai's dissertation at the Institute of Technology and Innovation Management at the Hamburg University of Technology, which was later modified and updated along with the coauthor Cornelius Herstatt. The research team at the institute, led by Cornelius Herstatt, has been exploring the area of globalization of innovation over the past decade.

We initiated this research at a time when many books and studies by practitioners and management scholars were throwing a spotlight on frugal innovations emerging from India, specifically in the healthcare sector. Hospital chains, like Aravind Eye Care and Narayana Hrudayalaya, are lauded for offering world-class treatment at affordable rates to low income patients. Several large companies, like GE Healthcare and Tata, have started to launch low-cost innovations for the Indian middle- and low-income segments to tackle the most pressing health issues. These are not only significant achievements in themselves but regarded as potential alternative solutions to addressing poverty through private sector involvement.

This motivated us to delve deeper into this phenomenon to understand how these companies are innovating for low income markets, also known as the Bottom of the Pyramid (BOP). The exploratory nature of this research allowed us to analyze the phenomenon at a micro-level. We tried to find answers to questions that were at first sight partly in contradiction with the literature. For example, the question of a general compatibility of frugal, low-cost innovations with the objective of profitability. Or whether large group companies can ever successfully implement disruptive and frugal innovations from within existing functions and how appropriate structures and processes would have be to designed in such companies to achieve this target.

These and other questions led to meetings and discussions with profoundly interesting personalities, experts, founders, managers, and doctors who are having tremendous impact on the Indian healthcare system and potentially revolutionizing healthcare. These meetings were fascinating and tremendously inspiring and allowed us to find answers for our research questions and finally create this book.

This book would not have been possible but for the support and openness of all the people and institutions involved. We are most grateful to the senior executives and managers of Aravind Eye Care Systems, Aurolab, GE Healthcare India, Narayana Hrudayalaya, and Tata Group who we interviewed and who gave us deep insight into their work.

We would also like to extend our gratitude to our colleagues at the institute for the multiple fruitful and thought provoking discussions along this journey. A special thank you goes to Dr. Rajnish Tiwari for reading through the manuscript giving us very helpful guidance. And finally, we would like to thank our families for their constant and unwavering support over the years.

Hamburg, Germany   Aditi Ramdorai
January 2015   Cornelius Herstatt

Contents

1 **Introduction** 1
  1.1 Research Problem and Relevance 1
  1.2 Research Objectives and Scope 2
  1.3 Structure of the Book 3
  References 4

2 **Bottom of the Pyramid Concept: Taking Stock** 7
  2.1 Background 7
  2.2 Characteristics of the BOP Market 8
  2.3 Business Strategies at the BOP 11
    2.3.1 Challenges in Doing Business at the BOP 11
    2.3.2 4As Framework 13
    2.3.3 Implications for the Firm 16
  2.4 Criticism of the BOP Approach 17
    2.4.1 Overestimation of Market Size 18
    2.4.2 Harming the Poor 18
    2.4.3 Undermining the State's Role in Development and Other Alternatives to Capitalism 19
    2.4.4 Inability of MNCs to Address the BOP 20
  2.5 Current State of BOP Scholarship 20
    2.5.1 Evolution of the BOP Approach 20
    2.5.2 BOP Approach and Other Tangential Areas 21
  2.6 Why It Is Interesting and Imperative to Conduct BOP Research 21
  References 22

3 **Disruptive Innovations Theory** 27
  3.1 Introduction 27
  3.2 Disruptive Innovation Theory 27
    3.2.1 Definition 27
    3.2.2 Extensions of the Disruptive Innovation Theory 29

3.2.3   Disruptive Innovation in the Context of Technological
        Discontinuities.. 32
3.2.4   Critique of Disruptive Innovation Theory............ 33
3.3   Challenges in Commercializing Disruptive Innovations....... 33
3.3.1   Resource Allocation Processes..................... 35
3.3.2   Inadequate Market-Facing Organizational Competency... 35
3.4   Recommendation to Established Firms Seeking to
      Commercialize Disruptive Innovations................... 35
3.5   Summary... 36
References.. 36

4   Methodology and Research Process......................... 39
4.1   Introduction.. 39
4.2   Methodology.. 39
4.2.1   Context... 39
4.2.2   Rationale for Case Study Research................. 40
4.3   Research Process.................................... 41
4.3.1   Case Study Selection............................. 42
4.3.2   Data Collection.................................. 43
4.3.3   Data Analysis.................................... 43
4.4   Quality and Reliability.............................. 44
References.. 45

5   Study 1: The Bottom of the Pyramid Market as a Source
    for Disruptive Innovations............................. 47
5.1   Introduction and Research Question..................... 47
5.1.1   Introduction.................................... 47
5.1.2   Research Question and Methodology................ 48
5.2   Embedding the BOP Phenomenon in Theory............... 49
5.2.1   Linking Disruptive Innovation Theory and BOP Markets... 49
5.2.2   How Frugal Innovations, Inclusive Innovations, Reverse
        Innovations, Gandhian Innovations and Disruptive
        Innovations are Interrelated..................... 50
5.3   Empirical Context................................... 53
5.3.1   Healthcare Challenges in India.................... 53
5.3.2   Case Studies: Aravind Eye Care System and Narayana
        Hrudayalaya Hospitals........................... 54
5.4   Analysis.. 60
5.4.1   How Are Low-cost Specialty Hospital Chains Potentially
        Disruptive?..................................... 60
5.4.2   What are the Drivers of Their Innovations?......... 63
5.4.3   Short Excursus: Reflections on the Lead User
        Characteristics of AECS and NH................... 66
5.4.4   Why is BOP an Appropriate Context for Disruptive
        Innovations?.................................... 68
5.5   Managerial Implications and Discussion................. 70
References.. 71

6 Study 2: Lessons from GE Healthcare: How Incumbents Can Systematically Create Disruptive Innovations 75
  6.1 Introduction 75
  6.2 Theoretical Context 76
  6.3 Research Question and Methodology 78
    6.3.1 Research Question 78
    6.3.2 Methodology 79
  6.4 Empirical Context 80
    6.4.1 GE Healthcare Case Study 80
    6.4.2 Characteristics of the Value Segment Products 85
  6.5 Analysis 88
    6.5.1 Disruptive Potential of GE Healthcare's Value Segment Products 88
    6.5.2 Overcoming the Innovator's Dilemma 90
    6.5.3 Ambidexterity in Action at GE Healthcare 95
    6.5.4 Other Measures in Combating the Unfavorable Characteristics of Disruptive Innovations 98
  6.6 Discussion 100
  References 101

7 Study 3: Lessons from Tata: How Leadership Can Drive Disruptive Innovations 105
  7.1 Introduction 105
  7.2 Theoretical Foundations 107
    7.2.1 Leadership and Innovation 107
    7.2.2 Leadership and Ambidexterity 109
  7.3 Research Question and Methodology 109
    7.3.1 Research Question 109
    7.3.2 Methodology 110
  7.4 Empirical Context 111
    7.4.1 About Tata Group and Tata Chemicals 111
    7.4.2 Tata Swach Project 112
  7.5 Analysis 118
    7.5.1 Disruptive Potential of Tata Swach 118
    7.5.2 Role of Senior Leadership 120
    7.5.3 Differentiating and Integrating: A Process View of Ambidexterity at Tata 123
  7.6 Discussion 127
  References 127

8 Addendum: Linking Paradox Resolution and Disruptive Innovations for the Bottom of the Pyramid markets 131
  8.1 Introduction 131
  8.2 Theoretical Foundations: Theory of Paradox 132
    8.2.1 What is a Paradox? 132
    8.2.2 Pursuing Social and Financial Goals: A Performance Paradox 133

8.3   Empirical Context.................................... 134
8.4   Analysis... 136
8.5   Discussion... 137
References... 138

9   Discussion of Findings and Conclusion...................... 141
9.1   Integration of Findings............................... 141
      9.1.1   Overview.................................... 141
      9.1.2   Organizational Conditions at Established Firms
              for Pursuing Disruptive Innovations................ 142
9.2   Theoretical Contributions............................. 146
      9.2.1   BOP as a Context for Disruptive Innovations......... 146
      9.2.2   Organizational Ambidexterity and Disruptive Innovation
              Theory..................................... 146
      9.2.3   Leadership and Disruptive Innovation Theory......... 148
      9.2.4   Paradox Theory.............................. 149
9.3   Implications....................................... 149
      9.3.1   Managing Disruptive Innovations Within Established
              Firms...................................... 150
      9.3.2   Policy Implications for Healthcare Sector........... 151
9.4   Limitations of the Research........................... 152
9.5   Future Research Agenda.............................. 153
9.6   Conclusion.. 153
References... 154

**Appendix A. Bottom of the Pyramid Innovations from India Mentioned
in Studies by C.K. Prahalad**.................................. 157

Appendix B. Interview List Study I............................ 159

Appendix C. Interview List Study II........................... 161

Appendix D. Interview List Study III and Addendum.............. 163

Appendix E. Interview Guidelines............................. 165

Executive Summary

Companies are increasingly seeking growth in the Bottom of the Pyramid (BOP)—that is, the roughly four billion people living in low-income markets. Disruptive innovations, which significantly open up markets by introducing large populations of nonconsumers by making products or services more affordable, more convenient or easier to use, have the potential to create growth.

Several examples of disruptive innovations for the BOP exist in India, which have also been dubbed as frugal innovations. Low-cost, specialty hospital chains like Aravind Eye Care and Narayana Hrudayalaya have managed to bring down the cost of care of certain medical procedures dramatically through process and business model innovations. Companies are also developing technologies that tackle pressing health issues. The Indian conglomerate, Tata Group, launched a water filter targeting low income consumers, and General Electric (GE) Healthcare has developed a low-cost electrocardiogram (ECG) machine called MAC i along with other medical devices targeting hospitals treating low income patients in India. These two cases exemplify how large established players have successfully launched disruptive innovations from within the organization, even as management literature proposes companies to spin off their disruptive projects to overcome the "innovator's dilemma."

The first part of this research explores the innovation capacity of the two low-cost specialty hospital chains in order to establish why BOP markets are a good context for disruptive innovations. The second part of this research involves exploratory case studies of General Electric (GE) Healthcare and Tata, which examine the organizational conditions that enable large companies to develop disruptive innovations. Secondary data, including company press releases, annual reports, and primary data in the form of interviews as well as internal company documentation have been analyzed.

A key element for an organization's long-term success is to be ambidextrous, i.e., capable of balancing exploration and exploitation. This study adopts the lens of ambidexterity on these organizations, as they have successfully launched disruptive innovations from within. GE Healthcare has adopted formal organizational structures and resource allocation mechanisms to integrate the development of frugal innovations for the emerging markets within its organization. In contrast, Tata does not have any formal structures, but a senior executive who incubated disruptive projects for the BOP projects before integrating them into existing business units.

This work will leverage these two contrasting cases to explore organizational structures and senior leadership role in enabling disruptive innovations. Thus, this work contributes not only to the ongoing development of disruptive innovation theory but also to organizational ambidexterity theory. Companies intending to develop disruptive innovations for low income markets can learn from these insights and build necessary organizational conditions, structures, and processes.

List of Figures

Fig. 1.1 Structure of the research 4
Fig. 2.1 Global poverty trends 9
Fig. 2.2 Cross-country comparison: Income distribution of BOP
population in Ukraine, India and Nigeria 10
Fig. 2.3 The 4A Framework 14
Fig. 3.1 Analytical representation of the evolution of disruptive
innovation. 28
Fig. 4.1 Research process 41
Fig. 5.1 Links between Bottom of the Pyramid concept and disruptive
innovation theory 50
Fig. 6.1 GE Healthcare ECG device product portfolio 90
Fig. 6.2 Change healthymagination brought to the New Product
Introduction process at GE Healthcare 93
Fig. 6.3 Comparison of Ambidextrous Organizational Design
by O'Reilly and Tushman (2004) and GE Healthcare's
Organizational Design 97
Fig. 7.1 Yield development of different crops in India from 1961
to 2011 117
Fig. 7.2 Evolution of the Tata Swach project 126

List of Tables

Table 3.1   Characteristics of disruptive innovations 31
Table 5.1   Key concepts related to Bottom of the Pyramid innovations 52
Table 5.2   Disruptive characteristics of low-cost specialty
hospital chains 61
Table 6.1   Disruptive characteristics of GE Healthcare's value segment
products 89
Table 7.1   Comparison of innovator roles from selected literature 108
Table 7.2   Disruptive characteristics of Tata Swach 119
Table 7.3   Mechanisms of differentiation and integration in the Tata
Swach project 125
Table 9.1   Cross-case comparison between Tata and GE Healthcare 143
Table 9.2   Comparison between early GE Healthcare projects
and Tata Swach 144

List of Abbreviations

AECS	Aravind Eye Care Systems
BOP	Bottom of the Pyramid
CSR	Corporate Social Responsibility
EA	Executive Assistant
ECG	Electrocardiogram
FMCG	Fast Moving Consumer Good
GE	General Electric
GGO	Global Growth Organization
ICFC	In Country For Country
IMR	Infant Mortality Rates
INR	Indian Rupee
JFWTC	Jack F. Welch Technology Center
JV	Joint Venture
MIC	Maternal and Infant Care
MNC	Multi National Corporation
NH	Narayana Hrudayalaya
P&L	Profit & Loss
PPP	Purchasing Power Parity
PT	Phototherapy
R&D	Research and development
RHA	Rice Husk Ash
TCL	Tata Chemicals
TCS	Tata Consultancy Services
TRDDC	Tata Research Development and Design Center
$	U.S. Dollar

Chapter 1
Introduction

"Any intelligent fool can invent further complications, but it takes a genius to retain, or recapture, simplicity."
—E. F. Schumacher, *economist and author of "Small is Beautiful"*

1.1 Research Problem and Relevance

An influential economist of the 1970s, Ernst Friedrich Schumacher, was a proponent of sustainability and simplicity. He also initiated the movement of 'appropriate technologies' (Schumacher 1973) as a development approach based on technology to address socio-economic problems in developing countries. About two and a half decades later, the Bottom of the Pyramid (BOP) approach was initiated by C. K. Prahalad, a management thinker, along with other colleagues. This approach argued for market-based solutions for poverty, by including billions of people into formal economy (Prahalad and Lieberthal 1998). He argued that addressing these markets would require "radical innovations in technology and business models" (Prahalad and Hart 2002, p. 3).

Prahalad and other scholars showcased several frugal, low-cost innovations, coming out of emerging markets, which provide essential functionality and fit the local environment (Prahalad 2004; Prahalad and Hammond 2002). This spawned immense academic and practitioner interest in the past decade and led to several concepts that highlight specific aspects of this phenomenon, for instance, frugal innovation (Tiwari and Herstatt 2012), Gandhian innovation (Prahalad and Mashelkar 2010) or inclusive innovation (George et al. 2012).

The four case studies, which are explored in this research, are exemplars of this phenomenon. Aravind Eye Care Systems and Narayana Hrudayalaya are two low-cost specialty hospitals from Southern India. Aravind Eye Care is a network of ophthalmology hospitals that serves a majority of its patients for free or at a steeply subsidized rate, yet remains financially sustainable. It has been able to do this by dramatically bringing down the cost of procedures and increasing productivity through a series of innovations. Similarly, Narayana Hrudayalaya that specializes in cardiology also aims to bring quality healthcare services to the poor.

Apart from healthcare delivery, this work also focuses on product innovations. GE Healthcare has shown strong commitment to developing BOP markets with

© Springer International Publishing Switzerland 2015
A. Ramdorai, C. Herstatt, *Frugal Innovation in Healthcare*, India Studies in Business and Economics, DOI 10.1007/978-3-319-16336-9_1

frugal innovations like the electrocardiogram (ECG) MAC i, priced at a fraction of high-end ECG devices from developed markets. Finally, the Indian conglomerate, Tata,[1] has developed a low-cost water filter that does not require running water or electricity and thus addresses consumers living in areas with poor infrastructure.

Such frugal innovations, particularly in healthcare, have the potential to touch and improve the lives of millions of people living at the BOP. However, while there has been considerable interest in BOP markets, little academic research has been published in this domain (Bruton 2010). Hence, research that explores different aspects of this phenomenon is valuable from an academic perspective and may also lead to insights that can impact lives.

1.2   Research Objectives and Scope

The first part of the research will embed the phenomenon of BOP innovations into existing innovation management theory, namely disruptive innovation theory. Disruptive innovations theory, established by Clayton Christensen, explores the mechanisms behind change brought by innovation to firms and industries (Christensen 1997, 2006; Christensen and Bower 1996).

Disruptive innovations, in contrast to sustaining innovations, underperform existing products in the market with respect to the primary performance attribute, but introduce new performance attributes. Previous work in this field has shown how incumbents have often failed in commercializing or responding to disruptive innovations (Christensen and Rosenbloom 1995). Christensen and other scholars (Hart and Christensen 2002; Hang et al. 2010) have also highlighted examples of disruptive innovations from emerging markets.

This research will build on their work to theoretically link the BOP concept with disruptive innovation theory. Further, it will explore case studies of the low-cost specialty hospitals described above to explain why BOP markets provide a rich context for disruptive innovations.

Following this, the research will delve into the BOP phenomenon to enrich disruptive innovation theory. Although Christensen's work, followed by other scholars, has contributed to our understanding of the impact of disruptive innovations and their underlying mechanisms, several gaps still remain (Danneels 2004). One such area is the question of how established firms can successfully commercialize disruptive innovations. Previous works by Christensen recommends established firms to spin-off disruptive projects into separate entities (Christensen 1997). This follows logically from the reasons why established firms fail to respond to disruptive innovations. To summarize briefly, Christensen's explanation for this failure is that the resource allocation processes within established firms tend to

---

[1] Tata refers to the Tata Group. The Tata Swach was initiated as a group level effort before becoming part of Tata Chemicals.

prioritize sustaining projects over disruptive projects (Christensen and Bower 1996).

However, more recently, management scholars have been discussing the value of ambidexterity, the ability of companies to simultaneously exploit existing markets and explore new opportunities (Tushman et al. 2010). While the concept of ambidexterity is applicable to several fields, such as, strategy, innovation management, organizational learning (Simsek 2009), in the scope of this research, ambidexterity would be defined as the ability to simultaneously pursue disruptive and sustaining innovations (Danneels 2006).

Drawing upon the case studies of GE Healthcare and Tata, this research aims to get an in-depth understanding of how established firms can leverage ambidexterity to pursue disruptive innovations from within the organization. Thus, this research hopes to contribute both to disruptive innovation theory and organizational ambidexterity within the context of BOP markets.

1.3 Structure of the Book

This book consists of eight parts. The first two parts lay the theoretical foundations to the research. The first chapter takes stock of research into BOP markets. It gives a comprehensive overview of the challenges companies face while addressing BOP markets and the strategies that are required to overcome these challenges. The chapter concludes with an analysis of why it is still interesting and imperative to do research in this field.

The following chapter explores disruptive innovation theory. The chapter focuses on what literature says about the challenges established firms face in commercializing disruptive innovations and what theory recommends established firms do.

Chapter 4 focuses on the methodology for this research. The subsequent chapter describes the overall research process and details of the exploratory qualitative research methodology adopted for this research.

The research results are classified into three studies and an addendum. The first study sets the theme of the research, linking the BOP concept and disruptive innovation theory. Through exploring the two cases of the low-cost specialty hospitals, Narayana Hrudayalaya and Aravind Eye Care Systems, this study explores why BOP markets are an appropriate context for disruptive innovations. This is done through analyzing the drivers behind the innovation capacity of these low cost specialty hospitals.

The next two studies explore under what conditions established firms can successfully commercialize disruptive innovations in the BOP context. While the success of the products in the market has not been measured, success in the context of this research is defined as the ability of the organization to develop disruptive innovations and bring it to market successfully from within its boundaries. The first study explores the GE Healthcare case. The emphasis of this case study is

Fig. 1.1 Structure of the
research

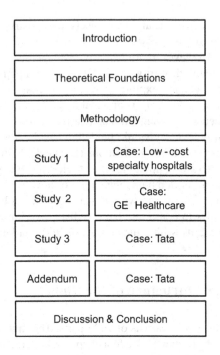

organizational design, structures and processes that enable GE Healthcare to systematically commercialize disruptive innovations from within (Fig. 1.1).

Subsequently the work explores the case study of Tata, where the emphasis is on the role leadership plays in enabling disruptive innovations. The final addendum explores a particular aspect of disruptive innovations from the BOP, namely how paradoxical thinking fuels and enables them. Through empirical insights, this contributes to the prevailing and active debate on paradoxes in organizations (Smith and Lewis 2011).

In the final part of the book, we summarize, contrast and integrate findings from the two case studies, GE Healthcare and Tata. The chapter concludes with theoretical contributions of the research, as well as managerial and policy implications that can be derived from this work.

References

Bruton, G. D. (2010). Letter from the editor: Business and the World's poorest billion–the need for an expanded examination by management scholars. *The Academy of Management Perspectives, 24*(3), 6–10.

Christensen, C. M. (1997). *The innovator's dilemma: When new technologies cause great firms to fail.* Boston: Harvard Business School Press.

Christensen, C. M. (2006). The ongoing process of building a theory of disruption. *Journal of Product Innovation Management, 23*(1), 39–55.

Christensen, C. M., & Bower, J. L. (1996). Customer power, strategic investment, and the failure of leading firms. *Strategic Management Journal, 17*(3), 197–218.

Christensen, C. M., & Rosenbloom, R. S. (1995). Explaining the attacker's advantage: Technological paradigms, organizational dynamics, and the value network. *Research Policy, 24*(2), 233–257.

Danneels, E. (2004). Disruptive technology reconsidered: A critique and research agenda. *Journal of Product Innovation Management, 21,* 246–258.

Danneels, E. (2006). Dialogue on the effects of disruptive technology on firms and industries. *Journal of Product Innovation Management, 23*(1), 2–4.

George, G., McGahan, A. M., & Prabhu, J. (2012). Innovation for inclusive growth: Towards a theoretical framework and a research agenda. *Journal of Management Studies, 49*(4), 661–683.

Hang, C.-C., Chen, J., & Subramian, A. M. (2010). Developing disruptive products for emerging economies: Lessons from Asian cases. *Research-Technology Management, 53*(4), 21–26.

Hart, S., & Christensen, C. (2002, Fall). The great leap. *MIT Sloan Managment Review.*

Prahalad, C. K. (2004). *The fortune at the bottom of the pyramid: Eradicating poverty through profits.* Upper Saddle River, NJ: Wharton School Publishing.

Prahalad, C. K., & Hammond, A. (2002). Serving the World's poor profitably. *Harvard Buisness Review, 89*(9), 48–59.

Prahalad, C. K., & Hart, S. (2002). The fortune at the bottom of the pyramid. *Strategy & Business, 26.*

Prahalad, C. K., & Lieberthal, K. (1998). The end of corporate imperialism. *Harvard Buisness Review, 76,* 68–79.

Prahalad, C. K., & Mashelkar, R. (2010). Innovation's Holy Grail. *Harvard Business Review, 7*(8), 132–142.

Schumacher, E. (1973). *Small is beautiful. A study of economics as if people really mattered.* London: Blond Briggs.

Simsek, Z. (2009). Organizational ambidexterity: Towards a multilevel understanding. *Journal of Management Studies, 46*(4), 597–624.

Smith, W. K., & Lewis, M. W. (2011). Toward a theory of paradox: A dynamic equilibrium model of organizing. *Academy of Management Review, 36*(2), 381–403.

Tiwari, R., & Herstatt, C. (2012). Assessing India's lead market potential for cost-effective innovations. *Journal of Indian Business Research, 4*(2), 97–115.

Tushman, M., Smith, W. K., Wood, R. C., Westerman, G., & O'Reilly, C. (2010). Organizational designs and innovation streams. *Industrial and Corporate Change, 19*(5), 1331–1366.

Chapter 2
Bottom of the Pyramid Concept: Taking Stock

2.1 Background

Bottom of the Pyramid or Base of the Pyramid (BOP) refers to the lowest socio-economic segment in the world. The Bottom of the Pyramid concept was established in a series of articles in practitioner journals by Prof. C. K. Prahalad and colleagues (Prahalad and Lieberthal 1998; Prahalad and Hammond 2002; Prahalad and Hart 2002), but the idea was popularized by his book "Fortune at the Bottom of the Pyramid" (Prahalad 2004).

It was a call to MNCs world over to create products and services for the four billion strong low income markets, which MNCs tended to ignore (Prahalad and Lieberthal 1998). The authors positioned this approach as having two key advantages: first, it meant creating new revenue streams for MNCs as they enter largely un-tapped markets and second, they viewed it as a new market-based approach to poverty alleviation for the world's poor.

To put this in perspective, around the turn of the millennium, when this concept was taking shape, management scholarship saw little potential for firms engaging with the poor in a mutually beneficial way other than corporate philanthropy (Kolk et al. 2013). The concept put forth by Prahalad, stirred this debate and spawned scholarship at the crossroads between poverty and business.

Companies are also increasingly interested in penetrating the BOP as they seek new markets (Karamchandani et al. 2011). As economies shrank during the financial crisis and growth stagnated post crises in most developed markets, companies continued their efforts within developing markets in search of growth. Even within predominantly BOP markets like India, growth is increasingly coming from lower down the pyramid. From 2009 to 2012, rural consumption outpaced urban consumption (rural consumption grew at 19.2 % vs. urban consumption at 17.2 % (Accenture 2013)).

This chapter provides an overview of this debate since its inception. The first part of the chapter deals with the characteristics of the socio-economic strata known

© Springer International Publishing Switzerland 2015
A. Ramdorai, C. Herstatt, *Frugal Innovation in Healthcare*, India Studies in Business and Economics, DOI 10.1007/978-3-319-16336-9_2

as BOP. Next, the challenges of doing business with the BOP and business strategies for firms engaging with the BOP are described. Following this, the criticism towards the BOP proposition is outlined. In the final section, the current state of BOP scholarship is reviewed and the linkage between the BOP concept and tangential bodies of work is discussed. The chapter concludes with comments on why scholarship in this field of management research is still relevant and interesting.

2.2 Characteristics of the BOP Market

The World Resource Institute, a global economics research organization, and the International Finance Corporation, define the BOP segment as people with an annual income in 2005 PPP terms of less than $3,260 (Hammond 2010). According to this definition, the BOP segment is about four billion people strong.[1]

Scholars and economists have put forth different definitions of the poverty line and thus the population size of 'the poor' is disputed. The World Bank draws two international poverty lines, at $1.25 PPP per day and at $2 PPP per day. According to World Bank Statistics, there are about 1.3 billion people living at under $1.25 PPP per day and about 2.4 billion people living at under $2 PPP per day in 2010 (World Bank 2012). While there has been a significant reduction in the number of extreme poor (people living under $1.25 a day at 2005 PPP rates) since the 1980s, the number of people living on less than $2 a day has remained relatively unchanged, as can be seen in the Fig. 2.1 (World Bank 2012).

BOP proponents distance themselves from this debate (Prahalad 2010). They emphasize the fact that vast populations of low-income segments world over have been largely ignored by the formal sector. This sector has limited or no access to various essential products and services and are thus underserved (Prahalad and Hammond 2002). They argue that the BOP constitutes a vast majority of the world population and should not be ignored (Prahalad 2010; Prahalad and Hart 2002). This research takes the same perspective and works with the definition of the BOP from a study conducted by the World Resource Institute in collaboration with the International Finance Corporation, a member of the World Bank Group.

The World Resource Institute estimates that the total household income of the BOP segment is $5 trillion, making it a significantly sized segment in the world market. While it is true that the collective purchasing power of the BOP is substantial, serving it is a challenge as the BOP segment is very heterogeneous and distributed (London and Hart 2010). According to the report published by the World Resource Institute, Asia has the largest portion of the BOP segment totaling

---

[1] The research conducted by the World Resource Institute was unique in terms of scale and depth. More recent figures for the distribution of the income pyramid at the income levels as defined by the World Resource Institute are unavailable.

World population size at two international poverty rates
billion

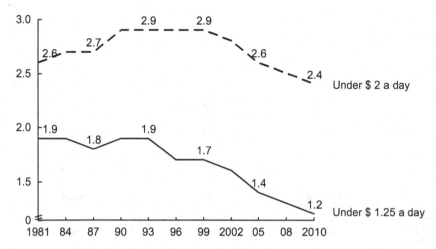

Fig. 2.1 Global poverty trends. *Source*: World Bank (2012)

to about 2.86 billion people and represents over 50 % of the purchasing power in the growing developing countries (Hammond 2010). Africa, Latin America and Eastern Europe also have large BOP populations.

Thus, the BOP market is distributed geographically across many countries. Also, each country has a different income distribution and the characteristics of the BOP vary vastly between different income groups within the segment.

Figure 2.2 illustrates this point well. In Ukraine, the largest BOP market after Russia in Eastern Europe, the BOP segments are concentrated in the higher income groups, i.e., above $1,500. In contrast, Nigeria has a vast majority of the population that lives under $1,000. In India, the income distribution is shaped like a diamond, with a majority of the population earning between $500 and $2,000 annually.

In some countries, a vast majority of the population falls under the BOP category (Hammond 2010). For instance, in India about 95 % of the total population (Hammond 2010). In nominal terms, the average income in India is roughly $3 per day and as such, a significant portion of the population falls under the BOP category.[2]

Several countries with large BOP segments have experienced significant growth in the past years and are also projected to continue growing even as developed markets stall or slump into recession. In India alone, the rising income is expected to vault current low-income segments into middle income population, quadrupling the aggregate consumption from INR 17 trillion in 2005 to INR 70 trillion by 2025 (MGI 2007).

---

[2] IMF World Economic Outlook 2013 Database.

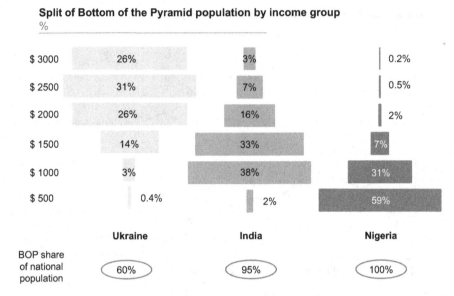

Split of Bottom of the Pyramid population by income group

Fig. 2.2 Cross-country comparison: Income distribution of BOP population in Ukraine, India and Nigeria. *Source*: Hammond (2010)

Food, housing, and household goods are the largest industries followed by transportation, education, communication and healthcare (Guesalaga and Marshall 2008). Food is the most sizable item on a BOP household budget (Hammond 2010), e.g., for lower socio-economic segments in India, it represents over 50 % of spend (MGI 2007). However, discretionary spending in this segment exists and studies have shown that even the extremely poor, i.e., those living under $1 per day, have the propensity to own goods such as television, mobile phone and radio (Banerjee and Duflo 2007).

One striking characteristic that this heterogeneous segment has in common is its vast unmet needs. Access to fundamental needs such as healthcare, water, sanitation and electricity is lacking or very poor (Hammond 2010). Over 2.5 billion people in the world are estimated to live without adequate sanitation (WHO 2008). Many people in the BOP segment do not have a bank account or other basic financial services. The unmet needs of the BOP are very fundamental, and addressing them is essential to raising their welfare.

The BOP market is dominated by an 'informal' and extralegal economy, defined as largely unregulated by legal institutions but governed by social ties (Godfrey 2011). This poses an additional challenge for established firms, especially MNCs, to become active in this segment.

A vast majority of the BOP lives a life of subsistence and many have low literacy levels. This is often compounded by the 'poverty penalty, the relatively higher cost borne by the poor, compared to those better off, in their participation in certain markets (Prahalad and Hammond 2002; Mendoza 2011). A classic example is the case of high interest rates faced by borrowers who have no access to financial institutions and are dependent on local money lenders (Prahalad and Hammond 2002).

2.3 Business Strategies at the BOP

As described above, the BOP market is vastly different from developed markets and thus companies intending to serve these markets need to adopt unique strategies in doing so (London and Hart 2004). Lack of knowledge and heterogeneity of this segment, the challenges in accessing these markets and low purchasing power of this segment have made established firms neglect these markets for long (Prahalad and Lieberthal 1998).

However, given the changing dynamics in the world economy, companies have been increasingly showing interest in addressing this untapped market. But addressing the BOP poses unique challenges to firms (London and Hart 2004). BOP literature offers companies different frameworks and guidelines for addressing the BOP market. The first set of principles was offered by Prahalad in his seminal book (Prahalad 2004). While these principles laid the fundamentals for research into this field, the 4As framework, introduced by Anderson and Billou (2007) provides a good overview. This framework was also later acknowledged and slightly modified by Prahalad (Prahalad 2012). This section first describes the challenges companies face while addressing the BOP market and then goes on to describe the 4As framework (Anderson and Billou 2007) and its implication for the firm's product development and organization.

2.3.1 Challenges in Doing Business at the BOP

As outlined in the section above, BOP markets are vastly different from mature markets that established companies currently serve. Doing business at the BOP poses several challenges to companies. These challenges can be grouped into three main categories: Market challenges, distribution challenges and organizational challenges.

2.3.1.1 Market Challenges

Several characteristics of the BOP market pose challenges for companies. BOP markets are dominated by **informal economies**. Informal markets are unregistered and function without the oversight of institutions, yet are not illegal (McGahan 2012). OECD estimates the size of the informal sector to be up to 38 % in Sub-Saharan Africa and 35 % in South Asia, relative to the GDP of the country

(Schneider et al. 2010). In some communities, especially in the BOP segments the percentage might be over 50 % (McGahan 2012). Companies that are used to dealing with proper paper work might find this environment challenging as local vendors and suppliers of products at the BOP may work in shadow economies and trade only in cash. Also companies that deal with competitors who work entirely in shadow economies, without regulations or quality standards, face higher transaction costs than their competitors (Karamchandani et al. 2011).

The other market challenge that companies face is the relatively **low purchasing power** and low demand in BOP markets. As individuals at the BOP have low income levels and large portions of their income is spent on basics like food and housing, they typically have very low buying power (Hammond 2010; Simanis 2012). This issue is compounded by irregular income flow. The other factor complementary to this is the lack of demand for products and services, which are deemed "necessary" from a Western perspective (Karamchandani et al. 2011). This makes it difficult for companies to gauge demand and has resulted in several missteps in the past (Simanis 2012).

Finally, BOP markets are characterized by **institutional voids** (Khanna and Palepu 1997). This means that key institutions and infrastructure, necessary for market formation and operation is often missing or not functioning effectively (Khanna and Palepu 1997). Companies engaging in the BOP have to often bridge these gaps in order to develop a functioning ecosystem. An example of this is Coca Cola, which has co-developed solar powered refrigerators with local suppliers in India and installed these at many of its vendors serving the BOP because of the lack of reliable electricity in those areas. Yet another example is that of large Indian IT companies who have inhouse training facilities for fresh graduates who go through one year training programs (Khanna and Palepu 2006). They have invested in these facilities to overcome India's underdeveloped education system and lack of certification providers.

Research into institutional voids has uncovered how large conglomerates in developing countries often imitate or substitute institutions in order to overcome institutional voids (Khanna and Palepu 1999). In the BOP context, cross-sector alliances with NGOs and other intermediaries has been highlighted as one way to reduce the negative effects posed by institutional voids for MNCs (Webb et al. 2010). Cross-sector partnerships can help companies respond to prevalent conditions in BOP markets, and partnerships with governmental organizations can help companies cope with challenges in the institutional environment (Schuster and Holtbrügge 2012, 2013).

2.3.1.2 Distribution Challenges

The BOP population in several countries is, to a very large extent, rural. For instance, in India, 78% of the BOP population lives in rural areas (Hammond 2010). This, combined with the fact that infrastructure to reach these areas is often poor, makes physical distribution of goods to the BOP segment challenging.

Again, taking the example from India, poor infrastructure not only causes long lead times for the logistics industry, but also results in higher costs. Coastal and rail logistics in India cost up to 70 % more than in the United States in purchasing power parity terms (Gupta et al. 2010). This is driven mostly by severe capacity constraints in rail and ocean freight transportation in India as well as hidden costs that arise from inefficient handling, long transit times and damages (Gupta et al. 2010).

While mobile phones have high penetration rates in rural India, internet penetration still remains quite low at about 4 % in 2012 (Roy 2012). This compounds not only infrastructure challenges but also hinders access to information. Informational asymmetries are a common problem for BOP producers, such as rural farmers and also for consumers (Vachani and Smith 2007).

This is why Prahalad termed distribution as "critical for developing the BOP market" and posited that "innovations in distribution are as critical as products and process innovations" (Prahalad 2004, p. 46).

2.3.1.3 Organizational Challenges

Beyond the external market challenges noted above, organizations also face internal pressures when championing BOP initiatives. BOP initiatives often require patient capital, and tolerance that the business will generate healthy returns after longer time periods (London 2008). Moreover, BOP projects require innovation that tend to be a significant departure from the companies' core activities (Karamchandani et al. 2011). These are the reasons why BOP projects typically face internal organizational challenges. Scholars Olsen and Boxenbaum (2009) identified internal organizational barriers for BOP initiatives at a Danish mulitnational. The root cause of these barriers lay both in the mindset as well as the processes of the organization, such as project evaluation criteria and managers' incentive system (Olsen and Boxenbaum 2009).

2.3.2 4As Framework

As the section above emphasizes, the challenges in doing business at the BOP are significant and vastly different from developed markets. This is why companies that intend to bring their products and services to this market need a differentiated approach. Scholars and practitioners exploring BOP markets have established several sets of guidelines for companies (Simanis et al. 2008; London and Hart 2010; Prahalad 2004). The 4As framework (analogous to the 4Ps of marketing) was initially articulated by Anderson and Billou (2007), and was later modified and adopted by Prahalad (2012). Although this framework risks oversimplification, it is succinct and captures the key managerial approaches required in tackling the BOP market. It can therefore be considered a relevant framework to discuss business strategy for the BOP market (Fig. 2.3).

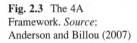

Fig. 2.3 The 4A
Framework. *Source*:
Anderson and Billou (2007)

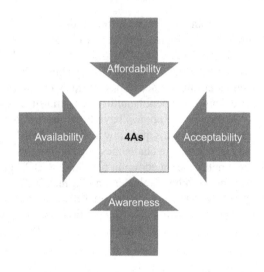

2.3.2.1 Affordability

Given the low purchasing power of the BOP segment, creating extremely afford-able products and services is critical. Successful BOP products and services have been priced 70–95 % lower than high-end products with similar, but reduced functionality (Prahalad and Mashelkar 2010). A widely cited example is prepaid mobile services by Bharti Telecom, an Indian mobile service provider, which was a pioneer in offering extremely low prices, as low as 1 cent per minute (Prahalad and Mashelkar 2010). The introduction of this service by Bharti Telecom changed the competitive landscape in the country and enabled millions of people to access mobile services. This made the Indian mobile market grow to over 930 million subscribers in 2012, from just 37 million in 2001, a $25 \times$ increase in about 11 years (Chattopadhyay 2013).

Besides innovating to bring down cost dramatically, companies have adopted other strategies to make their products more affordable. Procter & Gamble and Unilever offer their products like shampoos and soaps at very low prices in single-use sachets.

Individuals at the BOP very often do not have a regular monthly cash flow but an intermittent one on a daily or weekly basis, and sometimes only at the end of harvesting seasons (Basu and Srivastava 2005). Therefore, instead of an upfront investment model, companies have adopted a model that enables their customers to pay small amounts on a weekly basis. Selco, a company based in Southern India that sells photovoltaic cells to the BOP, works with micro financing agencies and offers its customers a flexible payment model that fits their cash flow stream (Rao et al. 2009; Sharma 2010).

Successful products for the BOP have shown a dramatic shift in price-performance points compared to developed markets. The approach has moved from seeking a cost reduction of current offerings by 10–20 % to newly developed bottom up solutions that seek to decrease prices so radically that BOP consumers have access to these offerings (Prahalad 2006).

2.3.2.2 Acceptability

An offering has to fit the needs of the BOP segment for it to succeed. While this may seem obvious, it is necessary to stress the uniqueness of the BOP context and how little developed-market firms who do not operate in this context know about this environment (Prahalad 2004; Hart and London 2005).

A deep understanding of the local context is necessary to create products and services that fit their unique needs. Nokia and Haier have launched successful products that were built on insights coming from these needs. Haier, the Chinese white goods company, developed a washing machine with extra wide drain pipes. The washing machine was built on the insight that customers in rural areas used these machines to also wash vegetables and hence, caused the drain pipes to clog (Anderson and Billou 2007). Similarly, Nokia introduced a very successful handset in India that had an in-built torch after its designers realized that Indians often use their phone as a source of light during the frequent power cuts (Austin-Breneman and Yang 2013).

These two examples highlight the need for deep local understanding for product development; however, this need extends to all aspects of commercializing and delivering products to the BOP. In order to create "contextualized" solutions for the BOP, MNCs need to develop "native capabilities" and embed themselves in the local environment (Hart and London 2005). Only through this can companies gain the deep insights necessary to target BOP segments.

2.3.2.3 Awareness

Selling products and services to the BOP most often involves market creation. Thus, managerial attention must be focused on market creation and awareness creation measures while addressing the BOP (Prahalad 2012).

Often, even if a company identifies a certain need, creating awareness and customer demand to satisfy the need can be a challenge. In order to create this demand and build a market, companies have to embed themselves in local BOP communities and forge alliances with local companies, NGOs, cooperatives and even public institutions (Seelos and Mair 2007). Such initiatives require substantial investment. These unconventional alliance partners bring with them deep local knowledge, capabilities and trust of the local communities (Hart and Sharma 2004).

Challenges in awareness building measures are often compounded by the fact that there is a low penetration of media in remote rural regions (Prahalad 2004). Companies are forced to find innovative ways at the grassroots to spread awareness. Hindustan Unilever (HUL), a subsidiary of the Fast Moving Consumer Good (FMCG) company, Unilever, has pushed awareness-raising campaigns at the grassroots for its Lifebuoy soap brand. Through extensive handwashing campaigns at schools in media dark areas, HUL is trying to change behavior that leads to increased hygiene as well as demand generation for its products (Rajan 2007). HUL went to extraordinary lengths to educate consumers about the benefits of handwashing and about germs and diseases under the Swasthya Chetna campaign (the campaign had a UV detector demo to show *invisible* germs) (Prahalad 2004). This was a much deeper educational effort rather than just transmission of information, which made it a success (Sridharan and Viswanathan 2008).

2.3.2.4 Availability

Bringing products to the BOP customer, especially in remote regions or in areas with poor infrastructure poses a significant challenge. Scholars Prahalad and Hammond (2002) emphasized this challenge by noting that the critical barrier to doing business in rural regions is distribution access.

To reach these customers, companies need to reinvent their distribution strategies. A few cases from successful companies in India show different strategies companies can adopt. Hindustan Unilever employs an army of women called Shakti Ammas to sell its goods to remote rural villages of 5,000 people or less. This has deepened the company's rural reach, especially in areas with low television penetration. Through these women entrepreneurs, HUL has created a reach of over 100,000 villages across the country. HUL has thus found a way to control distribution costs by outsourcing the 'last mile' to local entrepreneurs (Prahalad and Hart 2002).

Other companies also leverage technology, such as telemedicine to create pathways to reach remote corners. Aravind Eye Care has been a pioneer in telemedicine in India (Rangan and Thulasiraj 2007). Another strategy leveraged by ITC, an Indian conglomerate, is to share the distribution network they have built in rural areas with other players interested in these markets (Prahalad 2004).

While several strategies exist for companies to create access into BOP markets, it often necessitates a reinvention of their existing distribution systems (Vachani and Smith 2007). Companies often have to work with local communities and local entrepreneurs for a deep reach or piggyback on existing infrastructure to reach consumers at the BOP (Vachani and Smith 2007).

2.3.3 Implications for the Firm

2.3.3.1 Implications for Product Development

Tailored products and services that cater to the unique needs of the BOP markets are required to succeed in this segment (Prahalad 2004; Anderson and Billou 2007). In the past, companies have failed by just introducing a 'lower cost version' of their current product (London and Hart 2004). To create tailored products and services, it is essential to get a deeper and comprehensive grasp of the local needs through users and local partners when developing a new product of BOP markets (Prahalad and Hart 2002). Immersive methods, involving practitioners embedding themselves in the environment over a period of time, help generate this deep understanding (Nakata and Weidner 2012; Vishwanathan 2010). Scholars and practitioners also point out the advantages of co-creating products with partners or individuals at the BOP (Prahalad 2012; London and Hart 2004).

Another area that requires rethinking is pricing. As established above, affordability is a key consideration while developing products and services for BOP markets (Prahalad 2012). Companies cannot win by deriving the price for their product/service by adding a margin on top of their existing cost structure. Rather they have to develop a product/service that fits the buying power of the market. As Prahalad put it, moving away from the tradition logic of $Cost + Margin = Price$ to $Price—Margin = Cost$ (Prahalad 2004).

Prahalad extends this thinking by introducing the concept of the 'innovation sandbox' (Prahalad 2006). He contends that companies need to set constraints for innovating for the BOP. Reframing these constraints can facilitate innovations rather than hindering them, by serving as triggers and helping form new ideas and new opportunities (George et al. 2012). The Tata Nano, the world's cheapest car, came out of constraints set by the chairman of the Tata Group, including the price tag, space requirements and standards (Prahalad and Mashelkar 2010).

2.3.3.2 Implications for Organization

Research suggests that a key success factor of BOP ventures is the capability to build strong partnerships with non-conventional stakeholders such as NGOs, cooperatives, local government bodies and self-help groups. Scholars call this ability *social embeddedness*, which enables companies to get a "deep understanding of and to integrate with the local environment" (London and Hart 2004, p. 15). These partners help build trust and legitimacy in the local communities (Hart and London 2005). The ability of firms to identify and interact effectively with a diversity of non-traditional stakeholders is termed *radical transactiveness* (Hart and Sharma 2004) and is seen as a competitive advantage for BOP ventures (Seelos and Mair 2007). This also has significant implications for the way companies serving BOP markets are organized, how deep their local capabilities are and how their company boundaries are defined (Hart and London 2005).

2.4 Criticism of the BOP Approach

While the BOP concept has garnered popularity among scholars and universities, in addition to institutions and companies, this has not been without criticism (Walsh et al. 2005; Landrum 2007; Peredo 2012; Karnani 2007a, b, 2009; Jaiswal 2008).

This section will summarize key criticisms of the BOP approach and also briefly discuss the proponent's viewpoint.

2.4.1 Overestimation of Market Size

Aneel Karnani has been the most vociferous critic of the BOP approach (Karnani 2007a, b, 2009). One of his main theses is that the BOP market does not represent an attractive market for MNCs. Karnani estimates the market to be about $0.3 trillion in nominal terms, a fraction of what C.K. Prahalad and Hammond estimate. The difference in estimation mostly arises due to a different definition what constitutes poverty. Karnani uses the $2 per day PPP income whereas the WRI defines BOP as people with incomes less than $3,000 a year or roughly $8 per day PPP that includes the vast lower-middle class in large economies like India and China. This discrepancy has been acknowledged by Prahalad (2010).

Critics point out that BOP ventures are 'risky' (Karnani 2006), rather than representing 'untapped potential' waiting to be discovered (Prahalad and Hart 2002). Some authors argue that the potential exists but to tap it would require a long term commitment, innovative strategies and is resource intensive (Pitta et al. 2007; Seelos and Mair 2007).

2.4.2 Harming the Poor

One of Prahalad's core theses is that businesses can contribute to alleviating poverty by serving BOP markets (Prahalad 2004), as the subtitle of the book says, "Eradicating poverty through profits".

Opponents point out that this is an over optimistic view and that there is little empirical evidence to support this thesis (Jaiswal 2008; Karnani 2007a). In addition, they argue that viewing the poor as consumers alone will not lift them out of poverty. Viewing the BOP as a source of producers, and by generating income and employment, is the only way of fighting poverty (Karnani 2009).

Karnani extends this line of thought, by stating that in some cases the BOP approach might even harm the poor. Karnani supports this argument with the Fair and Lovely case, a whitening cream sold by HUL targeting the BOP market (Karnani 2007b). He argues that selling products to the poor without restriction can be harmful, as they "often lack the information and education needed to make well informed choices" (Karnani 2007a, p. 99). Bad consumption habits such as tobacco and alcohol consumption constitutes a significant portion of the expenditure of people living under $1 per day (e.g., rural poor in Mexico spend 8.1 % of their budget on tobacco and alcohol) (Banerjee and Duflo 2007).

Jaiswal compromises between Karnani and Prahalad's views on BOP (Jaiswal 2008). He proposes a framework for large companies that encourage selective consumption of the poor, i.e., avoiding products that are not suited for their well-being, and also emphasizes the role of the poor as producers. The key element of his paradigm is determining whether the company is responding to the basic needs and well-being of the BOP through its product or service. This approach avoids the dangers, mentioned by Karnani, of exploiting the poor. It also ensures that there is inclusion of the poor in the formal economy that Prahalad's approach to BOP argues for.

Echoing this proposition, Sethia argues for a strong value frame while designing products for the BOP to avoid pushing the group towards harmful consumption practices prevalent in the West (Sethia 2005).

As a counter note, Prahalad argues that the BOP approach, as conceptualized by him does integrate these approaches. He counters Karnani's argument that giving the poor access to products and services also contributes to their welfare, as it reduces their costs for services and alleviates their poverty penalty (Prahalad 2010). Echoing Prahalad's opinion, Fitch and Sorensen (2007) posit that while supply side development, i.e., developing the BOP market as producers creates larger number of jobs and thus contributes to poverty alleviation, initiatives that create access to products and services for the poor have many more benefits as they create opportunities indirectly through improved quality of life.

2.4.3 Undermining the State's Role in Development and Other Alternatives to Capitalism

Another core thesis of the BOP approach is that the private sector must play a role in development, as the State and other international institutions have failed to fulfill this mission in the last decades (Prahalad 2004).

Karnani opposes this claim and points out that "romanticizing the poor" is harmful as it dilutes the importance of the State's role in poverty reduction. He argues that providing basic services, such as water, healthcare, education, is the State's responsibility and the BOP view underemphasizes this responsibility, which could have negative moral implications (Karnani 2009). The BOP approach could potentially shadow these successes that can contribute to key learning on poverty reduction.

In an alternative line of argument, Peredo (2012) posits that the BOP discourse reinforces capitalistic hegemony. By homogenizing the poor and conceptualizing them as "homo economicus", she argues, that the BOP scholarship does not take into consideration alternative perspectives of capitalism.

2.4.4   Inability of MNCs to Address the BOP

A fundamental debate still exists on who is best fit to address the BOP market. While Prahalad and other proponents of the BOP approach argue that MNCs, with their capabilities and resources, are best suited to address BOP markets, critics argue that local companies or even social entrepreneurs are best equipped to do so.

Local companies are embedded in the market and have a deep understanding of it (Karnani 2007a). Further, while the BOP market might be large in numbers, it is still very fragmented and distributed across several low income countries, making it hard for an MNC to reach (Karnani 2007a). Out of the 12 cases put forward by Prahalad himself in his seminal book, only two companies were MNCs, the others were a mix of small and medium sized companies, NGOs and larger indigenous companies active in this space (Karnani 2007a).

2.5   Current State of BOP Scholarship

2.5.1   Evolution of the BOP Approach

The initial idea, set out by Prahalad and colleagues called for increased participation by MNCs in the BOP market (Prahalad and Lieberthal 1998). This first generation of BOP scholarship was successful in identifying companies, large and small, that conducted business at the BOP through innovative products/services and innovative business models.

While this idea spawned research as well as changes in business approaches towards the poor, several points of criticism were raised against the initial BOP concept. Consequently, the second generation of BOP research (London and Hart 2010; Simanis and Hart 2008; Simanis et al. 2008) was characterized by seeking "mutual value" for businesses as well as communities (London et al. 2010, p. 582). This stream of scholarship was built on work, which researchers had conducted along with companies that co-created business models at the BOP from scratch.

Beyond this effort, several works are beginning to question the 'fortune' at the BOP. While some scholars argue that serving the BOP is mired with challenges (Karnani 2009; Pitta et al. 2007), others point out that the BOP market can be interesting for companies provided that they have a long-range mindset, are willing to deal with informal markets, can find innovative ways to dramatically reduce costs and keep out legacy systems and cultures (Karamchandani et al. 2011). So rather than an open invitation, these practitioners' and scholars' recommendation is more tempered and they point out challenges as well as measures for managing risks at the BOP markets.

2.5.2   BOP Approach and Other Tangential Areas

The BOP approach is part of the discourse on the interaction between society and business. The dominant view in the 70s and 80s was characterized by Milton Friedman, who famously claimed "the only one responsibility of business towards society is the maximization of profits to the shareholders within the legal framework and the ethical custom of the country" (quoted in (Garriga and Melé 2004, p. 53)). However, in the 90s and turn of the century, the discussion of the social responsibility of companies shifted towards other stakeholders and highlighted their role in improving society as well as creating competitive advantage for themselves.

As part of this shift, Porter and Kramer (2011) established the concept of shared value, defined as policies and practices for companies to create competitive advantage while simultaneously improving society. These scholars posit that companies can do this in three ways, by reconceiving products and services for the poor, as the BOP approach also propagates, by redefining value chains, which can influence environmental sustainability and by strengthening local clusters, e.g., by improving local infrastructure or training future talent in communities that they operate in.

Thus, the BOP approach can be considered one form of creating shared value, because it gives millions of customers access to products or services that were previously unavailable or only available to a limited extent, while simultaneously creating new markets for companies. Other parallel concepts are inclusive business or inclusive capitalism, capitalism that 'includes' the poor and disenfranchised (Hart 2005).

Another group trying to address major social problems through innovatively using and combining resources, in a financially sustainable way, are social entrepreneurs (Mair and Marti 2006). Social entrepreneurship is gaining global support through networks, such as Ashoka, as well as foundations that support individuals (Mair and Marti 2006).

While the shared value approach and social entrepreneurship have the same aim to integrate social and economic value, the shared value and BOP approach address corporations whereas social entrepreneurship is practiced by individuals.

2.6   Why It Is Interesting and Imperative to Conduct BOP Research

The BOP discourse started with a range of papers first published around the turn of the century (Prahalad and Lieberthal 1998; Prahalad and Hart 2002; Prahalad and Hammond 2002). While C. K. Prahalad clearly popularized the idea, early co-authors, Stuart Hart and Allen Hammond went on to research and publish in the field together with Prahalad (Hammond 2010; Prahalad and Hart 2002; Prahalad and Hammond 2002) as well as independently (Hart 2005; Hammond 2010; London and Hart 2004).

At this time, the dominant logic in management was that corporations could address problems of low-income segments of society only through philanthropic efforts, not through economically viable business efforts (Kolk et al. 2013). The BOP approach challenged these views and pushed companies, especially MNCs, to view these segments as potential markets for growth (Prahalad 2004). Since then, research into this segment has painted a more complex and nuanced picture, highlighting not only the potential but also the challenges (Pitta et al. 2007).

While the idea of business at the BOP has been around for about one and a half decades, it has not been part of extensive academic research and has resulted in few journal publications (Bruton 2010). In terms of scholarship, many questions still need to be answered for companies to be able to address the segment (George et al. 2012). Scholars call this a "new frontier" of international strategy because it requires a fundamental rethink of existing products/services and business models (Ricart et al. 2004).

Research in this field holds promise. Renowned management scholars have been calling on the management research community to increase research in this area (Bruton 2010; McGahan 2012; George et al. 2012). Issues related to the BOP and the intersection between poverty and business involves and can affect a vast majority of the world population (Prahalad and Hammond 2002). Increased attention from management research into these issues is required for it to stay relevant and vital (McGahan 2012).

Finally, research into BOP issues also holds promise of unlocking the potential of the private sector to address the needs of the poor (Prahalad 2004). Mobile telephony is often exalted as a success story because of its proliferation in the last decade mostly driven by private sector's involvement in the BOP (Deloitte 2012). Low-income segments, however, have many more unfulfilled needs that could potentially be addressed with similar speed through the involvement of businesses. Research into past and current initiatives can offer companies insights into various opportunities and challenges in addressing the BOP markets. In turn, organizations can strive to offer life-enhancing products and services to millions of poor.

References

Accenture. (2013). *Masters of rural markets: Profitably selling to India's rural consumers.* Accenture.

Anderson, J., & Billou, N. (2007). Serving the World's Poor: Innovation at the base of the economic pyramid. *Journal of Business Strategy, 28*(2), 14–21.

Austin-Breneman, J., & Yang, M. (2013). Design for micro-enterprise: An approach to product design for emerging markets. In: *Proceedings of the ASME 2013 International Design Engineering Technical Conferences & Computers and Information in Engineering Conference.*

Banerjee, A. V., & Duflo, E. (2007). The economic lives of the poor. *Journal of Economic Perspectives, 21*(1), 141–167.

Basu, P., & Srivastava, P. (2005). Scaling-up microfinance for India's rural poor. *World Bank Policy Research Working Paper* (3646).

Bruton, G. D. (2010). Letter from the editor: Business and the World's poorest billion–the need for an expanded examination by management scholars. *The Academy of Management Perspectives, 24*(3), 6–10.

Chattopadhyay, U. (2013). Making India a telecom manufacturing hub: Emerging issues and challenge. *World Academy of Science, Engineering and Technology, 75*, 450–456.

Deloitte. (2012). What is the impact of mobile telephony on economic growth?

Fitch, B., & Sorensen, L. (2007). The case for accelerating profit-making at the base of the pyramid: What could and should the donor community be seeking to do, and what results should it expect? *Journal of International Development, 19*, 781–792.

Garriga, E., & Melé, D. (2004). Corporate social responsibility theories: Mapping the territory. *Journal of Business Ethics, 53*(1–2), 51–71.

George, G., McGahan, A. M., & Prabhu, J. (2012). Innovation for inclusive growth: Towards a theoretical framework and a research agenda. *Journal of Management Studies, 49*(4), 661–683.

Godfrey, P. C. (2011). Toward a theory of the informal economy. *The Academy of Management Annals, 5*(1), 231–277.

Guesalaga, R., & Marshall, P. (2008). Purchasing power at the bottom of the pyramid: Differences across geographic regions and income tiers. *Journal of Consumer Marketing, 25*(7), 413–418.

Gupta, R., Jambunathan, S., & Netzer, T. (2010). *Building India: Transforming the nation's logistics infrastructure*. New York: McKinsey & Company.

Hammond, A. (2010). *The next 4 billion: Market size and business strategy at the base of the pyramid*. Washington, DC: World Resource Institute.

Hart, S. (2005). *Capitalism at the crossroads: aligning business, earth, and humanity*. Upper Saddle River, NJ: Wharton School Publishing.

Hart, S., & London, T. (2005). Developing native capability. *Stanford Social Innovation Review, 3*(2), 28–33.

Hart, S., & Sharma, S. (2004). Engaging fringe stakeholders for competitive imagination. *Academy of Management Executive, 18*(1), 7–19.

Jaiswal, A. K. (2008). The fortune at the bottom or the middle of the pyramid? *Innovations: Technology, Governance, Globalization, 3*(1), 85–100.

Karamchandani, A., Kubzansky, M., & Lalwani, N. (2011). Is the bottom of the pyramid really for you? *Harvard Business Review, 89*(3), 107–111.

Karnani, A. (2006). Mirage at the bottom of the pyramid. *SSRN eLibrary*.

Karnani, A. (2007a). The mirage of marketing at the bottom of the pyramid. *California Management Review, 49*(4), 90–100.

Karnani, A. (2007b). Doing well by doing good—case study: 'Fair & Lovely' whitening cream. *Strategic Management Journal, 28*(13), 1351–1357.

Karnani, A. (2009). Romanticizing the poor. *Stanford Social Innovation Review, 7*(1), 38–43.

Khanna, T., & Palepu, K. (1997). Why focused strategies may be wrong for emerging markets. *Harvard Buisness Review, 75*(4), 41–51.

Khanna, T., & Palepu, K. (1999). The right way to restructure conglomerates in emerging markets. *Harvard Business Review, 77*, 125–135.

Khanna, T., & Palepu, K. (2006). Emerging giants. *Harvard Business Review, 84*(10), 60–69.

Kolk, A., Rivera-Santos, M., & Rufín, C. (2013). Reviewing a decade of research on the "Base/Bottom of the Pyramid" (BOP) concept. *Business and Society, 20*, 1–40.

Landrum, N. (2007). Advancing the base of the pyramid debate. *Strategic Management Review, 1*(1), 1–12.

London, T. (2008). The base-of-the-pyramid perspective: A new approach to poverty alleviation. In: Academy of Management, 2008. Academy of Management Proceedings (pp 1–6).

London, T., Anupindi, R., & Sheth, S. (2010). Creating mutual value: Lessons learned from ventures serving base of the pyramid producers. *Journal of Business Research, 63*, 582–594.

London, T., & Hart, S. (2004). Reinventing strategies for emerging markets: Beyond the transnational model. *Journal of International Business Studies, 35*(5), 350–370.

London, T., & Hart, S. (Eds.). (2010). *Next generation business strategies for the base of the pyramid*. Upper Saddle River, NJ: Pearson Education Inc.

Mair, J., & Marti, I. (2006). Social entrepreneurship research: A source of explanation, prediction, and delight. *Journal of World Business, 41*(1), 36–44.

McGahan, A. M. (2012). Challenges of the informal economy for the field of management. *The Academy of Management Perspectives, 26*(3), 12–21.

Mendoza, R. U. (2011). Why do the poor pay more? Exploring the poverty penalty concept. *Journal of International Development, 23*(1), 1–28.

MGI. (2007). The 'Bird of Gold': The rise of India's consumer market.

Nakata, C., & Weidner, K. (2012). Enhancing new product adoption at the base of the pyramid: A contextualized model. *Journal of Product Innovation Management, 29*(1), 21–32.

Olsen, M., & Boxenbaum, E. (2009). Bottom-of-the-Pyramid: Organizational barriers to implementation. *California Management Review, 51*(4), 100–125.

Peredo, A. (2012). The BOP discourse as capitalist hegemony. *Academy of Management Proceedings, 2012*(1), 1–1.

Pitta, D. A., Guesalaga, R., & Marshall, P. (2007). The quest for the fortune at the bottom of the pyramid: Potential and challenges. *Journal of Consumer Marketing, 25*(7), 393–401.

Porter, M. E., & Kramer, M. R. (2011). The Big Idea: Creating shared value. How to reinvent capitalism and unleash a wave of innovation and growth. *Harvard Business Review 89*(1–2).

Prahalad, C. K. (2004). *The fortune at the bottom of the pyramid: Eradicating poverty through profits*. Upper Saddle River, NJ: Wharton School Publishing.

Prahalad, C. K. (2006). The innovation Sandbox. *Strategy & Business, 44*, 1–10.

Prahalad, C. K. (2010). The big picture. In T. London & S. L. Hart (Eds.), *Next generation business strategies for the base of the pyramid: New approaches for building mutual value*. New York: FT Press.

Prahalad, C. K. (2012). Bottom of the pyramid as a source of breakthrough innovations. *Journal of Product Innovation Management, 29*(1), 6–12.

Prahalad, C. K., & Hammond, A. (2002). Serving the World's poor profitably. *Harvard Buisness Review, 89*(9), 48–59.

Prahalad, C. K., & Hart, S. (2002). The fortune at the bottom of the pyramid. *Strategy & Business, 26*.

Prahalad, C. K., & Lieberthal, K. (1998). The end of corporate imperialism. *Harvard Buisness Review, 76*, 68–79.

Prahalad, C. K., & Mashelkar, R. (2010). Innovation's Holy Grail. *Harvard Business Review, 7*(8), 132–142.

Rajan, R. (2007). Unilever's business in India's subsistence economies. *Advances in International Management, 20*, 259–277.

Rangan, V. K., & Thulasiraj, R. D. (2007). Making sight affordable. *Innovations, 2*, 35–49.

Rao, P., Miller, J. B., Wang, Y. D., & Byrne, J. B. (2009). Energy-microfinance intervention for below poverty line households in India. *Energy Policy, 37*(5), 1694–1712.

Ricart, J. E., Enright, M. J., Ghemawat, P., Hart, S. L., & Khanna, T. (2004). New frontiers in international strategy. *Journal of International Business Studies, 35*(3), 175–200.

Roy, O. (2012). *Internet in rural India*. Bright Angles Consulting

Schneider, F., Buehn, A., & Montenegro, C. E. (2010). *Shadow economies all over the World New Estimates for 162 Countries from 1999 to 2007*. The World Bank Development Research Group Poverty and Inequality Team.

Schuster, T., & Holtbrügge, D. (2012). Market entry of multinational companies in markets at the bottom of the pyramid: A learning perspective. *International Business Review, 21*(5), 817–830.

Schuster, T., & Holtbrügge, D. (2013). Benefits of cross-sector partnerships in markets at the base of the pyramid. *Business Strategy and the Environment, 23*, 188–203.

Seelos, C., & Mair, J. (2007). Profitable business models and market creation in the context of deep poverty: A strategic view. *Academy of Management Perspectives, 21*(4), 49–63.

Sethia, N. (2005). At the bottom of the pyramid: Responsible design for responsible business. *Design Management Review, 16*(3), 42–49.

Sharma, A. (2010). Sustainable social development through innovations: Understanding Indian cases. *International Journal of Business and Globalisation, 5*(1), 17–30.

Simanis, E. (2012). Reality check at the bottom of the pyramid. *Harvard Business Review, 90*(6), 120–125.

Simanis, E., & Hart, S. (2008). *The base of the pyramid protocol: Toward next generation BoP strategy*. Ithaca, NY: Cornell University.

Simanis, E., Hart, S., & Duke, D. (2008). The base of the pyramid protocol: Beyond "basic needs" business strategies. *Innovations, 3*(1), 57–84.

Sridharan, S., & Viswanathan, M. (2008). Marketing in subsistence marketplaces: Consumption and entrepreneurship in a South Indian context. *Journal of Consumer Marketing, 25*(7), 455–462.

Vachani, S., & Smith, N. C. (2007). Socially responsible distribution: Distribution strategies for reaching the bottom of the pyramid. *California Management Review, 50*(2), 52–84.

Vishwanathan, M. (2010). A micro-level approach to understanding BOP markets. In T. London & S. Hart (Eds.), *Next generation business strategies for the base of the pyramid*. Upper Saddle River, NJ: Pearson Education, Inc.

Walsh, J. P., Kress, J. C., & Beyerchen, K. W. (2005). *Book review essay: Promises and perils at the bottom of the pyramid*. Ml 48109–1234. Ross School of Business, University of Michigan, Ann Arbor.

Webb, J. W., Kistruck, G. M., Ireland, R. D., & Ketchen, D. J. (2010). The entrepreneurship process in base of the pyramid markets: The Case of Multinational Enterprise/Nongovernment Organization Alliances. *Entrepreneurship: Theory and Practice, 34*(3), 555–581.

WHO. (2008). World Health Organization and United Nations Children's Fund Joint Monitoring Programme for Water Supply and Sanitation. Progress on Drinking Water and Sanitation: Special Focus on Sanitation.

World Bank. (2012). *World Development Indicators 2012*. World Bank.

Chapter 3
Disruptive Innovations Theory

3.1 Introduction

Disruptive innovation theory was established by Clayton Christensen, through a series of scholarly articles (Christensen and Rosenbloom 1995; Christensen and Bower 1996) and popularized by his seminal book, 'The Innovator's Dilemma' (Christensen 1997a). The theory resonated among practitioners in several industries and also resulted in influencing thinking and research in the areas of innovation management, strategy, organization, etc. (Danneels 2004). Researchers consider disruptive innovations as "a powerful means for developing and broadening new markets" (Govindarajan and Kopalle 2006b, p. 190).

This chapter will primarily provide an overview of the theoretical foundations of disruptive innovations. It will begin by outlining the definition of disruptive innovations and embed it into research in discontinuous technologies. Following this, shortcomings of the theory will be discussed. The final sections concentrate on the challenges that established firms face in commercializing disruptive innovations.

3.2 Disruptive Innovation Theory

3.2.1 Definition

Christensen categorizes innovations into two types—sustaining and disruptive (Christensen 1997a). To attain growth, companies continuously improve product/service features that their mainstream customers demand through sustaining innovations. Sustaining innovations thus improve the product along the primary performance dimension that established customer segments value, in an incremental or radical manner.

© Springer International Publishing Switzerland 2015
A. Ramdorai, C. Herstatt, *Frugal Innovation in Healthcare*, India Studies in Business and Economics, DOI 10.1007/978-3-319-16336-9_3

Disruptive innovations, in contrast, initially appear inferior from the perspective of mainstream customers but are appealing to emerging customers in the low-end or new niche segments, as they perform better on an alternative dimension. As these innovations improve over time, their performance is sufficient to satisfy the more mainstream customers in the market.

A key concept in disruptive innovation theory is that of 'performance oversupply' to explain why customers adopt the disruptive product while a more sophisticated option is available (Christensen 1997b). Christensen argues that the performance demanded or utilized by customers increases at a rate lower than the rate of performance improvement of the technologies as shown in the Fig. 3.1. This happens because companies innovate for their most demanding customers but in reality this segment of the market is overserved. As a result, the sustaining innovation improves to provide greater functionality than what the majority of the market can absorb. Thus, when the disruptive innovation reaches an acceptable level of performance or becomes 'good enough' for the market, customers switch over to the new technology and disruption occurs (Christensen 1997a).

Christensen built this theory drawing on research on the rigid disk drive industry (Christensen and Rosenbloom 1995). He followed the technology changes in the disk drive industry over a span of 25 years, where he identified the process of disruption occurring three times. These disruptions occurred as the industry moved from a larger-sized to smaller-sized disk drives, for instance from 14 in. to 8 in. or 8 in. to 5.25 in. or 5.25 in. to 3.5 in.. In every case, the smaller-sized drive was a disruptive technology and the key performance attribute valued most by the customers was capacity (in bytes). The smaller sized disk drive always had lower capacity compared to the previous generation; however, it was smaller in volume and lighter. These secondary attributes were valuable for emerging and niche

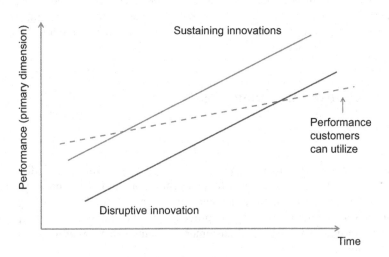

Fig. 3.1 Analytical representation of the evolution of disruptive innovation. Source: Christensen (1997a)

markets like mini-computers, desktops and notebooks but not attractive for existing customers of the disk-drive companies. For instance, the 3.5 in. disk drive technology established itself with notebook manufacturers, who appreciated the smaller size, lighter weight and decreased power consumption and were willing to trade-off off decreased capacity for these advantages. Over time as the capacity of the 3.5 in. disk drive improved, and became 'good enough', it was accepted by desktop manufacturers and went on to displace the 5.25 in. technology. Further, in each case of disruption, those firms that dominated the earlier technology did not manage to make the transition to the disrupting technology and were displaced by entrant firms.

Another example of disruptive technology is the table top photocopier (Govindarajan and Kopalle 2006a). In the 1970s, Xerox's high speed photocopier dominated the market. Canon, then a new entrant, introduced a cheaper table top printer that was smaller in size but made photocopies of lower quality. Due to its size, the table top was preferred by small businesses and households, then a niche segment in the printer market. However, as the quality of table top photocopying improved, the speed and performance was sufficient to satisfy mainstream market needs.

Disruptive innovations are distinct from radical innovations (Govindarajan and Kopalle 2006a). Radical innovations represent technological breakthroughs that offer substantially higher customer benefit relative to existing product/services (Sorescu et al. 2003). Disruptive innovations are generally simpler technologies (Christensen and Bower 1996). Moreover, while radical innovations address the mainstream market, disruptive innovations, with their lower performance and new features, appeal to emerging and niche segments.

Changes through disruptive innovations have occured several industries, including healthcare (Christensen et al. 2009), higher education (Christensen and Eyring 2011) and tourism (Guttentag 2013).

3.2.2 Extensions of the Disruptive Innovation Theory

Initial research into disruptive technologies spawned bodies of work by several researchers, including advances to the theory from Christensen and several colleagues he collaborated with. Christensen, in his sequel book, replaced the term disruptive technology with disruptive innovation to include service and business model innovations (Christensen and Raynor 2003). In this book, the authors also further categorized disruptive innovations into two types: low-end disruption and new-market disruption. In the case of low-end disruptions, initial customers of the disruptive technology are price-sensitive customers at the low end of the existing market for whom lower performance is acceptable. Low-end disruptions occur when current technologies are over-priced because their performance overshoots the performance expected by the market. Thus, lower-priced alternatives with "good-enough" performance have a chance to disrupt the existing technology.

Discount retailing is a low-end disruption vis-à-vis full-service retail stores. Christensen argues that at the time, customers in markets for hard goods like paint, hardware, toys were overserved in full-service retail stores as these segments did not require well-trained personnel and they could sell themselves. Thus, the entry of discount retailing in the USA with Wal-Mart became popular with more cost-sensitive customer segments as they changed their retailing business model (Christensen and Raynor 2003).

Alternatively, new-market disruptions "compete against non-consumption" as these enable new groups of people to begin using these products that previously lacked the money or skills to use them. The example of Canon's table-top photo-copiers, mentioned above, is an example of a new market disruptive innovation as it created new market segments (Christensen and Raynor 2003).

Govindarajan and Kopalle (2006b) contributed to this categorization by adding the concept of "high-end" disruptions. These disruptions refer to innovations that are typically more expensive than mainstream technologies but offer a secondary performance attribute. The authors present mobile phone technology as an example of high-end disruption. Similar to low-end disruptions, initially mainstream customer segments fail to see value in high-end disruptions. Consequently, they also pose a dilemma to incumbents. Incumbents also tend to underestimate the initial niche market and thus ignore the disruptive technology.

Markides (2006) argues for the refinement of the categories clumped within the term disruptive innovations. He proposes that technological, business-model and new-to-the-world product innovations be treated separately. He makes this argument because in some cases of business models, which are disruptive like budget airlines, are active in the mainstream market, yet have not displaced traditional airlines completely.

Adner (2002) analyzes this theory both from the lens of microeconomics and game theory. His model describes the underlying demand conditions that enable disruption. His examination of how customers evaluate performance offers a complementary view of the demand-side conditions when disruption occurs and also highlights the role of price in the process of disruption. While Christensen's model posits that disruption is enabled by sufficient performance, this model provides further refinement. Adner's demand-based view suggests that disruption is enabled by both sufficient performance as well as a sufficiently lower price.

Schmidt and Druehl (2008) offer a complementary framework for the disruptive innovation theory according to how technologies *diffuse* or *encroach* into the market. They refer to their term "high-end" encroachment as sustaining innovation, where the innovation is first caught on by the high-end of the market and then diffuses into the mass market. In contrast, low-end encroachment first displaces the existing technology in the lower-end of the market, i.e., customers with lower willingness to pay, and then diffuses to the higher-end of the market. The authors include fringe or detached market low-end encroachments, i.e., innovations where encroachment creates a new market, where the customer needs are different from the current low-end customers, as well as immediate low-end encroachment where low-end encroachment begins immediately upon introduction of the product.

Table 3.1 Characteristics of disruptive innovations

No.	Characteristic	Applicability	Sources
1	The disruptive innovation initially underperforms on the performance attribute valued by mainstream customers	All	Christensen (1997a)
2	The disruptive innovation, however, has features that are valued by fringe or new customers and introduces a secondary performance criterion	All	Christensen (1997a)
2a	A disruptive innovation can create new markets, as it attracts people who previously lacked the resources or skills to use it	New-market	Christensen and Raynor (2003)
2b	A disruptive innovation is typically simpler and lower cost	New market, Low-end	Christensen (1997a)
2c	A disruptive innovation can involve radical technology and attract high-end customers	High-end	Govindarajan and Kopalle (2006b)
3	Generally mainstream customers do not initially value these additional features and thus the disruptive innovation is commercialized in new market segment	All	Christensen and Raynor (2003)
4	The disruptive innovation initially seems to be financially unattractive for leading incumbents to pursue	All	Christensen (2006, 1997a)
5	The disruptive innovation steadily improves in performance and attracts mainstream customers to it; either it improves along the main performance attribute or market preferences shift towards the secondary performance attribute	All	Christensen (1997a), Henderson (2006)
6	The disruptive innovation takes significant share of the mainstream market	All	Christensen (1997a), Markides (2006)

These two categories refer to new market and low-end disruptive innovations respectively.

Building on the disruptive innovation theory by Christensen and its extensions, Table 3.1 summarizes the key characteristics of disruptive innovations and shows the type of disruptive innovation (low-end, new-market or high-end disruption) it applies to.

An important point to note is that disruption occurs over a period of time—"disruptive innovation is a process, not an event" (Christensen 2006, p. 46). In some cases, the process of disruption can take years, even decades (Christensen and Raynor 2003). Hence, it is difficult to determine a particular point in time when a certain product becomes disruptive. However, there remains a debate about when a technology vs. a business model gets disrupted. As, Markides (2006) argues, in several markets with a disrupting business model innovation, such as discount retailing or budget airlines, innovations acknowledged by Christensen as being disruptive (Christensen and Raynor 2003), the new business models "grow to a respectable size but never really replace the old ways" (Markides 2006, p. 21). This is why the final characteristic of disruptive innovations in the table above tempers the requirement for disruptive innovation to displace mainstream technology as proposed by some scholars (Danneels 2004) to gaining significant market share in the mainstream market.

3.2.3 Disruptive Innovation in the Context of Technological Discontinuities

Technology management has a long tradition of studying technological change and evolution. Schumpeter was among the earliest scholars to note how innovation can both create and destroy industries in waves of "creative destruction" (Schumpeter 1939). Successive bodies of research established the concept of S-curves (Foster 1986; Abernathy and Utterback 1978) and of technological trajectories (Dosi 1982) to explain how technology evolves and the underlying forces that lead to the decline of industries and firms. This section does not aim to give an elaborate history of scholarship around technological evolution. Instead, it aims to put the work of disruptive innovation in the context of research into technological discontinuities.

Cooper and Schendel's research was among the first to explore how new technologies are introduced outside the industry, often pioneered by start-up firms (Cooper and Schendel 1976). This work gave impetus to management scholars to explore why incumbents with financial strength and market knowledge often stumble in the face of technological change.

Research has turned to organizational theory to look at the resources and capabilities of firms to explain the reasons behind this puzzle (Hill and Rothaermel 2003). Tushman and Anderson (1986) explored organization competency as an explanation. These scholars argued that technology evolves through a series of incremental changes punctuated by technological discontinuities. These discontinuities may be competence-enhancing vs. competence-destroying. The authors posit that competence-destroying discontinuous technologies are initiated by entrant firms and lead to the downfall of established firms because these competence-destroying technologies render the skills and knowledge existing in the incumbent's obsolete.

Henderson and Clark lent nuance to this argument and explored other underlying factors of incumbent failure in the face of "seemingly minor improvements in technological products" (Henderson and Clark 1990, p. 9). Their model categorized innovations into modular and architectural innovation in addition to the existing categorization of incremental and radical innovation. They argued that architectural innovations, which change the architecture of the product pose challenges to established firms because they "destroy the usefulness of the architectural knowledge" that tends to be embedded in the structure of the firm (Henderson and Clark 1990, p. 9).

The technological evolution of the rigid disk-drive industry, Christensen's seminal case study, could not be explained by existing theory. The newer technology was not competence-destroying or an architectural innovation. Instead, the newer technology exhibited inferior performance compared to the mainstream technology. However, in every instance of technological change in the disk drive industry, the incumbent lost market share to entrants.

Christensen sought to explain the underlying factors of the incumbent's demise through the anomalies that could not be explained by these notable works on technological change evolution prior (Christensen 2006). Thus, Christensen's model of disruptive innovations sheds new light on why established companies are unable to deal with certain types of discontinuous innovations.

3.2.4 Critique of Disruptive Innovation Theory

Along with wide spread praise and traction in the practitioner world, disruptive innovation theory has also attracted criticism (Danneels 2004; Tellis 2006). The first front of criticism revolves around the definition of disruptive innovation and its lack of predictive ability. While disruptive innovations are defined as those that initially underperform vis-à-vis existing products/services, it is still unclear how exactly to distinguish these from other underperforming technologies. Thus, critics argue that disruptive innovation theory's inability to predict ex-ante makes it less valuable to managers. Great strides in this area have been made, while it is still unclear whether a particular disruptive innovation will be successful (Danneels 2004), scholars have developed frameworks that can better predict firms that are more likely to disrupt (Govindarajan and Kopalle 2006b) and markets that are more likely to be disrupted (Klenner et al. 2013).

The second attack on disruptive innovation theory is on the sampling for its empirical validation (Tellis 2006). Critics argues that Christensen chose limited and only successful cases to qualify his theory (Cohan 2000). Christensen defends this by noting that the choice of his case studies was aimed at pointing towards anomalies in existing theory and not for validating his theory (Christensen 2006).

Theory building of disruptive innovation theory is still an "on-going process" (Christensen 2006). While the theory has been continuously extended and applied to several different industries, there is still room for scholars to seek anomalies and refine the theory through theoretical and empirical research.

3.3 Challenges in Commercializing Disruptive Innovations

Prior research points to how established firms stumble in the face of technological change, which led to the coining of the term "incumbent's curse" (Foster 1986). Scholars have focused on a firm's capabilities (Tushman and Anderson 1986;

Henderson and Clark 1990) as well as managerial cognition to explain this (Tripsas and Gavetti 2000). Other quantitative research, however, shows that incumbent's curse may be overstated (Chandy and Tellis 2000). While their empirical data points to how several radical innovations have indeed been introduced by incumbents, it also acknowledges how incumbents underperformed with respect to lower cost innovations. While there has been ample evidence from history of technological evolutions, that entrants displace incumbents, it must be pointed out that there is also evidence to the contrary.

As pointed out in Sect. 3.2.3 above, technological discontinuities present established companies with challenges that lead to serious shifts in the industry. Disruptive innovations present another manifestation of this phenomenon, but have different characteristics and offer different explanations for why established firms fail to commercialize them (Christensen and Bower 1996; Rosenbloom and Christensen 1994).

Two inherent qualities of disruptive innovations differentiate them from other discontinuous innovation.

1. Lack of financial attractiveness: Christensen argues that disruptive innovations appear financially unattractive for companies to pursue (Christensen 2006), relative to their mainstream investments for three main reasons:

    I. Profit margins for disruptive innovations are typically lower (Christensen 1997a)
    II. Companies are unable to correctly estimate the size of the market for disruptive innovations since these innovations create completely new markets (Christensen and Raynor 2003).
    III. Companies tend to pursue large markets; however, markets for disruptive innovations are initially much smaller than mainstream markets and cannot provide volumes that make the business interesting for companies (Christensen et al. 2001).

2. Incompatibility with existing value network: Christensen uses the concept of value networks to explain attacker's advantage in commercializing disruptive innovations (Christensen and Rosenbloom 1995). Value networks are defined as the collection of upstream suppliers, downstream channels to market, and ancillary providers that support a common business model within an industry (Christensen 1997a). Disruptive innovations do not fit into the embedded value networks of the organization and new market disruptive innovations typically create new value networks with new performance attributes (Christensen and Raynor 2003).

These inherent qualities of disruptive innovations make them unattractive for established firms and they often fail to commercialize them (Christensen and Bower 1996). Disruptive innovations are not technologically challenging to established firms, in fact, Christensen's research shows that several established firms had already developed the technology. The key challenge they faced was in commercialization (Christensen and Bower 1996). Two underlying mechanisms have been identified by scholars as an explanation for this failure:

3.3.1   Resource Allocation Processes

Christensen and Bower (1996) argue that established firms fail to allocate resources to disruptive innovations because they do not address their current customer base. They base this argument on resource dependence theory by Pfeffer and Salancik (1978), where the authors posits that firms are governed by their resources and the sources of their resources, namely their existing and most profitable customers.

Because of this resource dependency, an incumbent's values and processes tend to favor sustaining innovations and this is where they invest their resources. The inherent qualities of disruptive innovations, stated in the previous section, make them unattractive to incumbents (Christensen and Overdorf 2000).

3.3.2   Inadequate Market-Facing Organizational Competency

Henderson contributed to the disruptive innovation theory by suggesting that another reason for companies unable to develop disruptive innovations is the lack of marketing competency (Henderson 2006). Exploring new, disruptive markets requires a major change in patterns of behavior and search (Danneels 2002). The lack of this competence in companies, which are focused on their current customers, hinders them from identifying emerging customer trends peripheral to their current business (Henderson 2006).

3.4   Recommendation to Established Firms Seeking to Commercialize Disruptive Innovations

In Christensen's research into the history of disk drives, he identified only three established firms, over three generations of technological change, which successfully managed a transition into the new technology. Two did so by spinning-out the technology into a different organization and the third through tremendous managerial effort from the CEO (Christensen and Bower 1996).

This led to Christensen and colleagues' most influential recommendation that established firms should set-up a separate organizational entity to develop and commercialize disruptive innovations (Christensen 1997a). Christensen went on to temper this recommendation by offering companies alternatives depending on the nature of innovation and how they fit the disruptive innovation project into the existing values and resources of the companies. His later recommendation notes that there are three options for companies to commercialize disruptive innovation (Christensen and Overdorf 2000). As stated earlier, companies can spin-out and have a distinct organizational entity focus on commercializing the disruptive innovation if the cost-structure does not fit with that of the companies', and if the initial market is estimated to be small. In case the innovation fits with the organization's processes, the innovation can be developed through internal heavy weight teams but requires a spin-off for the commercialization. And finally, established firms can acquire a company, which has the processes and capabilities to develop and commercialize the disruptive innovation. Other research also points to companies that initially created a separate organization to develop the disruptive innovation but then integrated it back into the mainstream business (Cohan 2000).

Research into understanding successful organizational responses by incumbents to discontinuous technologies, in a broader sense, also points to the role organizational design (Macher and Richman 2004). While spin-offs and acquisitions were identified as successful strategies, research also established the role of an internal venture in commercializing discontinuous technologies (Macher and Richman 2004). An internal venture is defined as a structure in which an organization sets up a venture with a set of routines and practices that are different and separate from the companies' core set of operations and have objectives that are different from the companies' core (Macher and Richman 2004).

However, in case of disruptive innovations, questions regarding the merits of spinning-out a distinct organization to pursue these disruptive projects still remain (Danneels 2004). Another open question is whether and how established firms can develop and commercialize disruptive innovations from within their boundaries (Danneels 2006).

3.5 Summary

Disruptive innovation theory has garnered attention over the past decade among practitioners and also generated debate among academics exploring technological change within industries. But, even while insights from the emerging disruptive innovation theory are being used to draw implications for managers, several questions at the core of the theory still remain unanswered.

Research into disruptive innovation continues to grow to build better theory (e.g., in improving the predictability of the theory (Klenner et al. 2013) and continues to be applied to different industries (e.g., tourism (Guttentag 2013), higher education (Christensen and Eyring 2011)). The ideas developed through the theory continue to be relevant for managers as digitization and other technologies pervade many industries and "disrupt" the status quo.

References

Abernathy, W. J., & Utterback, J. M. (1978). Patterns of Industrial Innovation. *Technology Review, 80*(7), 40–47.

Adner, R. (2002). When are technologies disruptive: A demand-based view of the emergence of competition. *Strategic Management Journal, 23*, 667–688.

Chandy, R. K., & Tellis, G. J. (2000). The incumbent's curse? Incumbency, size, and radical product innovation. *The Journal of Marketing, 64*, 1–17.

Christensen, C. M. (1997a). *The innovator's dilemma: When new technologies cause great firms to fail*. Boston: Harvard Business School Press.

Christensen, C. M. (1997b). Patterns in the evolution of product competition. *European Management Journal, 15*(2), 117–127.

Christensen, C. M. (2006). The ongoing process of building a theory of disruption. *Journal of Product Innovation Management, 23*(1), 39–55.

Christensen, C. M., & Bower, J. L. (1996). Customer power, strategic investment, and the failure of leading firms. *Strategic Management Journal, 17*(3), 197–218.

Christensen, C., Craig, T., & Hart, S. (2001, March/April). The great disruption. *Foreign Affairs* (pp. 80–95).

Christensen, C. M., & Eyring, H. J. (2011). *The innovative university: Changing the DNA of higher education from the inside out*. New York: John Wiley & Sons.

Christensen, C. M., Grossman, J. H., & Hwang, J. (2009). *The innovator's prescription: A disruptive solution for health care*. New York: McGraw-Hill.

Christensen, C., & Overdorf, M. (2000, March–April). Meeting the challenge of disruptive change. *Harvard Buisness Review*.

Christensen, C. M., & Raynor, M. (2003). *The innovator's solution: Creating and sustaining successful growth*. Boston, MA: Harvard Business Press.

Christensen, C. M., & Rosenbloom, R. S. (1995). Explaining the attacker's advantage: Technological paradigms, organizational dynamics, and the value network. *Research Policy, 24*(2), 233–257.

Cohan, P. S. (2000). The dilemma of the "innovator's dilemma": Clayton Christensen's management theories are suddenly all the rage, but are they ripe for disruption. *Industry Standard 10*.

Cooper, A. C., & Schendel, D. (1976). Strategic responses to technological threats. *Business Horizons, 19*(1), 61–69.

Danneels, E. (2002). The dynamics of product innovation and firm competences. *Strategic Management Journal, 23*(12), 1095–1121.

Danneels, E. (2004). Disruptive technology reconsidered: A critique and research agenda. *Journal of Product Innovation Management, 21*, 246–258.

Danneels, E. (2006). Dialogue on the effects of disruptive technology on firms and industries. *Journal of Product Innovation Management, 23*(1), 2–4.

Dosi, G. (1982). Technological paradigms and technological trajectories: A suggested interpretation of the determinants and directions of technical change. *Research Policy, 11*(3), 147–162.

Foster, R. N. (1986). *Innovation: The attacker's advantage*. New York: Simon and Schuster.

Govindarajan, V., & Kopalle, P. K. (2006a). Disruptiveness of innovations: Measurement and an assessment of reliability and validity. *Strategic Management Journal, 27*(2), 189–199.

Govindarajan, V., & Kopalle, P. K. (2006b). The usefulness of measuring disruptiveness of innovations ex post in making ex ante prediction. *Journal of Product Innovation Management, 23*(1), 12–18.

Guttentag, D. (2013). Airbnb: disruptive innovation and the rise of an informal tourism accommodation sector. *Current Issues in Tourism*, 1–26.

Henderson, R. (2006). The innovator's dilemma as a problem of organizational competence. *Journal of Product Innovation Management, 23*(1), 5–11.

Henderson, R. M., & Clark, K. B. (1990). Architectural innovation: The reconfiguration of existing product technologies and the failure of established firms. *Administrative Science Quarterly, 35*, 9–30.

Hill, C. W. L., & Rothaermel, F. T. (2003). The performance of incumbent firms in the face of radical technological innovation. *Academy of Management Review, 28*(2), 257–274.

Klenner, P., Hüsig, S., & Dowling, M. (2013). Ex-ante evaluation of disruptive susceptibility in established value networks—When are markets ready for disruptive innovations? *Research Policy, 42*(4), 914–927.

Macher, J. T., & Richman, B. D. (2004). Organisational responses to discontinuous innovation: A case study approach. *International Journal of Innovation Management, 8*(01), 87–114.

Markides, C. (2006). Disruptive innovation: In need of better theory. *Journal of Product Innovation Management, 23*(1), 19–25.

Pfeffer, J., & Salancik, G. (1978). *The external control of organizations: A resource dependence perspective*. New York: Harper & Row.

Rosenbloom, R. S., & Christensen, C. M. (1994). Technological discontinuities, organizational capabilities, and strategic commitments. *Industrial and Corporate Change, 3*(3), 655–685.

Schmidt, G. M., & Druehl, C. T. (2008). When is a disruptive innovation disruptive? *Journal of Product Innovation Management, 25*, 347–369.

Schumpeter, J. (1939). *Business cycles: A theoretical, historical and statistical analysis of the capitalist process*. New York: McGraw Hill.

Sorescu, A. B., Chandy, R. K., & Prabhu, J. C. (2003). Sources and financial consequences of radical innovation: Insights from pharmaceuticals. *Journal of Marketing, 67*, 82–102.

Tellis, G. J. (2006). Disruptive technology or visionary leadership? *Journal of Product Innovation Management, 23*, 34–38.

Tripsas, M., & Gavetti, G. (2000). Capabilities, cognition, and inertia: Evidence from digital imaging. *Strategic Management Journal, 21*(10–11), 1147–1161.

Tushman, M. L., & Anderson, P. (1986). Technological discontinuities and organizational environments. *Administrative Science Quarterly, 31*(3), 439–465.

Chapter 4
Methodology and Research Process

4.1 Introduction

This section introduces the methodological approach for this research. The first section describes the methodology and the rationale for the methods employed. The following section describes the data collection and the data analysis methods. The final section discusses the quality of the research methodology.

4.2 Methodology

4.2.1 Context

This book explores disruptive innovations from the Bottom of the Pyramid (BOP) markets. In the last decade, there has been increasing interest, from both academia and industry, in innovations for the BOP that have emerged from India. This interest was sparked by C. K. Prahalad's articles and seminal book, but was fired on by several other scholars who went on explore these innovations through different lenses (Govindarajan and Trimble 2012; Radjou et al. 2012; Prahalad and Mashelkar 2010).

While several case studies have been explored in practitioners' literature, very limited academic scholarship has dealt with these innovations from BOP markets, as the editor of the Academy of Management *Perspectives* noted (Bruton 2010). These innovations raise several interesting theoretical questions (Govindarajan and Ramamurti 2011; George et al. 2012). As George et al. (2012) have pointed out, there are several opportunities for developing theory around this phenomenon.

It was with this objective of applying an explorative theoretical lens on this phenomenon and embedding it in innovation management literature that this research was initiated. As the starting point was a phenomenon, which was not

© Springer International Publishing Switzerland 2015
A. Ramdorai, C. Herstatt, *Frugal Innovation in Healthcare*, India Studies in
Business and Economics, DOI 10.1007/978-3-319-16336-9_4

yet deeply studied by academic scholars, the research naturally developed into an inductive study.

While doing initial desk search and taking stock of examples of BOP innovations, it emerged that the health care sector offered several well-known and successful examples. Appendix A entails a collection of companies highlighted in some of the papers and in the book by C. K. Prahalad and his colleagues. The most prevalent industry in the list is the healthcare industry. Some of these companies, such as Aravind, NH and Jaipur foot had not only been successfully running for several years, but had also been able to scale up. To further assert this point, basic desk research was conducted into affordable healthcare solutions from India that have gained traction in the last few years.

Furthermore, health and poverty are intricately intertwined. Health, a central part of the Millennium Development Goals, is represented among three out of the eight goals and is key in the global agenda for fighting poverty (WHO 2005). These are the reasons why early in the research process, a decision was taken to focus on the healthcare sector.

4.2.2   Rationale for Case Study Research

Exploratory case study research methodology has been chosen for this research. Case study research is the method of choice when limited body of scholarly research is available in a given area and the objective is theory building (Eisenhardt 1989; Yin 1994).

Yin defines case study research as "an empirical inquiry that investigates a contemporary phenomenon in depth and within its real-life contexts, especially when the boundaries between phenomenon and context are not clearly evident" (Yin 2009, p. 18). Thus, when exploring phenomena where the context cannot be explicitly distinguished, the case study method is an apt choice. Furthermore when exploring complex situations and phenomena, case study research is recommended over alternative research methodologies such as survey and experiments (Yin 2009; Stake 1995). Miles and Huberman amplify this by stating that a strength of qualitative methods is their "richness and holism, with strong potential for revealing complexity" (Miles and Huberman 1994, p. 10).

Case studies have some shortfalls such as generalizability of results and building idiosyncratic theory. However, by virtue of the exploratory nature of this research seeking to understand different aspects of BOP innovations, case study is the preferred method.

4.3   Research Process

As mentioned earlier, an inductive and exploratory mode was chosen to approach the research questions. As one of the aims of this research was to embed the phenomenon of BOP innovations into existing theory within innovation management, namely disruptive innovation theory, the research process was iteration between data and theory right from the start.

The extended case method guided this research process (Burawoy 1998; Danneels 2002). In contrast to grounded theory that aims to generate social theory free from the influence of existing theory and contemporary emphasis (Glaser and Strauss 2009), extended case method is based on building existing theory.

Grounded theory was born at a time when few social theories existed, whereas the last decades have seen a proliferation of theories. The school of extended case method stemmed as a reaction to this (Burawoy 2009).

Extended case method encourages researchers to continually iterate between theory and data. As one of the aims of this study was to integrate a phenomenon into existing theory, this method was applicable as it also aims to integrate existing theories and bodies of work.

This method also forces the researcher to return to the field after going back and forth between the data and theory in order to continually refine results. The analysis of initial results and juxtaposing this with existing theories and frameworks reveals new areas of analysis. The research process is illustrated in the diagram below (Fig. 4.1).

The first step constituted identifying and describing the phenomenon to be explored and defining the research question. This was necessary to focus efforts into a narrower area of interest. At this step, several constructs from theory were also identified, such as characteristics of disruptive innovations and enablers of

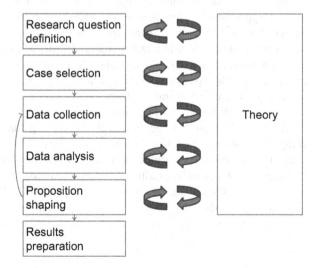

Fig. 4.1 Research process

disruptive innovations, which were later used in formulating the interview guide-lines during the data collection phase (Eisenhardt and Bourgeois 1988).

The next step was to select informative cases that could help in theory building. Also at this step, theory was looped into the process to identify which case studies could be relevant for extending existing theory. This step is described in detail in the next section. After this, field research was prepared and conducted. Also at this point, theory was revisited to inform and shape the interview guidelines.

The next step was data analysis that constituted content analysis, which also required going back and forth between theory and data. This analysis helped shape the propositions which were, in some cases, refined by further data collection with new sources or going back to interview partners to delve into selected topics. This also took place with looping theory and data to identify adjacent theoretical areas and new lenses to analyze the data with. Finally, the results were documented in form of working papers and also discussed and validated with key informants.

4.3.1 Case Study Selection

Case study research relies on theoretical and not statistical sampling (Eisenhardt 1989). This means that unlike statistical methods where sampling has to be repre-sentative, in case study method, the sample should be chosen for theoretical reasons, such as revelation of a new phenomenon, replication from other cases, to prove contrasting results, extension of emerging theory (Eisenhardt and Graebner 2007; Eisenhardt 1989).

To explore the question of why the BOP is a source for disruptive innovations, Aravind Eye Care Systems and Narayana Hrudayalaya hospitals were chosen as case studies. These were chosen from the list of frequently cited BOP innovations because of several reasons. Firstly, they were both in healthcare delivery and offered opportunity to compare across case studies. Secondly, these companies had been around for over 10 years and shown a successful track record of expan-sion, both domestically and internationally. Thirdly and most importantly, second-ary data showed that these companies had not only innovated in their core processes, but also spawned innovations in several adjacent areas, such as medical technology and microinsurance. Thus, they were illustrative cases of companies serving the BOP that were highly innovative.

To answer the other research question regarding the conditions under which companies can successfully commercialize disruptive innovations in the BOP context, two specific case studies were chosen among several options, namely GE Healthcare and Tata. GE Healthcare, with its low cost electrocardiogram (ECG) device, MAC 400 and MAC i, was often cited both in BOP literature as well as popular media. Also, Tata with its low cost water filter, Tata Swach, was often mentioned in literature (Ahlstrom 2010; Tiwari and Herstatt 2012a, b).

What makes these two examples special is also the fact that these two players are large established firms, which, contrary to existing management theory (see Sect. 3.3), developed these disruptive innovation primarily in-house. They also could offer two different perspectives because GE Healthcare is an American incumbent and Tata and emerging market multinational.

Another more practical consideration in the case selection was gaining access to the companies. Through my professional network and through recent networking activity at conferences, we were able to contact key people in each of these companies as well as convince them to participate in my research.

4.3.2 Data Collection

Primary data mainly consisted of interviews and internal firm documents. In addition to that, for the Aravind Eye Care and Narayana Hrudayalaya case studies, observations were conducted in the two companies for about 4–5 h each. Secondary data mainly consisted of business school case studies, media reports and company reports, such as annual reports.

The interviews were all semi-structured and for each interview a guideline was developed prior to the interview. The semi-structured nature of the interviews were in line with the explorative character of the research and allowed for flexibility as opposed to more structured guides or surveys, yet had sufficient focus as a predetermined list of topics was chosen to ensure key questions were covered.

To limit bias in interviews (Eisenhardt and Graebner 2007), multiple interviews were conducted at each company and with different stakeholders, at different hierarchical levels and different functions to gain different perspectives. We also sought to interview all key people involved in the projects in every company, from middle managers, right up to senior leadership. For each of the following chapters, details about data collection and interview partners, specific to the study, will be presented.

4.3.3 Data Analysis

As described in Sect. 4.3, data collection and analysis were developed together in an iterative process because it enabled theory development to be grounded in empirical evidence (Hartley 2004).

To analyze all the data collected in the interviews, content analysis method was chosen. Content analysis mainly consists of coding passages according to themes, and has been described by method scholars as the process of transforming raw data into a standardized form (Babbie 2001). Critically reading the interview transcripts to highlight and code passages by certain themes is the first step of content analysis (Miles and Huberman 1994). This resulted in pieces of insight, which were noted down in the form of memos. These memos also helped while searching for appropriate theory and comparing it with data as it was a more compact form of my analysis. This was very much in line with Daneels' study of dynamic capabilities in new product development (Danneels 2002). Coding and structuring was facilitated by the MAX-QDA Software.

The codes were developed inductively and there was no set schema for coding in the outset, given the inductive and explorative nature of the research. Thus, conducting the inter-coder reliability test was not possible, as the coding scheme and coding categorization was developed during the data analysis process. This is in line with inductive qualitative approaches such as grounded theory, "whose goal is to discover and describe social phenomenon rarely conduct systematic inter-coder reliability tests" (Lamont and White 2005, p. 31). After initial coding, the next step was to refine these codes and memos into themes or categories. These categories were developed inductively and within each category was a structure of codes. These categories also became the basis of my results described in Chapters 5 through 8.

4.4   Quality and Reliability

Since this work follows the case study method, certain quality and reliability checks were performed continuously.

To ensure reliability, i.e., the ability to replicate results, all interviews but three were recorded and all interviews were transcribed (Yin 1994). The three interviews were conducted on the phone without access to a recording device, but were transcribed based on notes immediately after the interview. This procedure ensured that the data collection was verbatim, and recorded without bias. The transcripts were all appropriately saved in a case study database (Yin 1994).

To ensure construct validity, multiple interviewees were questioned around a certain topic (Yin 1994). To test some of the main findings and to refine the results, we continuously checked the emerging insights with old interview partners or with new ones and sometimes both. This was often the basis for the next round of data collection. For the GE Healthcare case study every informant reviewed the case results and approved the final insights. For the other case studies only key informants were requested to do so keeping in mind the time constraints others faced. All key informants from the companies approved the findings after verbally communicating it to them as well as after reading the manuscript.

The trickier aspect of ensuring quality in case studies lies in checking for external validity. External validity deals with the generalizability of the case results. In other words, how applicable are the results found in one company to other companies (Yin 1994). This is one of the most cited criticisms for single case study (Yin 1994).

While the focus of this work was not to test hypothesis but to build on existing theory, the case studies have been appropriately chosen. The two companies, GE

Healthcare and Tata have been chosen because they represent exceptions not the rule. They have been chosen because insights from these companies can help in the development of disruptive innovation theory as well as to BOP or frugal innovation literature. This is why the results will be valid, at best, for companies focusing on healthcare for the BOP. Further research and exploring multiple companies is required for further generalizing the results from these case studies.

References

Ahlstrom, D. (2010). Innovation and growth: How business contributes to society. *The Academy of Management Perspectives, 24*(3), 11–24.

Babbie, E. (2001). *The practice of social research* (9th ed.). Belmont: Wadworth.

Bruton, G. D. (2010). Letter from the editor: Business and the World's poorest billion–the need for an expanded examination by management scholars. *The Academy of Management Perspectives, 24*(3), 6–10.

Burawoy, M. (1998). The extended case method. *Sociological Theory, 16*(1), 4–33.

Burawoy, M. (2009). *The extended case method: Four countries, four decades, four great transformations, and one theoretical tradition.* CA: University of California Press.

Danneels, E. (2002). The dynamics of product innovation and firm competences. *Strategic Management Journal, 23*(12), 1095–1121.

Eisenhardt, K. M. (1989). Building theories from case study research. *The Academy of Management Review, 14*(4), 532–550.

Eisenhardt, K. M., & Bourgeois, L. J. (1988). Politics of strategic decision making in high-velocity environments: Toward a midrange theory. *Academy of Management Journal, 31*(4), 737–770.

Eisenhardt, K. M., & Graebner, M. E. (2007). Theory building from cases: Opportunities and challenges. *Academy of Management Journal, 50*(1), 25–32.

George, G., McGahan, A. M., & Prabhu, J. (2012). Innovation for inclusive growth: Towards a theoretical framework and a research agenda. *Journal of Management Studies, 49*(4), 661–683.

Glaser, B. G., & Strauss, A. L. (2009). *The discovery of grounded theory: Strategies for qualitative research.* NJ: Transaction Books.

Govindarajan, V., & Ramamurti, R. (2011). Reverse innovation, emerging markets, and global strategy. *Global Strategy Journal, 1*(3–4), 191–205.

Govindarajan, V., & Trimble, C. (2012). *Reverse innovation: Create far from home, win everywhere.* Boston, MA: Harvard Business School Press.

Hartley, J. (2004). Case study research. In C. Cassell & G. Symon (Eds.), *Essential guide to qualitative methods in organizational research* (pp. 323–333). London: Sage.

Lamont, M., & White, P. (2005). *Workshop on interdisciplinary standards for systematic qualitative research.* National Science Foundation.

Miles, M. B., & Huberman, A. M. (1994). *Qualitative data analysis: An expanded sourcebook.* Thousand Oaks: Sage.

Prahalad, C. K., & Mashelkar, R. (2010). Innovation's Holy Grail. *Harvard Business Review, 7*(8), 132–142.

Radjou, N., Prabhu, J., & Ahuja, S. (2012). *Jugaad innovation: Think frugal, be flexible, generate breakthrough growth.* San Francisco, CA: Jossey-Bass.

Stake, R. (1995). *The art of case study research.* Thousand Oaks, CA: Sage.

Tiwari, R., & Herstatt, C. (2012a). Assessing India's lead market potential for cost-effective innovations. *Journal of Indian Business Research, 4*(2), 97–115.

Tiwari, R., & Herstatt, C. (2012b). *Frugal innovations for the 'unserved' customer: An assessment of India's attractiveness as a lead Market for cost-effective products.* Working Paper No. 69, TIM/TUHH.

WHO. (2005). *Health and the Millennium Development Goals.* Geneva: World Health Organization.

Yin, R. K. (1994). *Case study research* (2nd ed.). Thousand Oaks, CA: Sage.

Yin, R. K. (2009). *Case study research: Design and methods* (4th ed.). CA: Sage.

Chapter 5
Study 1: The Bottom of the Pyramid Market as a Source for Disruptive Innovations

5.1 Introduction and Research Question

5.1.1 Introduction

Innovations emerging from Bottom of the Pyramid (BOP) markets have been engaging scholars and practitioners in the last decade (Prahalad 2012). Several concepts have emerged to describe this phenomenon from different perspectives, such as frugal innovation (Tiwari and Herstatt 2012), Gandhian innovation (Prahalad and Mashelkar 2010), inclusive innovation (George et al. 2012), jugaad innovation (Radjou et al. 2012) and reverse innovation (Govindarajan and Ramamurti 2011).

This emerging phenomenon has the potential to enrich mainstream management theories (Govindarajan and Ramamurti 2011; George et al. 2012), however, the BOP phenomenon remains largely under-theorized in academic literature (Bruton 2010).

The aim of this study is to embed this phenomenon in disruptive innovation theory and highlight the similarities between these concepts. Further, this study will examine two case studies, namely Narayana Hrudayalaya (NH) and Aravind Eye Care Systems (AECS), two low-cost specialty hospital chains in India to explain why BOP markets can be considered a source for disruptive innovations (Hart and Christensen 2002).

Healthcare as a sector provides a good context to examine this phenomenon. As pointed out in Chap. 4, several BOP innovations are related to healthcare. The healthcare system in almost every nation is in a state of distress. Developed nations, like the USA, face spiraling healthcare costs (Reinhardt et al. 2004) or long waiting lists in countries with nationalized, single-payer models like the UK (Emmerson et al. 2000). Developing countries face severe challenges in providing accessible and affordable quality healthcare for their large low income populations (Howitt et al. 2012). Frugal innovations in healthcare, emerging from BOP markets like

© Springer International Publishing Switzerland 2015
A. Ramdorai, C. Herstatt, *Frugal Innovation in Healthcare*, India Studies in Business and Economics, DOI 10.1007/978-3-319-16336-9_5

India, have the potential to bring quality healthcare to millions of needy patients (Prahalad 2006).

The Aravind Eye Care System (AECS) and Narayana Hrudayalaya (NH) hospitals have pioneered a system of providing extremely affordable healthcare to the poor by establishing high volume focused hospital chains. These companies have innovated their business models and processes to enable delivery of highly standardized procedures at extremely low costs. AECS diagnoses a majority of its 2 million patients and conducts 370,000 cataract surgeries per year for free or at a steeply subsidized rate (AECS 2013). Similarly, NH hospital in Bangalore offers high quality cardiac care at significantly lower costs compared to its competitors as it leverages its economies of scale.

These companies have also innovated beyond their processes to create other product and business model innovations on their own as well as in cooperation with external partners. AECS established Aurolab to manufacture low cost Intra Ocular Lenses (IOLs); NH has setup a low-cost hospital in Mysore that has reimagined hospital construction. These are just a few examples of how these hospital chains have innovated beyond their boundaries. Thus, they provide a valuable empirical context to examine the innovation capacity of companies serving the BOP.

5.1.2 Research Question and Methodology

Management scholars have been calling for companies to address BOP markets not only because these markets present opportunities for growth, but also because this can have a social impact—as the adage goes, "doing well by doing good" (Prahalad and Hart 2002; London 2007).

However, while there has been interest and engagement from the academic community as well as companies, the BOP phenomenon has been largely under-theorized in mainstream management scholarship. As the editor for the Academy of Management Perspectives put it, "while Prahalad's conceptualization of the bottom of the pyramid has been widely discussed, it has not generated extensive academic research among management scholars" (Bruton 2010, p. 6).

To contribute to this growing interest in innovations from BOP markets, this study aims to analyze this phenomenon from the theoretical lens of disruptive innovations. Disruptive innovation theory is still evolving (Christensen 2006) and an opportunity exists to contribute to building this theory further (Danneels 2004). One such area is the question of where disruptive innovations emerge and why (Danneels 2004).

The main aim of this study is two-fold. Firstly, this study will embed the phenomenon of innovations from the BOP in mainstream innovation management literature, particularly within disruptive innovation theory. As an extension, this study will also clarify the interrelationships among the several concepts that describe this phenomenon. The second aim is to understand how and why BOP markets are a source for disruptive innovations, by exploring two cases in the healthcare segment viz. the specialty hospitals AECS and NH.

Primary data for these cases was compiled through interviews (see appendix C for a list of interviewees), field visits and observations. Secondary data including business school case studies, newspaper articles and company reports were also analyzed.

5.2 Embedding the BOP Phenomenon in Theory

5.2.1 Linking Disruptive Innovation Theory and BOP Markets

Hart and Christensen (2002, p. 51) recognized the intersections between the BOP proposition and disruptive innovation theory, by stating that, "disruptive innovations can pave the way, helping companies combine sustainable corporate growth and social responsibility". Prahalad recognized BOP markets as a source for "breakthrough innovations" (Prahalad 2012). He argues that these innovations that allow companies "to participate in BOP markets can often be leveraged in developed markets" (Prahalad 2012, p. 12). Other scholars have also commented on the synergies between these concepts (Jain 2013; Hang et al. 2010).

In this section, the link between these two concepts will be examined, by building on previous works. Also based on the literature review on BOP and disruptive innovations conducted in the previous chapters, the following section links these two concepts.

The BOP concept and disruptive innovation theory have many elements that fit together. Figure 5.1 illustrates the intersections between the theory and the BOP concept.

One of the characteristics of disruptive innovation is that it attracts non-consumers or low-end customers that are satisfied with "good-enough" performance (Christensen and Raynor 2003). Similarly, BOP markets have vast populations with limited or no access to fundamental services and goods and are, hence, willing to adopt products with acceptable performance (Hart and Christensen 2002).

Disruptive innovations initially take root in nascent segments and non-mainstream markets (Christensen 1997) and are largely ignored by incumbents (Christensen and Bower 1996). The BOP markets are nascent markets for MNCs and were, until recently, ignored by them since members of BOP markets don't have the level of buying power that developed markets do (Prahalad and Lieberthal 1998).

Disruptive innovations are typically simpler and are offered at a lower price (Govindarajan and Kopalle 2006; Christensen 1997). Creating products and services that are simple and affordable to low-income segments is crucial for adoption

Fig. 5.1 Links between Bottom of the Pyramid concept and disruptive innovation theory

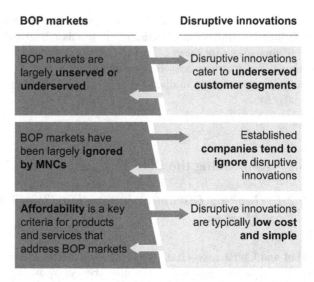

and success in the BOP (Prahalad 2004; Anderson and Billou 2007). Models created for the low-end can be profitably applied in the high-end as well (Hart 2010). Thus, scholars argue that products and services that succeed in BOP markets could be disruptive to dominant products and services in the higher-end of emerging markets as well as developed markets.

This section described the conceptual links between the BOP proposition and the disruptive innovation theory. Extending this line of thought, disruptive innovation theory can be an appropriate lens to examine this phenomenon. Further, empirical data from innovations for the BOP markets can also help to inform and enrich disruptive innovation theory.

5.2.2   How Frugal Innovations, Inclusive Innovations, Reverse Innovations, Gandhian Innovations and Disruptive Innovations are Interrelated

Following the success of the book 'Fortune at the Bottom of the Pyramid' and the establishment of the BOP concept by the scholar C. K. Prahalad, practitioner and academic interest increased in this field. The book included examples of several innovations—product, service, as well as business model innovations, which addressed low-income segments.

To describe this phenomenon, particularly to categorize the low-cost innovations emerging from the BOP or for the BOP, several terms have been coined. These concepts are 'reverse innovation' (Govindarajan and Trimble 2012; Immelt and Govindrajan 2009; Govindarajan and Ramamurti 2011), 'frugal innovation' (Tiwari and Herstatt 2012), 'jugaad innovation' (Radjou et al. 2012), 'Gandhian innovation' (Prahalad and Mashelkar 2010) and more recently 'inclusive innovation' (George et al. 2012). This section aims to clarify these concepts and explain how they are interrelated and also compare these concepts with disruptive innovation theory. In doing so, the works of the initiators of the concept (e.g., Govindarajan for Reverse Innovation) or those scholars who first published a definition for the phenomenon in academic literature was analyzed (e.g., Tiwari and Herstatt). This will contribute to elucidating these concepts, since they have similarities but little clarity exists on how they are interrelated.

The concept of reverse innovation was first described, using the case of GE Healthcare (Immelt and Govindrajan 2009). Govindarajan et al. use the term reverse innovation to describe this phenomenon of innovations first adopted in developing countries before being adopted by rich countries (Govindarajan and Ramamurti 2011). This reversal in diffusion of innovation, conventionally assumed to originate in developed countries, is the reason it is termed reverse innovation.

The concept of frugal innovation was popularized by a special report on 'innovations in the emerging markets' by the Economist. The magazine described the philosophy behind the development of frugal innovations—"Instead of adding ever more bells and whistles, they strip the products down to their bare essentials" (Economist 2010). Scholars Tiwari and Herstatt (2012) define frugal innovations as products or services aiming to reduce the total cost of ownership while providing 'good enough' quality by minimizing the use of resources along the complete value chain. A frequently cited example of frugal innovation is the car, Tata Nano. Another model discussed in literature, that is similar to frugal innovations is Resource Constrained Innovation (Ray and Ray 2010), which emphasizes labor-intensive, yet capital sensitive processes to develop affordable, functional products that are appropriate to the local environment.

The concept of jugaad innovation follows along these lines. 'Jugaad' is the Hindi term for a quick fix or improvisation. This concept also exists in other countries and can be translated to 'shanzhai' in Chinese (Sharma and Iyer 2012) and is associated with the more historical scholarly term from anthropology established by Lévi-Strauss, 'bricolage' (George et al. 2012), making do with what is at hand (Lévi-Strauss 1967). Authors Radjou et. al. have adopted this concept to illustrate an approach, that signifies a "unique way of thinking and acting in response to challenges" and "improvising solutions using simple means" (Radjou et al. 2012, p. 4). The authors also describe six principles that encompass this concept, to name a few, "do more with less" or "think and act flexibly". They also cite various examples related to jugaad, ranging from grassroots innovations (Gupta 2006; Praceus and Herstatt 2012) like the earthenware refrigerator to marketing innovations to classic frugal innovations like the Tata Nano (Radjou et al. 2012, p. 90).

Inclusive innovations or innovations for inclusive growth are "innovations that create or enhance opportunities to improve the wellbeing of those at the BOP" (George et al. 2012, p. 662). The emphasis in this case is the social impact towards the addressed market segment or the question of benefit. While low cost innovations like Narayana Hrudayalaya Heart hospital fall into the category, other social innovation practices like fair-trade are also considered examples of inclusive innovation because they affect the poor and the disenfranchised (George et al. 2012). Inclusive innovations can be considered a subset of social innovations, innovations aimed at solving 'societal problems' as poverty is one of many societal problems (Alvord et al. 2004).

Gandhian innovations is a term coined by Prahalad and Mashelkar to describe innovations emerging out of India, that "do more with fewer resources—for more people" (Prahalad and Mashelkar 2010). This concept emphasizes both the principles of affordability and frugality, like frugal innovations and that of inclusive growth, like inclusive innovations. It can thus be considered to be the intersection of frugal and inclusive innovations.

Table 5.1 shows how these terms are interrelated. The table lists the definition and the most frequently cited examples from above mentioned scholars to elucidate

Table 5.1 Key concepts related to Bottom of the Pyramid innovations

Name	Definition	Authors	Cited examples	Emphasis
Inclusive Innovation	"The development and implementation of new ideas, which aspire to create opportunities that enhance social and economic wellbeing for disenfranchised members of society"	George et al. (2012)	NH, Nestlé's nutrient fortified yogurt	Objective: Benefit to addressed market
Frugal Innovation	"They seek to minimize the use of material and financial resources in the complete value chain with the objective of reducing the cost of ownership while fulfilling or even exceeding certain pre-defined criteria of acceptable quality standards"	Tiwari and Herstatt (2012)	Tata Nano	Approach: Affordability and minimal use of resources
Jugaad Innovation	"A unique way of thinking and acting in response to challenges". Six principles of jugaad are: Seek opportunity in adversity, do more with less, think and act flexibly, keep it simple, include the margin, follow your heart.	Radjou et al. (2012)	Tata Nano, Ford Fiesta's marketing campaign	Approach: Improvising solutions with simple means
Reverse Innovation	"Where an innovation is adopted first in a poor country before being adopted in rich countries"	Govindarajan and Ramamurti (2011)	GE MAC400, NH	Locus: Country of first adoption
Gandhian Innovation	"How to do more with fewer resources—for more people"	Prahalad and Mashelkar (2010)	Aravind Eye Hospital, Tata Nano	Approach: Affordability and sustainability

these concepts. As shown in the table, each concept has a certain ontological emphasis.

How disruptive innovations fit into this picture is complex. Disruptive innovations that open up new markets can be considered inclusive innovations if they open up markets for non-consumers who could previously not afford the product or service and if it contributes to their well-being. Disruptive innovations also encompass the aspect of simplification and affordability like frugal innovations. Similarly, the aspect of "trickling up" to high-end markets is a characteristic that disruptive innovations share with reverse innovations. Reverse innovations that arise due to the income gap between developing and developed markets and seek affordable solutions may be disruptive. However, reverse innovations may emerge due to infrastructure gaps or sustainability gaps and these will not necessarily be disruptive (Govindarajan and Trimble 2009). So while these concepts do share aspects with disruptive innovations, they do not entirely overlap.

5.3 Empirical Context

This section provides a brief overview of the state of healthcare in India and the major challenges the country faces. This following section, elaborates on the two case studies AECS and NH.

5.3.1 Healthcare Challenges in India

Severe healthcare challenges burden developing countries like India, especially the country's poor. Creating access, improving availability and providing affordable quality healthcare services to the poor are critical to making healthcare inclusive in India.

About 69 %[1] of the population in India lives in rural and semi-urban areas. Access to healthcare for these populations is very limited, since 66 % of hospital beds are based in urban areas (Aitken et al. 2013). Further, the doctor-to-population ratio in rural areas is six times lower than in cities. As a result there is a major gap between health service accessibility in rural and urban India (KPMG 2011).

India also has a severe lack of doctors (about 6 per 10,000 population vs. 33 per 10,000 in Germany (WHO 2006, p. 190)) and shortage of hospital beds, at a level far below WHO guidelines (Gudwani et al. 2012). India has only 0.7 hospital beds for every 1,000 patients, while the world average is 2.6 (Deloitte 2010).

Moreover, affordability of quality healthcare services is also a challenge. Public spending on healthcare is very low and India ranks 171st in the world for public

---

[1] Source: India Census 2011.

healthcare spending as a percentage of GDP (Mullan 2006). Public hospitals that offer services for the poor are of low quality, typically understaffed and underfinanced (Gudwani et al. 2012). Lack of health insurance also results in high levels (over 70 %) of out-of-pocket health-care expenditure (Sherawat and Rao 2012). Often families become indebted if a member is hospitalized for long periods of time. Over 40 % of hospitalized Indians borrow heavily or sell assets to cover expenses and over 25 % of hospitalized Indians fall below the poverty line because of hospital expenses (NHRM 2005).

This urban focus and lack of affordable quality healthcare burdens India's poor disproportionately. Thus, there is an urgent need for developing inclusive models of healthcare for the poor in India (Balarajan et al. 2011).

5.3.2 Case Studies: Aravind Eye Care System and Narayana Hrudayalaya Hospitals

5.3.2.1 Introduction

Some hospitals in India are rising to the challenge of providing affordable healthcare to the poor. This section will describe innovations in healthcare delivery of two single specialty, low-cost hospitals, namely Aravind Eye Care hospital and Narayana Hrudayalaya.

The Aravind Eye Care System (AECS) is a network of ten hospitals in India, providing eye care to the poor. About half of the 370,000 surgeries performed in FY 2012–2013 were for free or at a steeply subsidized fee of about $10. In total AECS handled 3.1 million patients in FY 2012–2013 (AECS 2013).

AECS was setup by Dr. Venkataswamy in the late 70s with the mission to "eradicate needless blindness". It is still run mostly by Dr. Venkataswamy's family members, with the next generation now taking up leadership roles. Today, it is a concerted effort ranging from hospital management to consumables and equipment manufacturing to education and training. AECS is also working with other hospitals in India and around the world to help replicate the Aravind model. It is considered to be one of the largest eye-care hospitals and training centers for ophthalmologists in the world (Rangan and Thulasiraj 2007).

Narayana Hrudayalaya (NH) is a group of hospitals, headquartered in Bangalore, mainly focused on cardiac care and is most renowned for its world-class pediatric cardiac treatment unit. It was setup in 2001 by Dr. Devi Shetty in a mission to bring affordable healthcare to the masses. Since then NH has expanded to several cities, including tier-2 cities within India. Through a series of process innovations and leveraging its economies of scale, NH has managed to drive down the cost of an open-heart surgery (OHS) to about $2,000 (Khanna et al. 2005), which is a fraction of what a similar procedure in the USA would cost.

Driven by its mission, NH is striving to set new records for low-cost healthcare. In Mysore, a tier-2 city in India, NH has setup a new hospital that is said to set a new record for low-cost hospital construction in the industry. NH is taking its learnings to the developed world by launching a multi-specialty hospital in the Cayman Islands to serve locals in the region as well as under-insured Americans at a lower cost.

AECS and NH employ a range of strategies to bring down their cost and serve the poor profitably:

High Volumes and Operational Efficiency
AECS performed 3.1 million outpatient visits and 370,000 surgeries in the fiscal year 2012–2013 (AECS 2013). Such large volumes are generated mainly due to the large number of outreach camps that AECS organizes with the help of its partners such as Lion's Club and Rotary Club in districts around the state of Tamil Nadu. In each camp, thousands of patients are screened and those requiring further treatment, e.g., cataract surgery are brought to the closest AECS eye hospital.

At the hospital, patients are prepared in an "assembly line" fashion for the medical procedure (only for uncomplicated procedures like cataract surgery). Most of the preparatory work is done by trained nurses and assistants so that the surgeon concentrates on the most important steps of the surgery alone. As the surgeon is about to finish one surgery, the next patient is prepared and readied for surgery. This takes place in surgery halls with two or three beds that allow for fast movement.

This way of working ensures extremely high productivity of surgeons and a high utilization of medical equipment, which together entail a large portion of surgery costs. A surgeon at AECS performs five times the number of surgeries as a typical Indian ophthalmologist (Vickers and Rossen 2011).

Similarly NH is one of the largest hospitals focusing on cardiac care in the world. It seeks patients through its wide network of partner clinics connected through telemedicine facilities. This brings the per-patient costs down tremendously by increasing surgeon productivity and utilization of capital equipment. As Dr. Devi Shetty, the founder and Chairman of Narayan Hrudayalaya described the advantages of their scale:

> By doing more operations your result gets better, cost goes down, more people will be trained, and so when we scale up our operations we have got enough people trained to build new hospitals.
> (Interview 1A)

Clinical Efficacy
AECS and NH achieve lower costs by compromising on comfort (e.g., with shared rooms). However, they do not compromise on the quality of treatment—AECS has proven to have same if not better success rates compared to UK hospitals (Mashelkar and Borde 2010). Similar NH's quality is comparable with US based hospitals, measured in mortality rates with 30 days of surgery – NH hospitals have an average of 1.4 compared to US average of 1.9 (Govindarajan and Trimble 2012).

Narrow Clinical Focus
The narrow focus allows AECS and NH to specialize and streamline operations. The focus also hones expertise and allows doctors to specialize in rare and complex

operations. Even uncommon conditions are seen relatively often because of the large volume of patients. For instance, NH has experts who have performed the largest number of rare and complicated pediatric cardiac procedures in the world (Khanna et al. 2005).

Tiered-Pricing
Both NH and AECS are financially sustainable. In the Aravind model about 50 % of the paying patients subsidize the other half. Paying patients receive more comfortable treatment, e.g., private rooms and beds vs. shared dorms and floor mats and are charged slightly lower than market rates for their surgeries. However, the treatment remains the same, i.e., the same surgeons provide the same treatment to patients irrespective of their fees.

NH charges the majority of its patients rates that are lower than comparable Indian hospitals. Subsidized patients pay about $1,000 for an Open Heart Surgery (OHS) as compared to four times the amount in a comparable Indian hospital. NH charges its paying patients about $1,900 for the OHS procedure, which can cost over $ 40,000 in the United States (Khanna et al. 2005).

5.3.2.2   Innovation Capacity

AECS and NH have been scrutinized by various researchers through case studies (Rangan and Thulasiraj 2007; Khanna et al. 2005; Ibrahim et al. 2006; Prahalad and Hart 2002). Most case studies have focused on process innovation and the social impact of these hospital chains. During my interviews and field trips, we focused on the disruptive nature of their innovations as well as other innovations beyond process innovations that these two companies have spawned. Two aspects are highlighted below, namely, the innovative models these companies have implemented to reach their customers and product innovations these companies have developed themselves or co-created with partners.

New Models to Reach Customers

The mission of both NH and AECS is to provide quality healthcare access to the poor. They leverage economies of scale to bring down costs and thus serve the poor profitably. In order to attract a large number of patients, these hospital chains have formed innovative partnerships and models.

NH has created a microinsurance scheme with the State Government that covers surgeries in particular hospitals in the region of Karnataka. Farmers who are part of the co-operative, pay a premium of about $2 per year, which is then partially backed by the State Government of Karnataka (Maheshwari and Kiran 2009). This insurance model is innovative because it is a community based scheme and also a private public partnership (Kuruvilla et al. 2005). About one third of the hospital's patients are insured under this scheme (Anand 2009).

AECS partners with NGOs to organize remote rural screening camps. AECS and its partners send doctors and medical staff to villages to screen the elderly and young children. Those diagnosed with issues are brought to the nearest Aravind hospital. Their food and transportation is covered. This mode of community outreach has succeeded in removing barriers to affordable eye care (Natchiar et al. 1994). Through such camps AECS has been able to reach about 3.1 million patients in FY 2011–2012, continuously increasing the number of patients screened over the last decade (AECS 2013). AECS has also created a series of vision centers in remote areas that are permanent structures. They are connected to AECS hospitals via telemedicine facilities and a self-developed software for tele-ophthalmology (Bai et al. 2007).

These new models for attracting patients contribute to the success of the specialty, high volume business models of AECS and NH.

Product and Business Model Innovations

Through partnerships and through own development efforts, these companies have developed several innovations that have contributed to the cost-effectiveness of their procedures and helped in fulfilling their mission to bring affordable healthcare to the poor.

Product Innovations

AECS—Aurolab Aurolab was formed in 1992 with the aim of creating low-cost Intra-Ocular Lenses (IOLs). Before Aurolab, AECS depended on leading IOL manufacturers who would give them IOLs as charity. This was AECS's main bottleneck to scale. Aurolab brought down the cost of hard IOLs from $100 to about $5 (Ibrahim et al. 2006). Today Aurolab produces several types of IOLs, even sophisticated variants that only one or two other players in the world produce. It sells IOLs to 120 countries and has a world market share by size of about 10 %. It sells large volumes to NGOs, such as Christoffel Blinden Mission, and has thus opened up a new market for IOLs for charitable eye-care for the poor (Bhandari et al. 2008).

Aurolab is also one of the largest ophthalmological equipment suppliers in India. They have diversified into sutures, blades, pharmaceuticals and also equipment like laser photocoagulators. Aurolab products are CE and FDA certified and it also has ISO certification for its facilities.

Aurolab prioritizes investments into research and development (R&D) for new products by looking at the commercial aspect as well as the social impact of the innovations, i.e., which equipment/consumable is currently very expensive for AECS and how the cost could be driven down. Its close relationship with AECS enables it to leverage AECS's doctors both formally (in form of clinical workshops) as well as informally to come up with new ideas and identify new needs. As the CEO of Aurolab described this cooperation:

Usually it is based on some formal or informal interaction or when the doctor has some idea, usually they call us in to discuss and when we come up with some product ideas we take it to the doctors and then discuss with the doctors who are closely associated with that kind of product.
(Interview 1D)

AECS—Anti-fungal eye drops AECS's doctors encountered several patients from rural areas suffering from severe fungal eye infections. They were typically farmers growing certain crops like onions that required large doses of pesticide. Fungal eye infections are not common in developed countries; therefore, no appropriate medication was available on the market. AECS's doctors formulated a medication in form of an eye drop using medication for treating skin fungal infections. Thus, they created an off-label drug from dermatology in eye drop form. This solution was then taken up by Aurolab and rigorously tested. Aurolab then brought the eye drop for fungal infection, Vozole, into the market. This drug also does not require refrigeration. It is now sold all across India.

AECS—Low-cost retinal cameras In the rounds through AECS one notices several instances of retinal cameras that are built using ordinary digital cameras attached to the bodies of older models of ophthalmological equipment.

AECS has also tweaked an ordinary digital camera to operate as a stand-alone retinal camera, which they use in their telemedicine facilities for remote locations.

AECS—Forus Health Forus Health is a startup from Bangalore, which has, together with AECS, created an ophthalmology pre-screening device, 3nethra. This is a multi-functional imaging system that costs significantly less than similar devices in the market. The equipment is also designed to be portable (to be able to carry it to screening camps in remote regions) and to be easy to operate. It can be used to detect five major ailments that constitute about 90 % causes of blindness. It is also designed as a potential solution to the dearth of ophthalmologists in India.

Forus Health was founded by two engineers who were working for the Philips Innovation Center in Bangalore. As part of Philip's strategy to develop products for the emerging markets, Philips organized workshops with key local players and AECS was one of them. The idea to create a low-cost ophthalmological screening device was born while the founders were still at Philips. Philips showed initial interest, even flying down key executives from Netherlands to meet AECS in Madurai. However, despite the initial enthusiasm, the idea did not gain sufficient traction within Philips. As the founder of Forus Health put it:

So Philips obviously was working on very high end modalities. . .it's understandable that they may not want to start something in a space especially in India where we don't even know whether this will sell or not. . .So for whatever reason, it [the idea of co-developing a low cost ophthalmological screening device with AECS] slowly died
(Interview 1F)

The founders, still very motivated by AECS and with 'the urge to do something for the eradication for avoidable blindness', quit Philips and founded their own company. They are now primarily selling different versions of the pre-screening device 3nethra.

NH—Low-cost hospital constructions NH has setup a low cost hospital in the city of Mysore, a tier-2 city close to Bangalore. The aim of this hospital was to reimagine the construction of a hospital and to optimize on both the cost of the structure and the time for setting it up. The initial capex (capital expenditure) to construct a hospital and the operational fixed cost to run a hospital contribute heavily to the overall cost. In order to bring down these costs and pass on the benefit to patients, Dr. Shetty conceived a frugal hospital construction. The hospital in Mysore is constructed using prefabricated structures and light-roof construction. Further, the hospital also uses natural ventilation and restricts the use of air conditioning only to critical rooms like the Intensive Care Unit. The single-storey construction avoids the use of expensive concrete and steel structures and uses light-roof construction with tiles.

While the idea for this design was conceived by Dr. Shetty, the design and construction was undertaken by the Indian engineering firm L&T. With this frugal construction, NH has achieved a cost of INR 2,400 per square feet vis-à-vis hospital construction with comparable quality of INR 3,300 square feet, a reduction of 30 % in capex costs. Also, the design of the hospital with minimum air conditioning and using natural airflow will help the hospital cut down its operating costs.

Besides the innovative construction, the low cost hospital project in Mysore boasts of an innovative care companion program. This program was conceived by Dr. Shetty and designed together with the Stanford University Design School. The program aims to involve family members in post-surgery recovery of the patient. During the pre-operation stage a family member of the patient undergoes a training program that teaches the person how to perform basic but time-intensive tasks, such as nursing a wound. With this program, the hospital not only ensures continuity of care for the patient but also lowers the workload on hospital staff.

Business Model Innovations

NH—Trimedx NH has entered into a joint venture (JV) with Trimedx with the aim to increase the lifecycle of expensive medical equipment. Trimedx is a subsidiary of USA-based Ascension Health and specializes in helping hospitals reduce expenses and maximizing utilization of medical equipment. Ascension Health is the third largest USA-based non-profit health system focused on giving quality healthcare for the underserved.

The vice president responsible for this partnership from NH described this cooperation:

> Running a hospital is a very capital intensive service. We incur huge expenditures on medical equipment, about 50% of our capital expenditure is dedicated to equipment and building. These equipment also result in high maintenance costs. Spare parts for the machines are not available in the open market and biomedical companies also refuse to service equipment that is older than a few years. This way they force obsolescence. This also results in high service costs and high operational expenditure...
>
> Our aim with the partnership with Trimedx is to start a new standard. We will service equipment independent of the maker. We will use their resources and knowledge to source

products from South-East Asia, China—[these can be] spare parts or also cost-effective equipment.
(Interview 1G)

5.4 Analysis

5.4.1 How Are Low-cost Specialty Hospital Chains Potentially Disruptive?

Christensen and other colleagues have applied the disruptive innovation model to various industries, including healthcare (Christensen et al. 2000). Their research showed that innovations in healthcare have primarily been sustaining, i.e., helping doctors and hospitals solve ever more complex problems (Hwang and Christensen 2008). The healthcare sector in developed markets has not focused on affordability and simplicity, and this is considered one of the key factors in the rising healthcare costs in the USA and other developed countries (Smith et al. 2009; Howitt et al. 2012). Further, several procedures are so expensive, that they are out of reach for billions of people living in low and middle income countries. An industry that overshoots customer requirements is typically ripe for disruptive innovations (Christensen 1997). Christensen and colleagues claim this is the case for the healthcare industry (Christensen et al. 2000). A business model innovation, they believe, that can potentially disrupt the current market are focused care centers. Because single specialty hospitals concentrate on one procedure alone, they typically have lower costs compared to general hospitals and can also charge for outcome as opposed to a fee-for-service model (Hwang and Christensen 2008). Christensen, thus, considers specialty hospitals to be a disruptive innovation (Christensen et al. 2009).

The low-cost focused models of AECS and NH have been able to treat millions of patients who would otherwise not have any access to treatment. This is the hallmark of new market disruptive innovations (Christensen and Raynor 2003).

Table 5.2 captures the disruptive characteristics of these low cost hospital chains. AECS and NH have most of the characteristics of disruptive innovations, as can be seen in the table. The only criteria not satisfied is whether the existing market is "disrupted". This point warrants a deeper look.

To recap from disruptive innovation theory, the seminal work on the rigid disk drive industry by Christensen showed how disruptive "technology" replaced the previous generation of technology through several generations studied by him (Christensen 1993). In this case, success of disruption was defined as replacement of existing technology and in these cases the incumbent ran the risk of being completely ousted from the market.

However, as the definition of disruptive "innovation" came to include business models like budget airlines and discount retailers, disruption cannot be considered as a "replacement". Discount retailers and budget airlines have gained significant

Table 5.2 Disruptive characteristics of low-cost specialty hospital chains

No.	Characteristic	Type of disruptive innovation	Applicability to low-cost, focused hospitals
1	The disruptive innovation initially underperforms on the performance attribute valued by mainstream customers	All	Yes. Low-cost specialty hospitals focus on just one ailment and cannot solve complex health issues like general hospitals
2	The disruptive innovation, however, has features that are valued by fringe or new customers and introduces a new performance criteria	All	Yes, affordability is a feature valued by BOP customers
2a	A disruptive innovation can create new markets, as it attracts people who previously lacked the resources or skills to use it	New-market	Yes, many poor people are treated by NH and AECS who would otherwise have not been able to access quality healthcare
2b	A disruptive innovation is typically simpler and lower cost	New market, Low-end	Yes, AECS and NH offer treatment to the poor at a substantially lower cost
2c	A disruptive innovation can involve radical technology and attract high-end customers	High-end	No
3	Generally mainstream customers do not initially value these additional features and thus the disruptive innovation is commercialized in emerging markets	All	Affordability is not the main criteria in developed markets as healthcare costs are typically not borne by end-customer
4	The disruptive innovation is financially unattractive for leading incumbents to pursue	All	Yes, incumbents would not focus on treating many patients at cost or for free
5	The disruptive innovation steadily improves in performance and attracts mainstream customers to it; either it improves along the main performance attribute or market preferences shift towards the newly introduced performance attribute	All	Yes, Aravind model is being replicated in other countries and attracting mid and high income customers in the local market. NH is expanding to serve underinsured patients in the USA and Caribbean through its Cayman Island facility
6	The disruptive innovation takes significant share of the mainstream market	All	To be determined. Low-cost specialty hospitals are significant trend in Indian market but not outside India

market share in their respective industries, but have not completely replaced the original model. Thus, Markides argues that disruptive innovations are considered "disruptive" when they take over a significant market share from incumbents (Markides 2006).

There is evidence that the two low-cost specialty hospitals are moving up in the market and gaining market share:

- In India: AECS and NH are attracting mid and high income customers within India. AECS is now considered to be the largest provider of eye care services and trainer of eye care personnel in the world (Rangan and Thulasiraj 2007). It has proven to have world-class quality and has been awarded numerous awards, most recently the FICCI award for India's best private hospital.

  Single specialty hospitals have become a major trend in India, as they hold several advantages – they offer more affordable services and incur lower investments to set up (D'Souza 2012). Several other low cost single specialty hospital chains have come up in the previous decade, which focus on different areas, such as Lifespring for maternal care. Industry experts expect the number of such single specialty hospitals to grow and expect these to bridge the gap in affordable quality healthcare (KPMG 2011).

- Other developing countries: Medical tourism, where people travel outside their home country to seek medical services (Turner 2010), is growing at NH. NH is not only attracting low and middle income Indian patients to seek treatment in its centers because of it reputed and highly experienced doctors, but also attracts customers from abroad. These are typically patients from developing countries and the Middle East, where quality medical treatment is unavailable.

  Similarly AECS has setup a consultation and capacity building arm called LAICO and brought the Aravind model to over 230 eye hospitals in India and in other developing countries such as Egypt, China and Tanzania. LAICO's consultancy services to replicate parts or the entire AECS model has helped its partner hospitals increase their productivity and decrease their costs (Bhandari et al. 2008).

- Developed markets: NH has setup a health center in Cayman Islands to serve locals and under-insured American citizens. This could be potentially disruptive to the healthcare delivery systems in the USA. But, there remains the question whether low-cost specialty hospitals can gain significant market share in developed markets, where regulatory restrictions and entrenched value networks may restrict them (Christensen et al. 2009).

The aim of these low-cost specialty hospitals is to bring quality healthcare to the poor who are otherwise "non-consumers". The establishment and expansion of the low-cost specialty model is creating a market for quality healthcare at the BOP, a market that is otherwise underserved or unserved.

This could be pointed out as one major difference between disruptive innovations emerging in developed markets and those from the BOP. In developed markets, success of disruptive innovations could be defined as gaining significant market share in "mainstream" markets. In case of disruptive innovations from the BOP, question remains how the "mainstream" market is defined, particularly whether the mainstream market is the local (Indian) market, similar (India like countries) markets or even global markets. It can be argued that the former would suffice because these markets in themselves are of significant size. Further, breaking through or disrupting mainstream markets in developed countries might be very challenging due to several reasons, e.g., regulatory frameworks (in case of healthcare).

Thus, it can be argued that innovations in the BOP context could be considered disruptive if they create access to non-consumers, like new market disruptive innovations. In addition to this, the "disruptiveness" could be driven by a significant gain in market share in the local mainstream market or by shaping the market substantially.

Disruptive innovations are considered challenging for incumbents because established firms run the risk of losing market share to disrupting technologies and business models. In line with the argument above, in case of disruptive innovations in the BOP context, the risk could lie in losing market share but also in failing to capture new opportunities in the emerging BOP segment.

There is another point worth noting with respect to the differences in disruptive innovations that emerged in developed countries vs. those emerging from BOP markets. In developed markets, disruptive innovations introduce several secondary performance attributes such as portability, ease of use and widening of the application (Christensen 1997). Yu and Hang (2011) offer a comprehensive study exploring different disruptive innovations. Their research shows that cost-reduction is one of the secondary performance attribute of disruptive innovations from developed countries, but not the only one. In contrast, disruptive innovations for the BOP create new markets primarily because of the significant reduction in price that gives access to large number of people who previously could not afford the product. Other attributes also play a role, such as fit to the local environment, but the decrease in cost is a primary factor.

Thus, while the question remains whether low-cost specialty hospitals in secondary care can gain significant market share of the global market, there is already substantial evidence that these two hospitals are creating new markets at the BOP and similar low-cost specialty models in secondary and tertiary care is expanding in India and shaping the market for affordable healthcare (KPMG 2011). Thus, the two hospital chains and the model of low-cost specialty hospitals can be considered disruptive in the BOP context.

5.4.2 What are the Drivers of Their Innovations?

5.4.2.1 Drivers of Innovation Capacity

NH and AECS have gone beyond optimizing their processes to achieve quality healthcare at a low cost. As shown in Sect. 5.3.2, these two companies have created several product and business model innovations on their own or with partners. There are three main drivers of their innovation capacity.

1. Extreme Need for Cost-effectiveness
The main mission of these two hospital chains is bringing affordable healthcare to the masses. The large number of procedures done for free or at steeply subsidized

rates creates an extreme need for cost-effectiveness and efficiency, which in turn drives these companies to innovate at different levels.

AECS founded Aurolab in order to manufacture low cost IOLs, which enabled it to scale. NH and AECS are cooperating with different companies with the objective of making healthcare more cost-effective. AECS has cooperated with Forus Health to develop a low-cost fundus camera; similarly the cooperation between NH and Trimedx has led to the creation of a new business model with Trimedx.

These cooperations were based on the joint vision to make healthcare more affordable, as supported by the following quote by the founder of Forus Health:

> With Aravind we had a lot of brainstorming on the overall concept of screening device for five major eye problems and all well debated, discussed and finalized and approved because they [AECS doctors] were the authorities. ... I think the philosophy behind Forus, they [AECS] have been the biggest inspiration.
> (Interview 1F)

2. Clinical Volumes

These two hospitals have some of the largest volumes of patients in the world. This makes AECS and NH's doctors specialists in some areas. For instance NH performed twice the number of cardiac surgeries compared to the largest US hospital in 2008. It is also considered the largest pediatric cardiac hospital in the world (Anand 2009). Doctors at such large specialty hospitals may even encounter rare diseases at unprecedented rates because of the large number of patients they treat.

This advantage is mirrored in a comment by the CEO of Aurolab.

> I think one of the things which makes them unique.. they see quite a large volume of patients, they see a wide range of diseases and pathologies because of the volume, because of the scale
> (Interview 1D)

This also leads to a large amount of data, which can be useful for testing equipment and drugs. The founder of Forus mentioned this as one of the main reasons for developing the equipment in partnership with AECS.

> I go every two months to Aravind. Collect all the images they have taken using my equipment and go back and find out what was the diagnosis they did against that and then run my auto algorithms
> ...And then during the product development stage... on the clinical side, how to read a retina image, how to read a cornea image, how to write the auto algorithms, the collaboration with Aravind management helped greatly, whether it's Dr. Kim or Dr. Krishna Das. They were the ones who actually guided us to develop our auto analysis algorithms.
> (Interview 1F)

3. BOP-Specific Knowledge

Since these hospitals have been focusing on poor patients and working in a resource-constrained setting for several years, they have gained vast BOP market-specific knowledge.

For instance, it was a doctor at AECS who spotted the need for anti-fungal eye drops, when he identified several such cases among his patients and then developed a solution for it. Aurolab took this solution, extensively tested it and introduced it to the market.

The procurement team of NH has an in-depth understanding of making medical equipment function in their setting (with poor infrastructure and for such large volumes). They have extensive knowledge on spare part sourcing and design of equipment, especially with respect to wear and tear of parts. This is another reason why they are resourceful partners in the Trimedx JV. As the vice president responsible for this JV mentioned:

> There is a strong biomedical team at NH. We have very good knowledge about purchasing, especially in the Indian biomedical landscape. We also have a strong supply chain in place of sourcing local spare parts... Our procurement head Dr. Milind also has in depth knowledge of equipment, like which parts wear off faster and how to fix these parts.
> (Interview 1G)

5.4.2.2 Value Network Explanation for Innovation Capacity

As established in the previous section, several key characteristics of disruptive innovation theory apply to these low-cost specialty hospital chains and they can be deemed disruptive in the BOP context. In this section, another aspect of disruptive innovation theory is applied to the cases. As described in Sect. 5.3.2.2, these hospitals were responsible for spawning several innovations beyond their core processes. This phenomenon is explored through the disruptive innovation lens.

One key aspect of disruptive innovations is that they emerge in new value networks. A value network is defined as the collection of upstream suppliers, downstream channels to market, and ancillary providers that support a common business model within an industry (Christensen 1997).

Christensen describes the concept of value networks to explain the rise of disruptive innovations (Christensen and Rosenbloom 1995). Value networks are the context in which a company creates value for its customers constituting other stakeholders upstream as well as downstream. Companies do not only innovate depending on their capabilities or their organization, but also depending on what is relevant for their value network (Christensen and Rosenbloom 1995).

These low cost hospitals are creating new value networks for affordable healthcare by creating new downstream channels and partnering with companies with mutually compatible models. The business model of these two low cost hospital chains functions on volumes. To create large customer demand from low-income segments, these companies have established new and innovative downstream channels, namely the micro-insurance schemes and the rural screening camps.

These hospitals also established companies or partnered with companies with similar missions. Due to a lack of solutions outside, AECS started innovating on its own to create low cost consumables and equipment by establishing Aurolab. Similarly AECS worked with Forus to co-develop a low cost fundus camera.

Forus was inspired by AECS and was founded on the same principle of eradicating needless blindness by making eye care more affordable. Similarly, the partnership between NH and Trimedx was founded on the mutual vision of making healthcare affordable.

The vice president responsible for the partnership between NH and Trimedx commented about why these two companies came together:

> [It was] mostly because there is a philosophical match with Narayana Hrudayalaya. Trimedx has a mission to bring low-cost healthcare to people and also has a philanthropic arm.
> (Interview 1G)

Companies like NH and AECS, with their focused, low-cost approach, are introducing new attributes, namely extreme affordability in the healthcare value network. The current ecosystem of healthcare in developed countries focuses on comfort and complexity, but not on cost-effectiveness (Christensen et al. 2000). There are indeed very few examples of for-profit companies focusing on providing quality healthcare to the poor as a target group. Thus, NH and AECS are creating a new kind of value network based on making quality healthcare extremely afford-able and are innovating within this new value network.

5.4.3   Short Excursus: Reflections on the Lead User Characteristics of AECS and NH

NH and AECS have been forced to innovate beyond their realm to deliver cost-effective quality healthcare. They have done so by themselves or in cooperation with others. NH and AECS's doctors are intermediate users of many of these innovations, like the fungal drops or IOLs. In several industries, users have been identified as a critical source of innovation (Von Hippel 1994). There will be a brief digression from the main research question to look at the cases from the user innovation theory perspective.

Scholars have shown that users innovate because they have needs that are "sticky", i.e., difficult to transfer (Von Hippel 1994) or because they expect to benefit from these innovations (Von Hippel 2003; Herstatt and Von Hippel 1992). Users benefit in different ways from their innovations: while user firms have shown to build competitive advantages from their innovations (Von Hippel 1986), indi-vidual users have shown to benefit from using their innovations (Lüthje and Herstatt 2004), by selling them, by financially benefiting from them indirectly or even simply enjoying the process of innovation (Bogers et al. 2010). Von Hippel also argued that the actor (user or producer) who expects to benefit most from the innovation will be the locus of innovation (Von Hippel 1982).

Several studies have demonstrated the role of physicians, as intermediate users, in developing products and to some extent commercializing them (Von Hippel et al. 1999; Lettl et al. 2006). Studies have also looked at the role of clinicians in developing off-label drugs (DeMonaco et al. 2006).

The early recognition of this user innovation phenomenon, resulted in Von Hippel (1978) formulating the approach of "Customer-Active Paradigm" (CAP) in which a customer develops a product idea and initiates the transfer of the idea to the producer. The Lead User theory extended this by calling on producers to proactively involve Lead Users in their innovation process to develop breakthrough products as they are on the leading edge and are qualified and motivated to work with firms (Lüthje and Herstatt 2004; Von Hippel 1986; Herstatt and Von Hippel 1992).

Lead Users demonstrate two key characteristics that differentiate them from ordinary users (Lüthje and Herstatt 2004):

1. Capability: Lead Users face new needs earlier than the majority of the customers in a market segment
2. Motivation: Lead Users benefit from the innovations that provide a solution to their needs

An important and current trend in healthcare is towards affordability, in order to contain soaring medical costs (Feldstein 2011). AECS and NH's doctors have served large numbers of poor patients profitably by continuously striving to bring costs of procedures down for many years. Thus, they are ahead of this trend. In addition to this, they are regarded as the best specialists in the country. These capabilities qualify their Lead User capabilities further (Lettl et al. 2006). They can also be considered extreme users as they perform many more procedures than average surgeons. It has been argued that extreme users show lead user characteristics (Lilien et al. 2002).

These companies benefit from incurring lower costs and these doctors also benefit from addressing problems encountered by them. However, the driving force behind this is competitive advantage in terms of cost, in order to further their mission in bringing affordable healthcare to the poor. Their extreme need for cost-effective solutions and their ability to innovate make these companies Lead Users in their fields.

Aurolab exploits the close relationship with AECS to integrate doctors at AECS as Lead Users in the innovation process. Aurolab's product developers regularly interact with AECS's doctors in formal and informal ways to extract ideas. Aurolab's employees attend conferences and seminars organized by AECS's physicians or research teams. Similarly, AECS's doctors play an active role in Aurolab's innovation process, be it at the conceptualization or testing phase.

The main source of new product ideas and solutions that Aurolab brings out are AECS's doctors because of their close relationship. As the CEO of Aurolab said about this cooperation:

> Usually Aravind's doctors look at a large number of patients and they are also aware of, you know, the economic constraints, which people have. . . So when they see that something is really useful then they look at how that can be done in an alternate way through a less expensive product or process and they tell us to try it.
>
> (Interview 1C)

Or similarly:

So these ideas of cost reduction . . .. mostly they come based on their [Aravind's doctors'] need to make something available to the patient at a much lower price. So we have developed many products like that in the last three or four years where those products are specifically made because we had very strong request from Aravind's surgeons.
   (Interview 1D)

To summarize, this section briefly digressed to highlight the Lead User characteristics of Aravind and NH. These characteristics have made them a source of innovations for other companies and also made them innovators in their own right.

5.4.4   Why is BOP an Appropriate Context for Disruptive Innovations?

The previous sections explored the disruptive potential of two low cost hospital chains emerging from India and drivers of their innovation capacity. The healthcare sector in India presents unique challenges and opportunities. The lack of healthcare personnel and infrastructure as well as the low paying capacity of patients forces players delivering healthcare to the masses to be innovative. We have seen the examples of AECS and NH, who have, through a series of process and business model innovations, established themselves as low cost specialty hospitals serving the BOP.

NH and AECS have enabled millions of patients to be diagnosed and treated by making medical procedures more affordable − hallmarks of new market disruptive innovations. NH's move up the market is also evidence of disruption. However, the question does remain whether these innovations will disrupt developed markets.

These hospital chains have also been the locus of frugal product and business model innovations. They have created these innovations on their own (e.g., through vertical integration) or in collaboration with other companies. Hence, they can also be considered Lead Users for low cost or frugal innovations. The drivers behind their innovation capabilities were their extreme need for cost-effectiveness, the vast numbers of patients they treat as well as their BOP-specific knowledge.

Analyzing the primary subjects as well as these innovations has given us insight into why BOP is a rich context for disruptive innovations. The BOP segment consists of the lowest socio-economic segment in the world, defined as individuals earning less than about $ 8 per day. Average GDP per capita in countries like India is about 15 times less than that of developed countries like the USA. Thus, individuals in the BOP segment have limited financial resources and affordability is a key characteristic of products and services developed for individuals at the BOP.

Companies serving the BOP, like NH and AECS, continually strive to become ever more cost effective. Their aim to develop affordable solutions for BOP customers, who otherwise would not have access to quality healthcare, gives them incentives to continually innovate to bring down costs of their procedures. As shown in the examples above, they do so on their own or with external partners. Many of these innovations, which make services and products accessible to those who previously could not afford it, are potentially disruptive.

This quote by the current managing director of AECS, Dr. Aravind Srinivisan, in an external interview, summarizes this point well:

> In my experience, innovation does not come from abundance, it comes from scarcity. The large population we serve is spurring us to think innovatively and do things innovatively.
>   (Vickers and Rossen 2011)

Thus, these cases demonstrate how the resource constraints of the BOP market drive players addressing these markets to develop disruptive innovations.

Basic services like quality healthcare for the poor are, to a large extent, not met by public institutions. Government hospitals fail to provide quality healthcare, which leads to individuals seeking care from private players. Moreover, private institutions have failed to cater to the needs of large parts of the world population for many years (Prahalad and Lieberthal 1998). Especially in the pharmaceutical industry, the underinvestment in research for tropical diseases is a well-known case of market failure (Trouiller et al. 2002). This is what led AECS to develop a drug for BOP-specific diseases they encountered. Millions of patients were granted access to quality healthcare by players like AECS and NH, who would have otherwise not had resources to seek treatment.

Several studies have shown how basic needs for the BOP in areas outside healthcare such as sanitation, housing, food, etc. also go unmet (Pedro Olinto et al. 2013; Hammond 2010). Addressing non-consumers and underserved consumers with simple and affordable products that have 'good enough' quality is the basic premise of new market disruptive innovations (Christensen and Raynor 2003). These large unmet needs of the BOP also incentivize companies aiming to address these markets to innovate appropriately.

This quote by Dr. Devi Shetty, the chairman of Narayana Hrudayalaya, encapsulates this point:

> Necessity is the mother of invention. We need to do 2.5 million heart surgeries per year. And all the heart surgeons in the country put together perform about 130,000 heart surgeries a year, and the others die. So we have to do something.
>   (Militzer 2013)

These two characteristics of the BOP market incentivize companies addressing them to innovate towards low-cost, scalable innovations to reach the largely unserved or underserved segments or "non-consumers". This analysis leads to the formulated proposition below:

Proposition: Resource constraints and the large unmet needs of the BOP drive players addressing the BOP market to develop 'good enough' solutions through disruptive innovations.

5.5   Managerial Implications and Discussion

This chapter explored the links between the BOP concept and disruptive innovation theory. It also elaborated on the different concepts that are tangential to the BOP phenomenon, like frugal innovations, Gandhian innovations, etc. and described their interrelationships.

The focus of the chapter was the case studies of low-cost specialty hospitals, NH and AECS from India. The case studies highlighted how NH and AECS have been innovative because they have been forced to create new business models, products and services under immense resource constraints to meet the unserved needs of their target segment. These case studies show how the BOP markets' resource constraints and the large unserved needs of the market drive their innovative capacity for disruptive innovations. Thus, companies addressing the BOP market are well positioned to develop disruptive innovations as they fit the needs of the market.

Developed-market companies scouting for disruptive innovations could turn to the BOP markets or partner with local players serving BOP markets to co-develop disruptive innovations. This is especially salient in the domain of healthcare as a fundamental rethinking is needed in healthcare models in developed countries in order to make it more affordable (Feldstein 2011). Some insights for this rethinking could come from disruptive innovations emerging form BOP markets. For this, companies and policy makers in developed countries need to be attentive and learn from these innovations to address their rising cost of healthcare. Also companies can use BOP markets as test beds and labs to create disruptive innovations as they will be confronted with issues in resource constraint, institutional voids, etc. that will push their boundaries.

In line with recent research into lead markets (Tiwari and Herstatt 2012), the BOP market in India could be considered to be a lead markets for cost-effective innovations in the healthcare sector. This would have to be examined in more depth.

To sum up, this study embedded the BOP phenomenon into innovation management literature. The study helped to draw the conclusion that two characteristics of BOP markets, namely the resource constraints and the large unaddressed needs, make BOP markets an appropriate context for disruptive innovations. Disruptive innovations have the potential to make quality healthcare affordable to millions in countries like India. They could also offer alternate paradigms to tackle soaring healthcare costs in the West. Thus, this study echoes the recommendations of the Economist, in stating that global healthcare systems can "find inspiration" in BOP markets like India (Economist 2009).

References

AECS. (2013). *Activity report*. Madurai: Aravind Eye Care Systems.

Aitken, M., Backliwal, A., Chang, M., & Udeshi, A. (2013). *Understanding Healthcare Access in India: What is the current state?* Parsippany, NJ: IMS Institute.

Alvord, S., Brown, D. L., & Letts, C. W. (2004). Social entrepreneurship and societal transformation an exploratory study. *Journal of Applied Behavioral Science, 40*(3), 260–282.

Anand, G. (2009). The Henry Ford of heart surgery. *Wall Street Journal*.

Anderson, J., & Billou, N. (2007). Serving the World's Poor: Innovation at the base of the economic pyramid. *Journal of Business Strategy, 28*(2), 14–21.

Bai, V. T., Murali, V., Kim, R., & Srivatsa, S. K. (2007). Teleophthalmology-based rural eye care in India. *Telemedicine and e-Health, 13*(3), 313–321.

Balarajan, Y., Selvaraj, S., & Subramanian, S. V. (2011). Health care and equity in India. *The Lancet, 377*(9764), 505–515.

Bhandari, A., Dratler, S., Raube, K., & Thulasiraj, R. D. (2008). Specialty care systems: A pioneering vision for global health. *Health Affairs, 27*(4), 964–976.

Bogers, M., Afuah, A., & Bastian, B. (2010). Users as innovators: A review, critique, and future research directions. *Journal of Management, 36*(4), 857–875.

Bruton, G. D. (2010). Letter from the editor: Business and the World's poorest billion–the need for an expanded examination by management scholars. *The Academy of Management Perspectives, 24*(3), 6–10.

Christensen, C. M. (1993). The rigid disk drive industry: A history of commercial and technological turbulence. *Business History Review, 67*(04), 531–588.

Christensen, C. M. (1997). *The innovator's dilemma: When new technologies cause great firms to fail*. Boston: Harvard Business School Press.

Christensen, C. M. (2006). The ongoing process of building a theory of disruption. *Journal of Product Innovation Management, 23*(1), 39–55.

Christensen, C. M., Bohmer, R., & Kenagy, J. (2000). Will disruptive innovations cure health care? *Harvard Buisness Review, 78*(5), 102–112.

Christensen, C. M., & Bower, J. L. (1996). Customer power, strategic investment, and the failure of leading firms. *Strategic Management Journal, 17*(3), 197–218.

Christensen, C. M., Grossman, J. H., & Hwang, J. (2009). *The innovator's prescription: A disruptive solution for health care*. New York: McGraw-Hill.

Christensen, C. M., & Raynor, M. (2003). *The innovator's solution: Creating and sustaining successful growth*. Boston, MA: Harvard Business Press.

Christensen, C. M., & Rosenbloom, R. S. (1995). Explaining the attacker's advantage: Technological paradigms, organizational dynamics, and the value network. *Research Policy, 24*(2), 233–257.

D'Souza, N. (2012, April 13). Why single-speciality hospitals are Prospering. *Forbes India*.

Danneels, E. (2004). Disruptive technology reconsidered: A critique and research agenda. *Journal of Product Innovation Management, 21*, 246–258.

Deloitte. (2010). *Medical technology industry in India*. Deloitte and CII.

DeMonaco, H. J., Ali, A., & Hippel, E. (2006). The major role of clinicians in the discovery of off-label drug therapies. *Pharmacotherapy: The Journal of Human Pharmacology and Drug Therapy, 26*(3), 323–332.

Economist. (2009, April 18). Lessons from a frugal innovator. *The Economist*.

Economist. (2010). First break all the rules. *The Economist*.

Emmerson, C., Frayne, C., & Goodman, A. (2000). Pressures in UK Healthcare: Challenges for the NHS. *Institute for Fiscal Studies*.

Feldstein, P. J. (2011). *Health care economics*. Clifton Park, NY: Cengage Learning.

George, G., McGahan, A. M., & Prabhu, J. (2012). Innovation for inclusive growth: Towards a theoretical framework and a research agenda. *Journal of Management Studies, 49*(4), 661–683.

Govindarajan, V., & Kopalle, P. K. (2006). The usefulness of measuring disruptiveness of innovations ex post in making ex ante prediction. *Journal of Product Innovation Management, 23*(1), 12–18.

Govindarajan, V., & Ramamurti, R. (2011). Reverse innovation, emerging markets, and global strategy. *Global Strategy Journal, 1*(3–4), 191–205.

Govindarajan, V., & Trimble, C. (2009). *Is reverse innovation like disruptive innovation?* Harvard Business Review Blog Network.

Govindarajan, V., & Trimble, C. (2012). *Reverse innovation: Create far from home, win everywhere.* Boston, MA: Harvard Business School Press.

Gudwani, A., Mitra, P., Puri, A., & Vaidya, M. (2012). *India Healthcare: Inspiring possibilities, challenging journey.* New York: McKinsey & company.

Gupta, A. K. (2006). From sink to source: The Honey Bee Network documents indigenous knowledge and innovations in India. *Innovations: Technology, Governance, Globalization, 1* (3), 49–66.

Hammond, A. (2010). *The next 4 billion: Market size and business strategy at the base of the pyramid.* Washington, DC: World Resource Institute.

Hang, C.-C., Chen, J., & Subramian, A. M. (2010). Developing disruptive products for emerging economies: Lessons from Asian cases. *Research-Technology Management, 53*(4), 21–26.

Hart, S. (2010). Taking the green leap to the base of the pyramid. In T. London & S. Hart (Eds.), *Next generation business strategies for the base of the pyramid.* Upper Saddle River, NJ: Pearson Education, Inc.

Hart, S., & Christensen, C. (2002, Fall). The great leap. *MIT Sloan Managment Review.*

Herstatt, C., & Von Hippel, E. (1992). From experience: Developing new product concepts via the lead user method: A case study in a "low-tech" field. *Journal of Product Innovation Management, 9*(3), 213–221.

Howitt, P., Darzi, A., Yang, G.-Z., Ashrafian, H., Atun, R., Barlow, J., Blakemore, A., Bull, A. M. J., Car, J., & Conteh, L. (2012). Technologies for global health. *The Lancet, 380*(9840), 507–535.

Hwang, J., & Christensen, C. M. (2008). Disruptive innovation in health care delivery: A framework for business-model innovation. *Health Affairs, 27*(5), 1329–1335.

Ibrahim, M., Bhandari, A., Sandhu, J. S., & Balakrishnan, P. (2006). Making Sight Affordable (Part I): Aurolab Pioneers production of low-cost technology for cataract surgery. *Innovations, 1*(3), 25–41.

Immelt, J., & Govindrajan, V. (2009). How GE is disrupting itself. *Harvard Buisness Review, 87* (10), 56–65.

Jain, S. (2013). Frugal innovation and disruptive innovation theory. In L Toombs (ed.), *Academy of management conference 2013*, Lake Buena Vista, Florida, 2013. AOM.

Khanna, T., Kasturirangan, V., & Manocaran, M. (2005). *Narayana Hrudayalaya Heart Hospital: Cardiac care for the poor.* Boston, MA: Harvard Business School.

KPMG. (2011). *Emerging trends in healthcare—A journey from bench to bedside.* KPMG.

Kuruvilla, S., Liu, M., & Jacob, P. (2005). A case study of the Yeshasvini Health Insurance Scheme for the rural poor in India. *International Journal of Self Help and Self Care, 3*(3), 261–306.

Lettl, C., Herstatt, C., & Gemuenden, H. (2006). Users' contributions to radical innovation: Evidence from four cases in the field of medical equipment technology. *R&D Management, 36*(3), 251–272.

Lévi-Strauss, C. (1967). *The savage mind.* Chicago: University of Chicago Press.

Lilien, G. L., Morrison, P. D., Searls, K., Sonnack, M., & Von Hippel, E. (2002). Performance assessment of the lead user idea-generation process for new product development. *Management Science, 48*(8), 1042–1059.

London, T. (2007). *A base-of-the-pyramid perspective on poverty alleviation.* Ann Arbor, MI: William Davidson Institute.

Lüthje, C., & Herstatt, C. (2004). The Lead User method: An outline of empirical findings and issues for future research. *R&D Management, 34*(5), 553–568.

Maheshwari, S., & Kiran, V. S. (2009). Cardiac care for the economically challenged: What are the options? *Annals of Pediatric Cardiology, 2*(1), 91–94.

Markides, C. (2006). Disruptive innovation: In need of better theory. *Journal of Product Innovation Management, 23*(1), 19–25.

Mashelkar, R., & Borde, S. (2010). Value for money and for many. *MIT Technology Review*, India Edition Feb 2010 (pp. 32–36).

Militzer, J. (2013). Cracking the code on affordable health care—Part 2: An interview with Dr. Devi Shetty, founder of Narayana Hrudayalaya, next billion.

Mullan, F. (2006). Doctors for the World: Indian physician emigration. *Health Affairs, 25*(2), 380–393.

Natchiar, G., et al. (1994). Attacking the backlog of India's curable blind: The Aravind Eye hospital model. *Archives of Ophthalmology, 112*(7), 987–993.

NHRM. (2005). *National Rural Health Mission: Mission Document 2005–2012*. New Delhi: National Rural Health Mission.

Pedro Olinto, K. B., Sobrado, C., & Uematsu, H. (2013). The state of the poor: Where are the poor, where is extreme poverty harder to end, and what is the current profile of the World's poor? Poverty Reduction and Economic Management Network; The World Bank October 2013 (No. 125).

Praceus, S., & Herstatt, C. (2012). *Consumer innovation in the poor versus rich world: Some differences and similarities*. Working Paper, Technologie-und Innovationsmanagement, Technische Universität Hamburg-Harburg.

Prahalad, C. K. (2004). *The fortune at the bottom of the pyramid: Eradicating poverty through profits*. Upper Saddle River, NJ: Wharton School Publishing.

Prahalad, C. K. (2006). The innovation Sandbox. *Strategy & Business, 44*, 1–10.

Prahalad, C. K. (2012). Bottom of the pyramid as a source of breakthrough innovations. *Journal of Product Innovation Management, 29*(1), 6–12.

Prahalad, C. K., & Hart, S. (2002). The fortune at the bottom of the pyramid. *Strategy & Business, 26*.

Prahalad, C. K., & Lieberthal, K. (1998). The end of corporate imperialism. *Harvard Buisness Review, 76*, 68–79.

Prahalad, C. K., & Mashelkar, R. (2010). Innovation's Holy Grail. *Harvard Business Review, 7*(8), 132–142.

Radjou, N., Prabhu, J., & Ahuja, S. (2012). *Jugaad innovation: Think frugal, be flexible, generate breakthrough growth*. San Francisco, CA: Jossey-Bass.

Rangan, V. K., & Thulasiraj, R. D. (2007). Making sight affordable. *Innovations, 2*, 35–49.

Ray, P. K., & Ray, S. (2010). Resource-constrained innovation for emerging economies: The case of the Indian telecommunications industry. *IEEE Transactions on Engineering Management, 57*(1), 144–156.

Reinhardt, U. E., Hussey, P. S., & Anderson, G. F. (2004). US health care spending in an international context. *Health Affairs, 23*(3), 10–25.

Sharma, A., & Iyer, G. R. (2012). Resource-constrained product development: Implications for green marketing and green supply chains. *Industrial Marketing Management, 41*(4), 599–608.

Sherawat, R., & Rao, K. D. (2012). Insured yet vulnerable: Out-of pocket payments and India's poor. *Health Policy and Planning, 27*, 213–221.

Smith, S., Newhouse, J. P., & Freeland, M. S. (2009). Income, insurance, and technology: Why does health spending outpace economic growth? *Health Affairs, 28*(5), 1276–1284.

Tiwari, R., & Herstatt, C. (2012). Assessing India's lead market potential for cost-effective innovations. *Journal of Indian Business Research, 4*(2), 97–115.

Trouiller, P., Olliaro, P., Torreele, E., Orbinski, J., Laing, R., & Ford, N. (2002). Drug development for neglected diseases: A deficient market and a public-health policy failure. *Public Health, 359*(9324), 2188–2194.

Turner, L. (2010). "Medical tourism" and the global marketplace in health services: US patients, international hospitals, and the search for affordable health care. *International Journal of Health Services, 40*(3), 443–467.

Vickers, T., & Rossen, E. (2011). Driving down the cost of high-quality care: Lessons from the Aravind Eye Care System. *Health International, 11*. McKinsey & Company.

Von Hippel, E. (1978). A customer-active paradigm for industrial product idea generation. *Research Policy, 7*(3), 240–266.

Von Hippel, E. (1982). Appropriability of innovation benefit as a predictor of the source of innovation. *Research Policy, 11*(2), 95–115.

Von Hippel, E. (1986). Lead users: A source of novel product concepts. *Management Science, 32* (7), 791–805.

Von Hippel, E. (1994). "Sticky information" and the locus of problem solving: Implications for innovation. *Management Science, 40*(4), 429–439.

Von Hippel, E. (2003). *Democratizing innovation* (Vol. 1). Cambridge, MA: The MIT Press.

Von Hippel, E., Thomke, S., & Sonnack, M. (1999). Creating breakthroughs at 3 M. *Harvard Buisness Review, 77*, 47–57.

WHO. (2006). *The World Health Report 2006—working together for health*. Geneva: World Health Organization.

Yu, D., & Hang, C. C. (2011). Creating technology candidates for disruptive innovation: Generally applicable R&D strategies. *Technovation, 31*(8), 401–410.

Chapter 6
Study 2: Lessons from GE Healthcare: How Incumbents Can Systematically Create Disruptive Innovations

6.1 Introduction

Bottom of the Pyramid (BOP) markets can offer a ripe context for potentially disruptive innovations. Companies could enter BOP markets by creating new market disruptive innovations to address the large unserved or underserved populations with simple and affordable products and services (Hart and Christensen 2002).

Addressing the vast, fast-growing, four-billion-people-strong market segment poses unique challenges to MNCs and also requires new thinking in the field of international strategy (Ricart et al. 2004). Companies seeking to serve the BOP segments have to deal with market creation issues, working in informal economies with institutional voids, with broader and diverse set of partners (London and Hart 2010) as well as internal organizational barriers (Halme et al. 2012; Olsen and Boxenbaum 2009). These are some reasons why MNCs have either failed to successfully enter BOP markets (Jaiswal 2008) or have largely ignored them (Prahalad and Lieberthal 1998).

Similarly, established incumbents generally fail to successfully commercialize disruptive innovations. Their internal processes and values force them to focus on their existing customers, thereby ignoring projects targeted at new emerging markets that lack a customer base (Christensen and Bower 1996; Christensen 1997).

A counter example to this is the American incumbent GE Healthcare,[1] which has been creating several frugal innovations targeted at emerging markets for the past years (Immelt and Govindrajan 2009). This study will look at organizational structures and processes that GE Healthcare has in place, which enable it to create disruptive innovations systematically. The study aims to contribute towards building disruptive innovation theory (Christensen 2006), where questions pertaining to selective success and failure of incumbents to create disruptive innovations remain

---

[1] GE, Healthymagination, MAC, Marquette, Lullaby are all Trademarks of GE.

© Springer International Publishing Switzerland 2015
A. Ramdorai, C. Herstatt, *Frugal Innovation in Healthcare*, India Studies in Business and Economics, DOI 10.1007/978-3-319-16336-9_6

unanswered (Danneels 2004). Literature on disruptive innovations recommends incumbent firms to create a separate entity for commercializing disruptive innovations (Christensen and Bower 1996). However, scholars have been calling upon firms to explore new markets and exploit existing opportunities simultaneously by being ambidextrous (Tushman and O'Reilly 1996).

The ability to successfully drive disruptive innovations in a sustained manner from within the organization will be analyzed through the lens of organizational ambidexterity. Ambidexterity is the ability of organizations to successfully balance exploration and exploitation. The manifestation of this act of balancing exploitation and exploration is the company's ability to initiate multiple innovation streams, in this case sustaining innovations and disruptive innovations (Danneels 2004; Tushman et al. 2010). Key proponents of organizational ambidexterity, O'Reilly and Tushman, consider it a "solution to the innovator's dilemma" (O'Reilly and Tushman 2008, pg. 202); however, present their thesis only conceptually. This is a general gap in the research of organizational ambidexterity, as noted by scholars of organizational ambidexterity where consensus exists on the need for ambidexterity, but the underlying mechanisms and the 'how' are far from understood (Gupta et al. 2006). This work will look at the mechanisms of ambidexterity at GE Healthcare to help explain its ability in successfully hosting both sustaining and disruptive innovations from within its boundaries.

The next section will focus on the theoretical background of this research, delving in greater detail into organizational ambidexterity. The following section describes the research methodology and research question. Section 6.4 narrates the empirical data from the GE Healthcare case study after which the main findings will be analyzed and the study will be concluded.

6.2   Theoretical Context

To recap Chap. 3, the theory of disruptive innovation contends that incumbents struggle to commercialize disruptive innovations because of their resource allocation processes that systematically favor sustaining innovations (Christensen and Bower 1996). Further, Christensen and Raynor (2003) state, that companies generally lack processes for dealing with disruption as it has a recurrent task. Christensen's main recommendation for established players is to set up autonomous units or spin-offs to incubate disruptive innovations (Christensen and Bower 1996; Christiansen and Raynor 2003).

In contrast to this recommendation, other scholars promote organizational structures that are loosely coupled with each other and enable organizations to simultaneously host evolutionary and revolutionary innovations from within (Tushman and O'Reilly 1996). Thus, questions remain on what makes some incumbents successful while others fail and whether companies always need to spin-off their disruptive projects (Danneels 2004) and also how established companies can systematically commercialize disruptive innovations, not just a one-off project.

Although a spin off can successfully protect projects, it also isolates the project from crucial company resources and capabilities and the ability for the company to learn (McDermott and OConnor 2002). This is why authors O'Reilly and Tushman (2008, p. 202) posit that "ambidexterity is one solution to the innovator's dilemma".

Organizational ambidexterity is an organizations' ability to successfully explore and exploit simultaneously. Researchers have diversely defined organizational ambidexterity and its importance has been noted across different fields of management research, including strategic management, innovation management, organizational learning and organizational behavior (Simsek 2009). This study operationalizes ambidexterity as the ability of organizations to simultaneously host different innovation streams (Tushman et al. 2010), in our case, sustaining and disruptive innovations (Simsek 2009; Danneels 2006).

Research points to three antecedents of ambidexterity, structural ambidexterity, which is achieved by creating separate structures for the different kinds of activities, contextual ambidexterity, which resides in an individual's ability to allocate time between exploration and exploitation (Raisch et al. 2009) and leadership-based antecedents of ambidexterity (Raisch and Birkinshaw 2008). As this work concerns mechanisms at an organizational level, this study will focus on structural ambidexterity. The main proponents of this school are O'Reilly and Tushman (O'Reilly and Tushman 2004; Tushman and O'Reilly 1996; Tushman et al. 2010).

Structural ambidexterity is achieved through distinct units within the organization held together by a common strategic intent, an overarching set of values, and a leadership team that can manage differentiated sub-units with clearly defined interfaces that leverage existing assets (O'Reilly and Tushman 2008). Structural differentiation of the different activities in distinct units ensures that exploratory units enjoy the necessary freedom and flexibility, while exploitative units can carry on uninterrupted with their ongoing business (Jansen et al. 2009). However, to reduce the risk of isolation and decreased coordination, targeted integration mechanisms between these units are necessary (Gibson and Birkenshaw 2004; Sirmon et al. 2007). These distinct units can help firms maintain multiple competencies that address competing demands (Gilbert 2005). The role of the top management is also considered crucial for reconciling the tensions and contradictions arising from managing multiple innovation streams (Smith and Tushman 2005).

While several works have confirmed business performance enhancement through ambidexterity (Gibson and Birkenshaw 2004; He and Wong 2004), there remains a gap in the understanding of the mechanisms by which organizations achieve ambidexterity. As Gupta et al. (2006, pg. 697) noted, "although near consensus exists on the need for balance, there is considerably less clarity on how this balance can be achieved".

Few works have empirically studied organization designs required to deal with multiple innovation streams, with the exception of a handful (Tushman et al. 2010; O'Reilly and Tushman 2004). From analyzing innovation episodes within 13 business units, organizational ambidexterity scholars identified the nature of ambidextrous organizational design—high structural differentiation of exploitative and exploratory units with targeting structural linkage (Tushman et al. 2010). In studying the cases of USA Today and Ciba vision, the authors O'Reilly and Tushman (2004) also identified the need for strategic intent and an overarching vision that permits the otherwise contradictory units to coexist. However, these case studies explore incremental vs. architectural innovations (Henderson and Clark 1990) or discontinuous innovations, which involve fundamental competence destroying technological changes (Tushman and Anderson 1986) and do not deal with disruptive innovations. As shown in Sect. 3.3, disruptive innovations have certain inherently unfavorable characteristics specific to them. Thus, empirically exploring the role of ambidexterity in hosting disruptive innovations is still an open field (Danneels 2004).

6.3   Research Question and Methodology

6.3.1   Research Question

This research brings together three fields of management research, namely BOP research, disruptive innovation theory and organizational ambidexterity. Analysis of strategy for MNCs in low-income markets is an emerging field of international strategy research (Ricart et al. 2004). Two of the most important aspects of products developed for BOP markets are the need for extreme affordability and adaptation to local needs (Tiwari and Herstatt 2012; London and Hart 2004; Prahalad 2004). By developing disruptive innovations to seize the opportunities of the BOP, companies could potentially "give themselves a chance for sustained corporate growth while also helping to lift the poor out of poverty" (Hart and Christensen 2002, p. 56).

However, questions regarding how large companies can successfully develop disruptive innovations from within their boundaries remain, as alluded to in Chap. 3. As Daneels (2006, p. 3) noted in the introduction to a special issue on Disruptive Innovations in the Journal of Product and Innovation Management:

> A question of great interest is whether the barriers to ambidexterity can be avoided by organizational separation, such as the formation of a spin-off unit to pursue disruptive technology, as recommended by Christensen.

Authors O'Reilly and Tushman posit that "ambidexterity is one solution to innovator's dilemma" (O'Reilly and Tushman 2008, p. 202). This research will attempt to answer this question by analyzing the case of GE Healthcare and its innovations for the Indian mass market. GE Healthcare is one of the few MNCs committed to developing products for low-income markets and has been developing several products over the last few years (Immelt and Govindrajan 2009). Thus, the key research question for this study is: What organizational structures and processes would enable incumbent firms to systematically create disruptive innovations for the BOP markets?

6.3.2   Methodology

Exploratory case study methodology has been chosen for this research as explained in detail in Chap. 4. This section provides a brief description of the methodology that is unique to this study.

This is a single case study of GE Healthcare and was chosen because it was a unique case of an MNC deeply committed to creating affordable innovation in healthcare and considerably investing in BOP markets (for further details see GE's healthymagination initiative[2]). GE Healthcare has demonstrated this commitment through several measures that have been highly publicized.[3]

Single case study research can richly describe the existence of a phenomenon (Siggelkow 2007) and extend and refine theory (Eisenhardt 1989). Therefore, this single case with GE Healthcare has been chosen.

Primary data in the form of interviews as well as internal company documentation have been analyzed. In total, 13 interviews were conducted with management at GE Healthcare involved in low-cost innovations, including senior executives. The interviews lasted between 30 and 90 min and were semi-structured in nature. Most interviews were conducted in person and some follow-up interviews were conducted over the telephone. All interviews were recorded and transcribed. Notes of the meeting and impressions, over and above the interviews were written the same day, conforming with the "24-h rule" (Yin 1994). All other processes for coding and data analysis are described in Chap. 4. Appendix D consists of the list of all interviews and the interview numbers. Secondary data, including company press releases, and annual reports were used to verify and triangulate the primary data.

Finally, the insights arising from the case study were played back to all the interview partners in form of a written manuscript, as per the confidentiality agreement signed with GE Healthcare. All interview partners were in complete agreement with the findings and implications drawn.

---

[2] For information about GE's healthymagination see: www.healthymagination.com/; Accessed on 15.11.2013.

[3] See the following papers and newspaper articles. 1. Bahree, M (2011). "GE Remodels Businesses in India", The Wall Street Journal, Apr 26th 2011. 2. Economist (2009) Lessons from a frugal innovator. Apr 26th 2009. 3. Immelt & Govindarajan (2009) "How GE is disrupting itself." Harvard Business Review.

6.4   Empirical Context

6.4.1   GE Healthcare Case Study

6.4.1.1   About GE Healthcare

GE Healthcare is a division of the American conglomerate, General Electric. General Electric was ranked number 9 in the Fortune 500 list in 2014 and is involved in diverse business segments constituting energy, technology, infrastructure, industrial and consumer goods and capital finance.

GE Healthcare is a subsidiary of GE and accounted for revenues of $18.2 bn in 2013 (GE 2013). GE Healthcare's main revenue streams are medical equipment and services in medical imaging, diagnostics, IT and patient monitoring systems.[4]

GE Healthcare has a long history in medical technology, and over the last few years has acquired several players around the world to establish itself as one of the main global players in healthcare technology.

6.4.1.2   Early Days and Early Successes

In the 90s, GE started targeting growth outside the USA through strategic acquisitions and alliances (Mitchell 2008). In 2000, GE established the Jack F. Welch Technology Center (JFWTC) in Bangalore to capitalize on the R&D talent available in the country (GE 2010b). It is GE's largest R&D center and the first one to be built outside the USA. Healthcare is one of the focus areas of JFWTC and a center of software excellence was established for GE Healthcare. Since its inception, the engineering teams at the JFWTC, working together with GE's global teams, were solely focused on developing GE's premium products.

However, the premium devices that the local Indian R&D teams were working on had penetrated only a handful of top tier hospitals in India's metropolitan cities. The main reason for this was the high price tag of GE Healthcare's premium products. It became apparent that GE Healthcare would not be able to penetrate these emerging markets with its existing product portfolio and would need to develop products especially for these markets. Indian sales teams were also starting to demand lower priced products.

Around 2001, the R&D team in India tried to push the idea for a low-cost electrocardiogram (ECG) device for India and India-like markets, but only after three years did they receive a positive response from the global GE Healthcare leadership. In fact, GE Healthcare in the early 2000 gave little importance to developing products for the emerging markets and as Immelt and Govindarajan noted:

---

[4] www.gehealthcare.com; Accessed on 15.08.2014.

India accounted for just 1 % of GE's revenues at the time and occupied roughly the same mindshare of managers with global responsibility.
(Immelt and Govindrajan 2009)

After many years of promoting the idea within the company, the head of the Diagnostic Cardiology business unit at the global level bought into it. This was in 2005, when the focus was shifting towards emerging markets.

The senior business unit leader, with backing from executive leadership, decided to invest in a team to develop a low cost ECG device for emerging markets. He also brought in technology experts from Germany to help the Indian team with knowledge transfer. The senior business unit leader also noted the difficulty and dilemma he faced while making this decision:

It is not easy to take out engineers from projects that are sure to give high returns.
(Interview 2E)

Nevertheless, he backed the project and the result was the MAC 400, which was priced at about $1,000, compared to premium segment ECGs that cost about ten times as much and about 30 % of the least expensive GE Healthcare ECG sold in the Indian market.

The value proposition of the MAC 400 was not only the cost advantage but also portability and robustness to work in an environment with power fluctuations and dust. Portability was an important feature as doctors in India, especially in tier 3 cities and rural areas have multiple practices and travel to smaller clinics in more remote regions. While this is a B2B product, and its direct customers, i.e. doctors and clinics outside tier-1 cities cannot be considered as part of the BOP segment, their patients, to a large extent, are low income individuals. However, also high income individuals may seek treatment in clinics that are target segment of GE Healthcare's MAC i. For these patients the question is not around cost but around bridging the infrastructure deficit.

The cost advantage was achieved by creating a smaller device that retained only key functionalities. Standard and commercially available subsystems were chosen, e.g., a standard, off-the-shelf charging system used for mobile phones was used instead of a custom-made power supply system and a more commonly used printer system was chosen, like those used for bus ticketing systems.

Around the same time, a project to develop a low-cost, portable ultrasound was initiated and was underway in GE's R&D labs in China. Both these projects required targeted effort and oversight from GE Healthcare's senior leadership. These projects were organized within product development teams directly reporting to senior leadership and were viewed as strategic investments for the company by the leadership. The leader who championed the MAC 400 project commented:

This is an area where we have accepted that the return on investment will be more long term than short term. This is an investment where when you invest a dollar now, the return is actually less than in some other areas...So it a strategic investment
(Interview 2E)

The MAC 400 project put innovations from the Indian R&D Labs on the map at GE. Two key events in 2006–2007 helped elevate the status of such frugal projects. In 2006, GE launched a commercial called health re-imagined, which was aired in the US. This commercial showcased the MAC 400 project in a rural Indian setting. Further, in 2007, two full pages in the annual report were dedicated to feature the MAC400 project.

The program leader commented on the significance of these events:

> MAC 400 launched first . . .it was given a lot of visibility internally in GE. So this is the first product developed at such a low cost. In 2008 [in the] GE annual report, there were two full pages dedicated for this product. . . . We, especially [the program manager] were very good in marketing this within GE and there were a lot of things that we could tell about the features and cost-effectiveness and ruggedness, reliability. So this came in GE annual report. . . [Also through the] GE corporate funded advertisement of this product we had a huge campaign in the US. . .that made this product quite famous and that triggered this thinking within many of the segments.
> (Interview 2B)

The next version, the MAC i (I stands for India), with a price tag of $535, was launched in 2009. This had an even more cost optimized design than the MAC 400, e.g., reduced printer size. Nevertheless, the MAC 400 and MAC i run the Marquette 12SL analysis program that runs on all high-end ECG devices. This way, the clinical efficacy of the device is not compromised. As noted by the GE senior executive responsible for the MAC i and MAC 400 development:

> One of the fundamental things is that a value product does not mean old technology. But many companies do this. They would sell the last generation products cheaper in emerging markets. That is nonsense. In our case, the value product means high-tech engineering but cost optimized
> (Interview 2E)

The MAC 400 and MAC i were considered breakthrough products at GE. It was not only because GE Healthcare had managed to develop such a low-cost ECG device, but it was also a breakthrough in terms of the value network GE Healthcare had to create to sell these products. GE Healthcare's portfolio until then only consisted of sophisticated and expensive devices and its sales, servicing teams were geared towards such a high-end product portfolio. Thus, these products were considerable departures from the norm at GE Healthcare. GE Healthcare faced and is still facing challenges in commercializing these innovations. One of the challenges lies in bringing these products to the end-customer in remote areas and GE Healthcare in India is trying out alternative distribution models for these products to reach tier-2, 3 cities and remote areas.

However, as the leader noted, GE Healthcare is taking a long range mindset for these projects. The MAC 400 and MAC i projects are considered as a long-term strategic investment for the company. This quote also underscores the commitment and the support from senior leadership the MAC 400 project got.

> They are strategic investments. . .that are shielded, which means that these are investment for the long term and in the short term, if there is a catastrophe in one business area, we would never take the investment from these shielded projects to help fix the other
> (Interview 2E)

6.4.1.3 Raising the Stature of Everything Global

These initial successes in product development led to major shifts within GE by 2009. In the 2009 annual report, GE's Chairman announced a push for reverse innovation to capture new opportunities that "takes a low-cost, emerging-market business model and translates it to the developed world" (GE 2009, p. 5). GE Healthcare also announced the healthymagination initiative in May 2009, with the commitment to invest $ 6 bn in the next 6 years to develop products with a goal "to provide better health for more people at lower cost" (GE 2010a). The healthymagination initiative was a key component in the GE's 2009 Renewal Model with a focus on creating market solutions for the society at large (GE 2011).

In late 2009, GE also decided to give India its own Profit and Loss (P&L) responsibility (Mahajan-Bansal and Goyal 2009b). Traditionally, GE's regional business leaders reported to their respective GE product business leaders. Under the new structure, the business unit leaders reported to John Flannery, the then CEO of GE India, who would in turn report to GE's vice chairman, someone with extremely high seniority within the organization. This was done to ensure India had the empowerment to develop products for its own markets. Jeff Immelt, Chairman of GE in the official press statement described it as:

> With an integrated team, we can develop products and services designed specifically to meet local needs and, potentially, for export to other markets.
> (Mahajan-Bansal and Goyal 2009a)

This was the first time a country, other than the USA had its own P&L. This also meant that it was in charge of its own growth strategy and its own budgeting processes.

In 2010, GE established the Global Growth Organization to oversee operations in high-growth markets. Thus, GE continued to push its emerging markets strategy by "raising the stature of everything global in GE" as the CEO, Jeff Immelt, put it in a press statement (Lemer and Crooks 2010).

6.4.1.4 Pushing Further Down the Pyramid

Moving beyond cardiology, GE Healthcare in India launched a new range of products in infant-care under the brand of Lullaby. The Lullaby warmer was launched first in 2009 at a price tag of $3,000, about 60–70 % lower than premium segment warmers. Next in the range, the Lullaby LED Phototherapy (LED PT) Device, developed in India for India-like markets was launched in 2011. The LED PT's value proposition of low Total Cost of Ownership, energy savings (up to 80 % energy saving due to use of LED technology), ease of use and serviceability, helped sales not only in India but also outside India, in total over 60 countries.

Even with the new range of Lullaby infant care products, the Maternal and Infant Care (MIC) team in India realized that the $3,000 warmer could sell in top-end clinics in the metros, but not in rural areas where the problems in infant mortality were deeper and where there was potential to impact infant mortality rates (IMR). In their current markets, for which their product portfolio was designed for, the aim of infant care was saving premature babies born very early, e.g., at 24 weeks. In contrast, in countries like India, the problems were more basic and the majority of cases were of infants born at a later stage. In the words of the MIC marketing executive:

> In the current state of the portfolio, we had some fantastic incubators and warmers, which are best in class. . ... but the products are made for those markets where the core issue of IMR is under control, whereas in countries like India, IMR is very high. We needed something, which is at a price point that can make an impact to the IMR [in India and countries like India]
> (Interview 2K)

To target this issue, the MIC India team in 2012 was working on a range of products that caters to segments in tier-2 and tier-3 cities and villages, mostly local clinics and government hospitals. These hospitals currently have low quality warmers that are often broken or overused or use naked 200-W bulbs to keep babies warm, according to MIC team's research. The MIC team aims to sell its new range of cost-effective products to these segments and push towards selling to clinics that have not adopted any warmers yet. As part of this effort, GE Healthcare India launched the Lullaby Warmer Prime in December 2013.

To cater to segments further down the pyramid, which mostly involves home births that occur outside a hospital or clinic (home births represent about 51 % of births in rural India (Chandramouli 2011)), the MIC India team has partnered with Embrace. Embrace is a non-profit organization that has developed an innovative, low-cost warmer priced at $250 that looks like a sleeping bag for a baby. It is portable and does not require a continuous supply of electricity.

The MIC team is working on an end-to-end solution that not only includes products at significantly lower price points but also a go-to-market strategy that includes collaborations with the government and NGOs.

GE Healthcare is also partnering with East Meets West, an international development agency focused on neonatal health, to distribute and service GE Healthcare's infant care products in developing and rural regions. While GE provides its products, servicing and technical expertise, East Meets West provides monitoring and training for the medical personnel. The MIC team in India is also starting a concerted effort to work with the government as they realize that only through such partnerships they can have an impact on national IMR.

This new approach is highlighted in this quote from the MIC marketing executive:

> We have dropped our—what should I say, reluctance—and we are more than willing to form partnerships with Embrace and to work with East Meets West to address the BOP market. So these are the different efforts of establishing a performance [value] segment. And my role is to facilitate the creation of low-cost value products in all these different ways. . .so it is a very concerted strategy.
> (Interview 2L)

However, this is not without challenges. As mentioned earlier, these initiatives required and still require an overhaul of GE Healthcare's existing processes and business models. The management candidly shared some of these challenges, as this quote by the senior leader in the Diagnostic Cardiology Unit highlights:

> We had a great show to launch the product, great press releases but nobody knew how to sell it...In the end we had to hire our own people. And this was more difficult than engineering. In the purchasing department of hospitals it is more professional. In this case you have doctors who give you cash. Big companies don't take cash... so how do you sell it? So these are the issues...we found out all this later. I completely underestimated this
>
>   (Interview 2E)

6.4.2   Characteristics of the Value Segment Products

These low-cost innovations are categorized in GE Healthcare as value or performance segment products. Within GE Healthcare, every product business unit has a dedicated value segment team. The value segment leader is typically based in an emerging market, such as India or China. The main task of the value segment leader is to develop and market value products in emerging markets and globally. The segment leader has functions related to product development reporting to him, e.g., marketing, engineering. Local sales teams who sell these products are organized regionally. However, not all product categories in the value segment were pursuing BOP markets. For instance high-end technologies like Computer Tomography (CT) had a value segment team based out of India, developing a low-cost CT scanner that aims to be 30–40 % cheaper than those currently in GE Healthcare's portfolio in India. However, CT scanners are still extremely expensive devices that only premier hospitals in countries like India would possess (in India there were 45 CT Scan centers in 2010 (Dutta 2010)). While this is a value segment product it cannot be termed as an innovation for the BOP market.

Although price is the main differentiator, the value proposition of these products goes beyond cost-effectiveness. Products developed for the BOP and in general for emerging markets need to be well adapted to local needs (London and Hart 2004). GE Healthcare's value segment products fit this mantra, as supported by this quote by the CTO of GE Healthcare India talking about the considerations behind the MAC i:

> [In places where the MAC i was to be deployed], there was no technician who knew where the leads had to be attached to get a reliable ECG so ease-of-use became an important criterion. Most of our devices sit in air conditioned rooms like this, they are plugged into the wall with back-up power. Then you look at places [where MAC i was to be deployed] that get three hours of power a week. So that became another consideration. If the patient cannot get to where the ECG machine is because it is 50–100 km away, the ECG machine has to get to the patient. So something that can be carried around. While the first thing on the surface always seems to be cost, that is really not the whole story and sometimes not even half the story. In fact most of what is in the MAC i has nothing in common with most of the

ECG machines we have except for the algorithms and the software, which is kind of the
legacy that we have and that we built over a period of time
(Interview 2F)

The other "half of the story" of GE Healthcare's value segment products, which
the above quote mentions, entails other product characteristics summarized in this
section:

1. Low complexity: The value segment products are stripped of non-essential
   features and focus on satisfying critical user needs. The products would compromise on unused features or even on convenience in order to keep the
   complexity and the cost of the product low. In case of the MAC i, the team
   decided to build a single-channel ECG without a display, which meant that it
   would be more inconvenient for doctors to read the ECG in comparison to
   3-channel digital displays, but the information would be the same.
2. Ease of Use: In many cases, the technicians operating medical devices in Indian
   clinics are minimally trained, especially in more remote regions. To ensure that
   they can properly operate the devices, ease of use is an important aspect in
   product development. The MAC i is designed with a minimum number of
   buttons and its regular usage requires only the on/off button. Similarly the
   MIC team, on one of its immersive market research field trips, heard a story of
   how a baby died because the nurse thought that the warmer was on when only its
   observation lamp was lit. This had a deep impact on the team and it decided to
   make its products "absolutely foolproof". The engineering lead of the MIC team
   recalled this incident and said:

   See it is very easy for me to say at least this basic knowledge should be there with the nurse,
   or that we should train them... but now we say we need to make the product foolproof for
   untrained people too
   (Interview 2M)

3. Reliability and serviceability: Products sold to remote parts of India would be
   difficult to service because of poor infrastructure to reach these places. Keeping
   this in mind, GE's products are also designed for serviceability by ensuring those
   parts that break down most often are avoided or extra components are sold along
   with the product. In general the engineering teams try to minimize the number of
   parts, especially the number of movable parts.
4. Environmental fit: BOP products generally have to function amidst harsh conditions, for instance high levels of dust and humidity and large fluctuations of
   voltage. Besides this, hospitals are generally not equipped with high-quality
   infrastructure. An example is the lack of wall oxygen supply in most hospitals,
   which is recommended for resuscitation (breathing) equipment for premature
   babies. To counter this, GE Healthcare's resuscitation device, currently under
   development in India, will work under both conditions, with wall oxygen supply
   or with an external oxygen cylinder. The device is able to function even with
   power breakdowns and time lags. As the leader of the MIC segment put it:

So this is the environment in which we work. Now, you cannot try to say, okay, get me reliable power and I'll give you a product, that doesn't work. . . then you're not in the game and you'll continue to create products that don't work. So now when you have [these conditions], you need to come up with some other innovative way of doing things
(Interview 2K)

5. Local use cases: Doctors in India adopt medical equipment for different use cases. For instance, in India several hospitals and clinics conduct large scale screening camps (as described in Chap. 5), often for free in rural areas or even urban areas, in order to pull in customers. Thus, the MAC i is designed in such a way that it can take 500 ECG's in a single charge. Also its requirement for portability came up because doctors in India sometimes have to travel between clinics.

6. Cost-effectiveness: The basic requirement of these products, "the right to play" is to make value segment products affordable for the mass market. This does not mean a 20 % or 30 % reduction in cost but typically 70 % and 90 % reduction. If one compares the MAC i and premium ECG devices sold in developed markets, there is difference of a factor of 20 in price. Not just the initial investment but the total cost of ownership must be kept low, as exemplified by GE's LED PT.

7. Clinical efficacy: In all GE Healthcare's products, clinical efficacy is not compromised. All products go through rigorous certification processes just like premium segment products do. The MAC 400 and MAC i run the same Marquette 12SL analysis program as the high-end ECG devices to interpret the ECG. This is the core of their technology, built on several years of testing and experience. Similarly, the MIC segment products all have high clinical efficacy but are geared towards saving late-stage premature babies vs. the premium segment incubators that are designed to save extremely premature babies.

In some cases, designing for one feature brings advantages in cost at the same time. For instance, in case of the LED PT, the team decided early on to do away with the cooling fan, which was a feature in previous generations of PT devices. This decision was taken in order to ensure reliability of the product as the fan system is generally very susceptible to breakdowns. Thus, the team designed the product with vents and natural airflow. This had the positive side effect of removing complexity and cost simultaneously.

These characteristics are very much in line with the characteristics of frugal innovations identified by authors Tiwari and Herstatt (2012). Beyond the points mentioned in the paper, clinical efficacy and product adaptation towards local use cases are additional characteristics of GE's frugal medical technology developed for India.

6.5   Analysis

The previous section described the successes and the challenges that GE Healthcare faced in introducing and selling value segment products. The section also summarized the characteristics of these value segment products. This section summarizes the disruptive characteristics of the value segment products and analyzes the organizational conditions in place at GE Healthcare and GE at large.

6.5.1   Disruptive Potential of GE Healthcare's Value Segment Products

As seen in the section above, GE Healthcare's value segment products trade-off features and convenience for price. With drastic price reductions, these products can be sold to new segments that were previously not using the product or using only a poor substitute. Value segment products have other features that make it attractive for mass markets in emerging economies, such as ruggedness, reliability and fit to the environment. Thus, while price is the main factor, the new performance attributes of these value segment products are also portability, reliability and ease of use (Table 6.1).

There is also emerging evidence of disruption upmarket. The India team has developed the MAC 600, a more sophisticated version of the MAC 400. Similar to the MAC 400, this is also a 3-channel ECG, but includes additional features, such as a color display and memory to store readings. It is sold in India as a mid-range product and as a low-end product in China, Eastern Europe as well as in more developed markets like Germany and France. In the developed markets it is marketed as the "digital camera of the ECG family", highlighting its ease-of-use.

Another later version developed by a team in China, the MAC 800, is built on similar principals as the MAC 400. It is a 6-channel portable ECG that can work in an additional mode and offers several communication options. This is priced at about $2,000 and also sold in the USA. The MAC 600 and MAC 800 have opened up new markets for ECG devices. These devices are sold to rural clinics, primary care physicians for whom high-end version would be too expensive as well as in emergency rooms where their small size and portability is an advantage (Immelt and Govindrajan 2009). Figure 6.1 depicts this product evolution.

Also a significant portion of Lullaby range warmers and the LED PT device are selling in more developed markets. The Lullaby warmer is currently selling in emerging markets and the LED PT device is also selling in parts of Central Europe and in the USA. These warmers and PT devices could potentially enable hospitals to purchase multiple units rather than just a few units traditionally purchased only for the Neo-Natal Intensive Care Units.

Table 6.1 Disruptive characteristics of GE Healthcare's value segment products

No.	Characteristic	Applicability	GE's value segment products
1	The disruptive innovation initially underperforms on the performance attribute valued by mainstream customers	All	Yes. MAC i has fewer features compared to premium segment ECGs. Also innovation on premium segment incubators addresses problems of ever younger premature babies. Value segment incubators focus on basic functionalities for premature babies at a more advanced stage.
2	The disruptive innovation, however, has features that are valued by fringe or new customers and introduces a new performance criteria	All	Yes, cost, ease of use and operability in harsh conditions
2a	A disruptive innovation can create new markets, as it attracts people who previously lacked the resources or skills to use it	New-market	Yes, these products can be afforded by hospitals and clinics in smaller towns and rural areas
2b	A disruptive innovation is typically simpler and lower cost	New market, Low-end	Yes, all value segment products are 60–80 % cheaper than premium equivalents and are of lower complexity
2c	A disruptive innovation can involve radical technology and attract high-end customers	High-end	No, not-applicable
3	Generally mainstream customers do not initially value these additional features and thus the disruptive innovation is commercialized in emerging markets	All	Yes, created for tier-2 and rural clinics in BOP markets
4	The disruptive innovation is financially unattractive for leading incumbents to pursue	All	Yes, value segment products cost a fraction of premium segment products
5	The disruptive innovation steadily improves in performance and attracts mainstream customers to it; either it improves along the main performance attribute or market preferences shift towards the newly introduced performance attribute	All	More sophisticated version, MAC-800 is creating new target segments like rural clinics and physician practices in developed countries.
6	The disruptive innovation takes significant share of the mainstream market	All	No evidence available yet

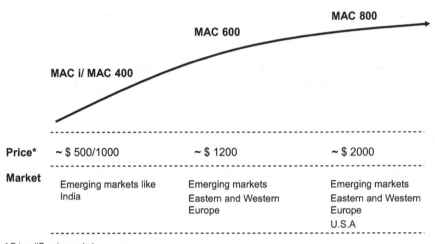

	MAC 800	
	MAC 600	
MAC i/ MAC 400		
Price*	~ $ 500/1000	~ $ 1200	~ $ 2000
Market	Emerging markets like India	Emerging markets Eastern and Western Europe	Emerging markets Eastern and Western Europe U.S.A

* Price differs by market

Fig. 6.1   GE Healthcare ECG device product portfolio

This quote by the manager responsible for ICFC products in the beginning of 2014 cements this trend:

> Since 1 year we are seeing increasing global uptake for our value products. We are seeing a trend towards value and affordability in healthcare systems across the globe. This is primarily driving this demand.
> (Interview 2J)

While it is true that these low-cost devices open up new markets, e.g., in rural India, the question does remain regarding the extent to which these low-cost devices will disrupt developed markets or how they will shape BOP markets. It is worth re-emphasizing, that disruption is a process and not an event (Christensen 2006) and the evolution of the healthcare industry in developed markets and other factors will play a role in this disruption process.

6.5.2   Overcoming the Innovator's Dilemma

In Chap. 3 the inherent qualities that make disruptive innovations unattractive for established firms were described, along with the underlying organizational mechanisms that prevent them from investing in disruptive innovations. To recap, disruptive innovation theory offers two sets of explanations for the failure of incumbents to commercialize disruptive innovations. The first explanation, put forward by Christensen and Bower (1996), points to the resource allocation processes at companies that tend to favor sustaining innovations because they address the needs of their current customers. The second explanation, put forth by Henderson (2006), emphasizes the lack of market-related capabilities that a firm needs to respond to emerging customer segments and disruptive innovations.

This section will elaborate on how GE Healthcare is countering these mecha-nisms with structures and routines that enable it to systematically invest in and commercialize disruptive innovations. The analysis shows that there are four mea-sures that counter the innovator's dilemma, namely ensuring dedicated processes for disruptive innovations, reconfiguring the value system, ensuring dedicated resources for disruptive innovations and building the required market-facing competencies.

6.5.2.1 Dedicated Processes

GE has created dedicated processes by putting new organizational structures in place to allocate resources to disruptive projects. The main structure is the GE India P&L. Until 2009, GE Healthcare was organized along product groups, where each product group was responsible for its P&L. In late 2009, GE introduced its "one GE" strategy in India, where it gave GE India its own P&L. This also meant own control of budget processes. As John Flannery, the previous CEO of GE India put it in an interview to a newspaper:

> The change to direct reporting is monumental as it fundamentally changes in many ways the business operations. . .The decision making is faster and so is spotting opportunities and acting upon them. India for a lot of MNCs is 3–5 % of business, but for myself and the team here it's 150 % of our business. So, the sense of urgency is very different in that context.
> (Sinha 2010)

GE India has control of budget and product development for the local market. Thus, if opportunities for the BOP are identified, those projects get funded from GE India directly, rather than having to apply for funding at the headquarters.

GE India reported into the Global Growth Organization (GGO), headed by John Rice, the vice chairman of GE. The GGO was setup to empower the emerging markets with resources and give it more autonomy to make decisions. The GGO is responsible for funding "In Country for Country" (ICFC) programs. This stands for products designed and developed in a country for that country. The program manager for ICFC programs in India summarized the advantages of these structures:

> What that gives you is the ability to seek funding for opportunities that are highly relevant in the Indian marketplace. So you go to John and tell him, 'Here's this market opportunity'. If I look at the overall number, it may not get prioritized within the Healthcare business because it's still a small number. It's an infant market. We need to create this market, grow this market. Whereas for India, it's all the more relevant because [GE's operations in] India can grow only if we invest the kind of money that we need for such products that are extremely relevant and designed solely for Indian requirements.
> (Interview 2H)

GE Healthcare India has setup this unique role of a program manager for ICFC programs who pivots between GE Healthcare India and the GGO. He is responsible for ensuring ICFC project ideas from India get appropriate access to funding from the GGO. In a broad sense, he is the ambassador for frugal innovations from India to the GGO or GE's headquarters. He described his role as:

On one hand I work with healthcare folks [in India] to determine what the market needs are, what the commercial pain points are, what the product portfolio gaps are. I then go back to GGO and explain to them why these are the gaps, [and] why we need the money to fill these gaps

(Interview 2H)

Thus, GE Healthcare India has put in place decision-making processes that give disruptive innovations a special status. Disruptive projects coming out of GE India for the Indian market run through dedicated processes (under ICFC program) that fall under the responsibility of GE India. As the quote by John Flannery emphasized, these projects are given special importance. These processes also ensure that these projects do not get lost as part of the overall business for whom these might be perceived as low priority. The ICFC program is also headed by a senior manager whose responsibility is to ensure that the disruptive projects for the Indian market get the resources they need from different sources within the company.

6.5.2.2 Reconfigured Values

The healthymagination initiative has brought the need to improve access and affordability of healthcare to the forefront within GE Healthcare. GE Healthcare has been able to operationalize the healthymagination vision by changing its innovation process. Cost, access and quality are now the three evaluation criteria in the companies' New Product Introduction (NPI) process. The value propositions of new product introductions are evaluated against the three axes of cost, quality and access to determine whether or not to pursue the project. As the erstwhile CEO of GE Healthcare Systems, Omar Ishrak noted about the healthymagination vision translating into its product development process[5]:

All new products must be designed in a way that a value proposition for those products must be considered during the initial phase of design...and by value proposition, we mean that whether that product is going to provide an improvement in cost to the health care system... whether it will increase access...or whether it will improve quality. So every new product will have to be gauged and assessed as to what value it will provide in terms of cost, quality, and access

Prior to healthymagination, there was a strategic filter in place for evaluating new product introductions that tried to determine whether the new product or technology could demonstrate a substantial improvement in imaging quality that a clinician would recognize (Kumar and Rangan 2012). This demonstrates the classical sustaining innovation mindset that most incumbents have (Christensen and Raynor 2003), which is improving quality for current customers.

With healthymagination, all projects are evaluated upfront in terms of value creation along the three axes. This is done upfront, before the New Product

---

[5] Interview available online on GE's official website: http://www.ge.com/audio_video/ge/health/healthymagination_vision.html.

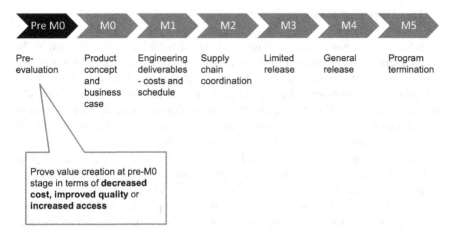

Fig. 6.2 Change healthymagination brought to the New Product Introduction process at GE Healthcare

Introduction process starts. It ensures that disruptive innovations, which previously couldn't have fulfilled the strategic filter criteria of demonstrable quality improvement, get priority because of their value proposition to increase access or decrease costs substantially vis-à-vis status quo (Fig. 6.2).

Thus, disruptive innovations for the BOP that can increase access or decrease cost compared to status quo fit well into the healthymagination framework and do not get rejected in the resource allocation processes for new product development. This is supported by this comment made by the CTO of GE Healthcare in Bangalore:

> The healthymagination framework fits almost perfectly. It's almost scripted for India. Every dimension is interrelated and is important... So for us actually it ends up being a perfect framework to articulate the challenges, to help evaluate opportunities, to help take products to market.
> (Interview 2G)

GE claims that impact of healthymagination initiative is beyond just the product development process, although this is most relevant for the purposes of this study. As this quote from Jeff Immelt, the Chairman of GE in the letter to their investors, points out, the initiative has led to a transformation in various aspects of the company:

> This commitment has transformed our entire approach to health—from the way we motivate and engage employees and consumers, to the way we collaborate with partners and develop new products. Today, healthymagination serves as a rallying cry for meaningful innovation to address the world's biggest health issues. It's a call for better products at more price points in more regions... In short, it's a call for better health worldwide.
> (GE 2011)

6.5.2.3   Dedicated Resources

GE's healthymagination initiative has also set aside $3 bn out of the total $6 bn commitment to launch products that improve cost, access and quality of healthcare. This involves not just in-house development but also acquisition or partnerships with external companies. Thus, the healthymagination initiative also provides dedicated funds for disruptive innovation ideas that might come from within or outside the firm. Projects like the cooperation with Embrace, to distribute very low cost baby warmers to rural areas, fall into this category.

Projects within GE Healthcare, which fit into the framework of healthymagination, can seek funding from healthymagination resources. Thus, disruptive projects that otherwise might not get resources from existing business units, have opportunities to seek resources elsewhere. As an example, the MIC team in India is receiving support from the healthymagination initiative to fund its macroeconomics research. This research helps the team to understand fundamental healthcare challenges in the maternal and infant care space in India and other emerging markets. As this is a new market for GE, building this market knowledge is crucial for their success.

Over and above the healthymagination initiative, GE India and Global Growth Organization, with their mandate to increase GE's presence in emerging markets, have a dedicated budget for developing products for the local markets. Tapping into these funds that are dedicated for BOP markets and value segment products, enables disruptive innovation projects to find resources. This way, mechanisms in established firms that would favor sustaining innovations over disruptive innovations are overcome.

6.5.2.4   Building Market-Related Competencies

By dedicating resources, processes and reconfiguring values to accommodate disruptive innovations within its organizational structures, GE Healthcare is combating the tendency of resource allocation processes to ignore disruptive innovations.

GE Healthcare has also taken steps to counteract the lack of market-facing organizational competency, Henderson's explanation for incumbent failure to respond to disruptive innovations (Henderson 2006).

Appropriate market-related capabilities are essential for successful product development and commercialization (Li and Calantone 1998; Danneels 2002). Exploring disruptive innovations that target new and emerging customer segments requires major changes in patterns of behavior and search by established firms (Danneels 2002). Established firms have market-related competencies for their existing markets or markets close to theirs and consequently may fail to develop or respond to disruptive innovations that target new customer segments or new customer preferences (Henderson 2006). It is, therefore, essential for companies to develop these new market-related competencies.

In the case of GE Healthcare, this translates to building local BOP market-related competencies. The BOP market is different from developed markets and has several characteristics and challenges that are unique to it as seen in Chap. 2. GE Healthcare has understood this and over the last few years, it has built local capabilities in India and other key emerging markets for product development for their value segments. Besides the engineering capability that it already had in place through the R&D center, GE Healthcare has created teams with product management, upstream marketing and market research skills in key emerging markets such as India for certain business areas. For instance, in the MIC space, there are product managers in India, China, Latin America and the Middle East. The MIC space in India has a complete marketing and product development team involved in various aspects—market research, development as well as managing local partnerships and government engagement. The importance of this was emphasized by the MIC value segment leader:

> So this is one of the most important things—setting up the organization such that the team has the empowerment to do things, the team has experienced people to do it, and the team has the right people sitting here to actually identify what exactly the need [of the local market] is. So you need qualified people who have different skill sets. You can't just run this whole thing with an R&D/engineering mindset.
> (Interview 2K)

Along similar lines, the manager of the ICFC program made the following statement:

> Since the launch of the Lullaby Warmer Prime, we have seen significant traction from the Government and small nursing homes. We can attribute this significant commercial demand to our investment in co-creation efforts with these new customer segments during the product development phase.
> (Interview 2J)

6.5.3 Ambidexterity in Action at GE Healthcare

These value segment innovations targeting the BOP represent emerging market opportunities, where firms need to diverge from the ongoing business and invest into exploration. As literature points out, it is vital for companies to balance exploitation and exploration, i.e., to be ambidextrous (O'Reilly and Tushman 2011; Raisch et al. 2009).

While the previous section concentrated on measures in place at GE to protect potentially disruptive innovations, this section describes how GE Healthcare achieves ambidexterity in simultaneously hosting both sustaining and disruptive innovation streams within its boundaries.

6.5.3.1   Structural Differentiation and Integration

GE Healthcare has adopted an ambidextrous design to balance its exploitation and exploration activities (O'Reilly and Tushman 2004). The existing high-end product segments serving developed markets are organized under the "premium segment" whereas the emerging-market products developed to make technology affordable are organized under the "value segment". The premium segment is responsible for developing products for GE Healthcare's existing high-margin customers, which represents sustaining innovations. The value-segment caters to low-income markets, representing disruptive innovations.

This organizational design ensures that the value segment leader is autonomous and empowered to develop products for BOP markets. The value segment is not a sidelined or neglected division within the company, but one with legitimacy and authority. The CTO of GE Healthcare described this empowerment:

> Each of these businesses today inside of the company has a general manager for value and that person, even though their business might be one-twentieth of the premium business, they [the value segment general manager and the premium segment general manager] are peers and at the same level of the staff
> (Interview 2F)

While structural differentiation is necessary to clearly delineate exploration from exploitation, organizations run the risk of isolating explorative activities and under-utilizing existing assets. Thus, structural differentiation needs to be combined with targeted integration activities (O'Reilly and Tushman 2008; Jansen et al. 2009). With an ambidextrous design, GE Healthcare ensures integration through the ambidextrous manager who is responsible for both segments (Tushman et al. 2010). The premium segment and the value segment also share a common CTO who oversees key product development decisions. These managers need to ensure that newly created value segments can leverage knowledge and expertise that exists within the company. After all, GE Healthcare is a market leader within several product categories. The MIC engineering leader described the integration as:

> It's extremely important that you don't lose the global connect...You have to leverage the existing platform; otherwise it's completely inefficient...So, for example, the heating system [in the baby warmer], we do leverage a premium platform for our heating because that is very crucial [part] and we have 30 years of experience in heating... Of course, we have reduced cost, we have changed the material, [etc.]
> (Interview 2M)

As seen in the figure below, the organizational design of GE Healthcare is very similar to the ambidextrous organization described by O'Reilly and Tushman (2004). All functions related to product development fall under the segments, whereas sales is a regional function and does not fall under this matrix, thus slightly different from the model (Fig. 6.3).

As demonstrated above, GE Healthcare achieves structural ambidexterity by putting in place differentiated entities with integrative mechanisms within an

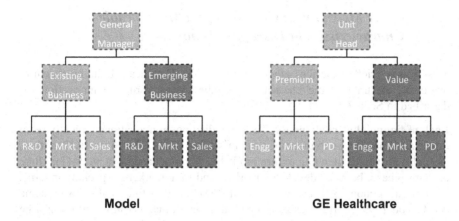

Model   **GE Healthcare**

Fig. 6.3 Comparison of Ambidextrous Organizational Design by O'Reilly and Tushman (2004) and GE Healthcare's Organizational Design

ambidextrous organizational design to ensure disruptive innovation streams can simultaneously be hosted along with existing sustaining innovation streams.

6.5.3.2 Overarching Vision and Strategic Intent

Research points out the need for strategic intent to pursue exploratory units as well as an overarching vision across the exploration and exploitation units (O'Reilly and Tushman 2011; O'Reilly and Tushman 2008). GE's strategic intent of being a global organization legitimizes the need to create strong local capabilities in emerging markets. At the same time, the healthymagination initiative provides a common vision across GE Healthcare.

The three healthymagination pillars have resulted in a reconfiguration of values within the company. GE Healthcare has traditionally been a technology leader in its industry. Improving the quality of healthcare is what GE Healthcare historically has been innovating towards. With the goals of improving access and decreasing cost, the initiative explicitly aims at shifting GE Healthcare's focus towards low-income emerging markets and disruptive innovations. The healthymagination initiative is, thus, able to create an overarching vision for units serving existing developed markets as well as new emerging markets within GE Healthcare.

Proposition: Established firms can ambidextrously manage disruptive and sustaining innovations through structural differentiation and integration as well as an overarching vision and strategic intent that reconciles both innovation streams.

6.5.4 Other Measures in Combating the Unfavorable Characteristics of Disruptive Innovations

This section briefly describes other approaches GE Healthcare India has taken to overcome the unfavorable characteristics inherent to disruptive innovations as described in Sect. 3.3.

Lack of financial attractiveness To recap, disruptive innovations typically seem financially unattractive to incumbents (Christensen 2006). Moreover, BOP markets have also proven challenging to turn profitable (Karamchandani et al. 2011). There is a large chasm between developed markets and BOP markets, especially in terms of informal economies (Banerjee and Duflo 2007), and institutional voids (Khanna and Palepu 1999). Further, as mentioned in Chap. 2, markets in the BOP must be created as opposed to addressing existing markets in developed economies. Thus, BOP markets pose new risks to MNCs and are sometimes viewed as being financially unattractive. Even at GE prior to 2009, proposals for low-cost innovations targeting BOP markets were often met with fear of cannibalization and dragging down profit margins (Immelt and Govindrajan 2009).

GE Healthcare's management tries to counter this by accounting for the cost for creating markets while evaluating projects for the BOP and emerging markets. As the CTO of GE Healthcare in India mentioned:

> Then we also look at if there is an element of market creation that has to happen, which means new users, different categories of applications, etc. That may take some more time. And we factor that in.
> (Interview 2F)

In terms of product portfolio, the value segment teams in India are substantially diverging from the norm by building some of the lowest cost equipment within GE Healthcare, in some cases about 80–90 % cheaper than the high-end products in their portfolio. In order to manage risks involved in the development and commercialization process, GE Healthcare has begun to assess many of these market risks and technical risks upfront. This approach is summarized well by this quote by the MIC value segment leader:

> So what we are trying to do is, try to move risks up to the front of the program, do things as early as possible...Can we find out the customer needs before even we embark on a New Product Introduction, which means can we fund a small team to go and identify needs even though it's not part of any NPI process, so that once a need is identified then we can put it to the NPI process very quickly. Can we mitigate technology risks earlier in the process as a separate activity, not as part of the NPI process... So, for example, can we get a heater head at 20 % of the cost of the current heater head? ... All of those [go to market] strategies have to be thoroughly thought of. So the entire supply chain piece, the entire commercialization piece, the service piece... all this has to form the go/no go for the product development
> (Interview 2K)

Further, GE Healthcare exploits these value segment products by selling more sophisticated versions in less price-sensitive markets around the world at a higher price. Many of GE Healthcare's ICFC products are being sold outside India, for instance in Eastern Europe, the Middle East and Latin America. The MIC value segment leader explains the success of selling its products outside India:

> If you can succeed with decent margins in an extremely price sensitive market like India, then when you go outside India you can potentially extract more value and get a better [profit] margin
> (Interview 2K)

This is one of the basic tenets of reverse innovation, taking innovations first adopted by emerging markets to more mature markets (Govindarajan and Ramamurti 2011). GE Healthcare, with its disruptive innovations, wins by keeping the cost low and exploiting higher margins when selling these products in more mature markets.

Thus, by accounting for increased risk and time requirement due to market creation, moving risks upfront in the product development process and leveraging reverse innovation, GE Healthcare is able to mitigate some of the financial risk of disruptive innovations.

Incompatible Value Networks As explained in Sect. 3.3, disruptive innovations do not fit into the embedded value networks of the organization and new market disruptive innovations typically create new value networks (Christensen and Raynor 2003). GE Healthcare faced—and is still facing—similar challenges of embedding their low-cost innovations into their existing value network. This quote from the MIC marketing executive summarized the problem well:

> Today we sell premium products to premium hospitals... Now once you decide to go to the bottom of the pyramid, once you decide to serve primary healthcare it's a completely different ball game. So it means you're going to the rural areas, you're going to mom and pop sort of entrepreneurs...
> (Interview 2L)

Also this quote by the GE executive responsible for the MAC 400 and MAC i emphasizes the point above:

> We thought we could use our distributors. But when we asked them they said 'No, I can't send my guy to the villages for the small margin of 80$. I have my rep in Mumbai and I have him sell big equipment. That gives me much more money'. They refused to do that [sell the low-cost ECG devices]
> (Interview 2E)

This forced GE Healthcare India to change their distribution strategy. They are learning from, and partnering with distribution channels of other industries like the pharmaceutical industry and consumer goods industry to build their own distribution network for their low-cost products. Besides the distribution channel, GE Healthcare is learning to work with different types of customers, including governments in developing countries because they are mainly responsible for procuring equipment for primary health centers in more remote areas. GE Healthcare is also innovating on other business process fronts in order to change their current upstream value network, e.g., by providing financing to purchase equipment by tying up with local banks, so as to ensure doctors in rural areas, who are generally managers/entrepreneurs of their practice, have access to loans.

Further, the MIC value team has defined its vision as "making an impact on IMR". This vision, rather than a one-dimensional mandate to create products for the BOP, forces them to take a more holistic approach and innovate along the entire value network. This not only affects their go-to-market strategy, e.g., partnering with NGOs such as East meets West to provide a more comprehensive support to providers, but also how they develop their products.

6.6 Discussion

Companies are increasingly looking at creating new markets for their products in low-income segments in emerging economies (Prahalad and Hart 2002). However, serving these markets poses new challenges to MNCs from developing affordable, "good enough" products to commercializing these innovations. This chapter explores GE Healthcare's ventures into serving low-income markets in India with disruptive innovations. In particular, this study explores organizational conditions that have enabled this incumbent to successfully and systematically develop and commercialize potentially disruptive innovations to serve BOP markets.

As shown through GE Healthcare's efforts, companies can create measures to protect disruptive innovations within the boundaries of the organization, namely by creating dedicated processes and resources for disruptive innovations, reconfiguring values to help prioritize disruptive innovations and building market-related competencies for exploring these new markets. The healthymagination initiative has reconfigured the values of GE Healthcare, right down to what products GE Healthcare brings to the market. GE has also ensured dedicated resources, processes and built BOP-related market competencies for enabling disruptive innovations, through corporate initiatives, structures and processes.

The study also shows that GE Healthcare's ambidextrous organizational design creates the right conditions to host disruptive and sustaining innovation streams within its boundaries. The structural separation of premium and value segments as well as the overarching healthymagination vision of improving quality as well as cost and access to healthcare gives value segment products legitimacy within the organization. Thus, the two elements of ambidexterity of differentiated and integrated structures as well as an overarching vision and strategic intent have been shown to be enablers.

GE Healthcare's structural changes in its organizational design have laid the foundations to help the company systematically create potentially disruptive innovations. GE Healthcare has adopted a permanent ambidextrous design by separating all its product units into premium and value segments. This fixed structure is an integral part of GE Healthcare's organization, as opposed to transitional organizational structures put in place for temporary innovation episodes (Tushman et al. 2010).

Thus, this work contributes to emerging disruptive innovation theory (Christensen 2006), by exploring organizational designs required by incumbent firms to deal with strategic challenges associated with disruptive innovations in the context of BOP markets (Danneels 2004). It also contributes to organizational ambidexterity theory by providing empirical evidence from the GE Healthcare case to show how a company has adopted an ambidextrous design to deal with hosting contradictory innovation types (Gupta et al. 2006).

Companies like GE Healthcare are leading the way to create disruptive innovations in medical technology by focusing on BOP markets. These disruptive innovations have the potential to not only shape the healthcare industry at the BOP by making quality healthcare accessible to those who previously could not afford it, but also help in tackling the global health care crisis.

References

Banerjee, A. V., & Duflo, E. (2007). The economic lives of the poor. *Journal of Economic Perspectives, 21*(1), 141–167.

Chandramouli, K. (2011). *Family welfare statistics in India.* India: Ministry of Health and Family Affairs.

Christensen, C. M. (1997). *The innovator's dilemma: When new technologies cause great firms to fail.* Boston: Harvard Business School Press.

Christensen, C. M. (2006). The ongoing process of building a theory of disruption. *Journal of Product Innovation Management, 23*(1), 39–55.

Christensen, C. M., & Bower, J. L. (1996). Customer power, strategic investment, and the failure of leading firms. *Strategic Management Journal, 17*(3), 197–218.

Christensen, C. M., & Raynor, M. (2003). *The innovator's solution: Creating and sustaining successful growth.* Boston, MA: Harvard Business Press.

Christiansen, C. M., & Raynor, M. (2003). *The innovator's solution: Creating and sustaining successful growth.* Boston, MA: Harvard Business Press.

Danneels, E. (2002). The dynamics of product innovation and firm competences. *Strategic Management Journal, 23*(12), 1095–1121.

Danneels, E. (2004). Disruptive technology reconsidered: A critique and research agenda. *Journal of Product Innovation Management, 21*, 246–258.

Danneels, E. (2006). Dialogue on the effects of disruptive technology on firms and industries. *Journal of Product Innovation Management, 23*(1), 2–4.

Dutta, R. (2010). India requires 100 PET CT Centres. *Express Healthcare.*

Economist. (2009, April 18). Lessons from a frugal innovator. *The Economist.*

Eisenhardt, K. M. (1989). Building theories from case-study approach. *Academy of Management Review, 14*, 532–550.

GE. (2009). *GE 2009 Annual Report.*

GE. (2010a). *GE healthymagination annual report 2009.*

GE. (2010b). *GE's Technology Center celebrates ten years of innovation in India.* GE News Center.

GE. (2011). *GE healthymagination annual report 2010.*

GE. (2013). *GE Annual Report 2013.*

Gibson, C., & Birkenshaw, J. (2004). The antecedents, consequences and mediating role of organizational ambidexterity. *Academy of Management Journal, 47*(2), 209–226.

Gilbert, C. G. (2005). Unbundling the structure of inertia: Resource versus routine rigidity. *Academy of Management Journal, 48*(5), 741–763.

Govindarajan, V., & Ramamurti, R. (2011). Reverse innovation, emerging markets, and global strategy. *Global Strategy Journal, 1*(3–4), 191–205.

Gupta, A. K., Smith, K. G., & Shalley, C. E. (2006). The interplay between exploration and exploitation. *Academy of Management Journal, 49*(4), 693–706.

Halme, M., Lindeman, S., & Linna, P. (2012). Innovation for inclusive business: Intrapreneurial Bricolage in multinational corporations. *Journal of Management Studies, 49*(4), 743–784.

Hart, S., & Christensen, C. (2002, Fall). The great leap. *MIT Sloan Managment Review*.

He, Z.-L., & Wong, P.-K. (2004). Exploration vs. exploitation: An empirical test of the ambidexterity hypothesis. *Organization Science, 15*(4), 481–494.

Henderson, R. (2006). The innovator's dilemma as a problem of organizational competence. *Journal of Product Innovation Management, 23*(1), 5–11.

Henderson, R. M., & Clark, K. B. (1990). Architectural innovation: The reconfiguration of existing product technologies and the failure of established firms. *Administrative Science Quarterly, 35*, 9–30.

Immelt, J., & Govindrajan, V. (2009). How GE is disrupting itself. *Harvard Buisness Review, 87* (10), 56–65.

Jaiswal, A. K. (2008). The fortune at the bottom or the middle of the pyramid? *Innovations: Technology, Governance, Globalization, 3*(1), 85–100.

Jansen, J. J. P., Tempelaar, M. P., Van den Bosch, F. A. J., & Volberda, H. W. (2009). Structural differentiation and ambidexterity: The mediating role of integration mechanisms. *Organization Science, 20*(4), 797–811.

Karamchandani, A., Kubzansky, M., & Lalwani, N. (2011). Is the bottom of the pyramid really for you? *Harvard Business Review, 89*(3), 107–111.

Khanna, T., & Palepu, K. (1999). The right way to restructure conglomerates in emerging markets. *Harvard Business Review, 77*, 125–135.

Kumar, V., & Rangan, K. (2012). *Healthymagination at GE Healthcare Systems*. Harvard Business School Case Study.

Lemer, J., & Crooks, E. (2010, November 9). Rice to lead GE in emerging markets. *Financial Times*.

Li, T., & Calantone, R. J. (1998). The impact of market knowledge competence on new product advantage: Conceptualization and empirical examination. *The Journal of Marketing, 62*, 13–29.

London, T., & Hart, S. (2004). Reinventing strategies for emerging markets: Beyond the transnational model. *Journal of International Business Studies, 35*(5), 350–370.

London, T., & Hart, S. (Eds.). (2010). *Next generation business strategies for the base of the pyramid*. Upper Saddle River, NJ: Pearson Education Inc.

Mahajan-Bansal, N., & Goyal, M. (2009a). Jeff Immelt: "India Will Be a Centrepiece in Our Growth". *Forbes India*.

Mahajan-Bansal, N., & Goyal, M. (2009b). GE has its finger on the Indian pulse, at last. *Forbes India*.

McDermott, C. M., & OConnor, G. C. (2002). Managing radical innovation: An overview of emergent strategy issues. *Journal of Product Innovation Management, 19*(6), 424–438.

Mitchell, W. (2008). Transforming a successful company: General Electric's organizational strategy Duke University.

O'Reilly, C., & Tushman, M. (2004). The ambidextrous organization. *Harvard Business Review, 82*(4), 74–81.

O'Reilly, C. A., & Tushman, M. L. (2008). Ambidexterity as a dynamic capability: Resolving the innovator's dilemma. *Research in Organizational Behavior, 28*, 185–206.

O'Reilly, C. A. I., & Tushman, M. L. (2011). Organizational ambidexterity in action: How managers explore and exploit. *California Management Review, 53*(4), 5–22.

Olsen, M., & Boxenbaum, E. (2009). Bottom-of-the-Pyramid: Organizational barriers to implementation. *California Management Review, 51*(4), 100–125.

Prahalad, C. K. (2004). *The fortune at the bottom of the pyramid: Eradicating poverty through profits*. Upper Saddle River, NJ: Wharton School Publishing.

Prahalad, C. K., & Hart, S. (2002). The fortune at the bottom of the pyramid. *Strategy & Business, 26*.

Prahalad, C. K., & Lieberthal, K. (1998). The end of corporate imperialism. *Harvard Buisness Review, 76*, 68–79.

Raisch, S., & Birkinshaw, J. (2008). Organizational ambidexterity: Antecedents, outcomes, and moderators. *Journal of Management, 34*(3), 375–409.

Raisch, S., Birkinshaw, J., Probst, G., & Tushman, M. L. (2009). Organizational ambidexterity: Balancing exploitation and exploration for sustained performance. *Organization Science, 20*(4), 685–695.

Ricart, J. E., Enright, M. J., Ghemawat, P., Hart, S. L., & Khanna, T. (2004). New frontiers in international strategy. *Journal of International Business Studies, 35*(3), 175–200.

Siggelkow, N. (2007). Persuasion with case studies. *Academy of Management Journal, 50*(1), 20–24.

Simsek, Z. (2009). Organizational ambidexterity: Towards a multilevel understanding. *Journal of Management Studies, 46*(4), 597–624.

Sinha, V. (2010, June 1). We'll now produce what India wants: John Flannery, GE India. *The Economic Times*.

Sirmon, D. G., Hitt, M. A., & Ireland, R. D. (2007). Managing firm resources in dynamic environments to create value: Looking inside the black box. *Academy of Management Review, 32*(1), 273–292.

Smith, W. K., & Tushman, M. L. (2005). Managing strategic contradictions: A top management model for managing innovation streams. *Organization Science, 16*(5), 522–536.

Tiwari, R., & Herstatt, C. (2012). Assessing India's lead market potential for cost-effective innovations. *Journal of Indian Business Research, 4*(2), 97–115.

Tushman, M. L., & Anderson, P. (1986). Technological discontinuities and organizational environments. *Administrative Science Quarterly, 31*(3), 439–465.

Tushman, M. L., & O'Reilly, C. A. (1996). Ambidextrous organizations. *California Management Review, 38*(4), 8–30.

Tushman, M., Smith, W. K., Wood, R. C., Westerman, G., & O'Reilly, C. (2010). Organizational designs and innovation streams. *Industrial and Corporate Change, 19*(5), 1331–1366.

Yin, R. K. (1994). *Case study research* (2nd ed.). Thousand Oaks, CA: Sage.

Chapter 7
Study 3: Lessons from Tata: How Leadership Can Drive Disruptive Innovations

7.1 Introduction

Disruptive innovations, especially new market disruptive innovations, have the potential to reshape existing markets and create new growth opportunities for companies (Christensen and Raynor 2003). Bottom of the Pyramid (BOP) markets offer ideal grounds for commercializing disruptive innovations since they have large, unaddressed needs, seek extremely affordable solutions that fit local needs and are largely ignored by MNCs (Prahalad 2004; Hart and Christensen 2002). However, as discussed in the previous chapters, disruptive innovation theory posits that established companies are not able to successfully commercialize disruptive innovations because their internal resource allocation processes favor sustaining innovations that focus on existing markets and profitable customers. Disruptive innovation theory thus recommends that companies spin-off disruptive projects (Christensen and Raynor 2003; Christensen 1997).

The previous chapter on GE Healthcare in India sheds light on how an established firm can leverage structural ambidexterity to systematically develop and commercialize disruptive innovations for the BOP and emerging markets at large. Similarly, the Tata Group is another conglomerate that has developed products and services for the BOP market. Tata Swach (*Swach* mean *pure* in Hindi), a low cost water filter, was developed and launched for the BOP market in India, a market that faces enormous healthcare challenges due to the unavailability of safe drinking water.

In 2009, when Tata launched the Swach, a large version was priced at INR 999 and a smaller version was priced at INR 499, approximately $21 and $11 respectively.[1] The closest competitor was Hindustan Unilever (HUL), Unilever's Indian arm, whose Pureit storage water filters were priced at INR 2,000 [$43[2]]. The

---

[1] Using $1 = INR 46.78 exchange rates on 30th Dec 2009.

[2] Using $1 = INR 46.78 exchange rates on 30th Dec 2009.

© Springer International Publishing Switzerland 2015
A. Ramdorai, C. Herstatt, *Frugal Innovation in Healthcare*, India Studies in Business and Economics, DOI 10.1007/978-3-319-16336-9_7

other more established players in the market offered water purifiers above $100, which were not only unaffordable to poorer segments but also required running water and electricity that is reliably available to only a minority of the Indian population. Thus, Tata Swach targeted an entirely new market segment, the BOP market, by virtue of its affordable price tag and without the requirement of electricity and running water.

Tata Swach had its genesis within Tata Consultancy Services' (TCS) R&D center, Tata Research Development and Design Center (TRDDC), in Pune. The initial prototype, Sujal, was built using widely available natural material, Rice Husk Ash (RHA). However, the filtration performance was only about 85 %, i.e., only about 85 % of the harmful microbes were destroyed in the filtration process. Development of the technology stalled because of lack of resources and the project was subsequently relegated to a Corporate Social Responsibility (CSR) initiative of TCS. The project was re-catalyzed when Mr. R. Gopalakrishnan, the then vice chairman of Tata Chemicals (TCL), visited the R&D labs and was introduced to Sujal. RG, as he is known in the company, marshaled resources for the project and invested in developing Swach into an affordable consumer product.

The Tata Swach case study helps unravel the role a senior leader plays in commercializing disruptive innovations from within the boundaries of an established firm. While disruptive innovation literature talks about how CEOs and top leaders have played a critical role in helping the company respond to disruptive innovations successfully (Christensen and Bower 1996), it is relatively silent on exactly what role the leader assumes.

This chapter will take a deeper look into the process of development and commercialization of the Tata Swach. It will focus on the role played by leadership in the innovation process. This longitudinal study will also lend a perspective to understanding ambidexterity over time. Few studies have looked at these mechanisms as they evolve over time (Westerman et al. 2006; Raisch et al. 2009). With this perspective, this study aims to deepen our understanding by taking a process view of ambidexterity and exploring how mechanisms of differentiation and integration unfold over a period of time.

The first part of the chapter sets the theoretical foundation of leadership and ambidexterity. This is embedded in the classical innovation management literature of individual roles in the innovation process. The next section, presents the gap in literature and the research question this chapter focuses on. The empirical section that follows presents the case study and gives an overview of the Tata Swach project and other BOP projects at Tata. Subsequently, the analysis section presents findings from the case study, followed by concluding remarks at the end of the chapter.

7.2 Theoretical Foundations

7.2.1 Leadership and Innovation

Senior leadership plays a crucial role in the facilitation of innovations and in creating an environment within an organization that is conducive to organizational learning (Van de Ven 1986). Several studies have concluded that support from senior management has a positive effect on the success of a project (Cooper and Kleinschmidt 1995, 2007; Ernst 2002). Support from senior management in the form of freeing up resources and people for the project (Cooper and Kleinschmidt 2007), general commitment to new products (Cooper and Kleinschmidt 2007) and involvement on a day-to-day basis has been proven necessary (Johne and Snelson 1988). To put their role into context, this section will borrow from the long tradition in innovation management scholarship that describes individual roles in the innovation process.

Research in the area of individual support during the innovation process has roots in both Anglo-American as well as German literature. Schon (1963) and later Chakrabarti (1974) identified the pivotal role of individuals in the product development process. Schon (1963) used the term "champion" to describe the role of these key individuals. Maidique (1980, p. 64) defines a champion as "a member of an organization, who creates, defines and adopts an idea for a new technological innovation and who is willing to risk his or her position or prestige to make possible, the innovation's successful implementation".

Almost in parallel to Schon and Chakrabarti, a new strain of research emerged in the German scholarly community through Witte (1973), where he described the existence of promoters in the innovation process (Rost et al. 2007). Witte's research identifies a dyad of promoters: the power promoter, who uses his hierarchical power to gain support for the innovation and to remove hindrances within the organization and the technology promoter who contributes with his technological expertise to the project. In contrast, a champion's role is not a particularly senior one within an organization, but that of a middle manager (Rogers 2003; Smith 2007). The role of a champion or multiple promoters is considered a success factor for the innovation process (Brockhoff et al. 1999; Hauschildt and Chakrabarti 1989). Several works have explored these roles and parallels can be made between the German and Anglo-American literature of roles played by individuals in the innovation process. Table 7.1 shows the interrelationships among the different scholarly works.

The role of the executive champion, in line with the power promoter, is one of a senior leader, who exerts his/her authority to realize the project (Chakrabarti and Hauschildt 1989). The main role of the executive champion or power promoter is to provide guidance (Rhoades et al. 1978), exert hierarchical power to protect innovation against organizational opposition (Hauschildt and Kirchmann 2001), and channel resources towards the innovation (Maidique 1980). The executive champion's or power promoter's exertion of power and influence can be crucial for the success of a novel idea or innovation (Howell et al. 2005).

Table 7.1 Comparison of innovator roles from selected literature

| | Source | | | |
Role	Rothwell (Rothwell et al. 1974)	Roberts (Roberts and Fusfeld 1980; Rhoades et al. 1978)	Maidique (Maidique 1980)	Witte/Hauschildt (Witte 1973; Hauschildt and Kirchmann 2001)
Sponsorship	Chief Executive	Sponsor/Coach	Executive Champion	Power promoter
Championing	Product Champion	Champion	Product Champion	Process promoter
Technical expert	Technical innovator	Chief Scientist	Technologist	Expert promoter

In subsequent research on radical innovations, Leifer (2000) termed the role that one or more key senior executives play as 'patrons'. Patrons provide "organizational protection, resources and encouragement" to radical innovation projects (Leifer 2000, p. 162). Another metaphor used in the role played by senior executives is "Godfather" (Smith 2007). Smith analyzes the political aspects of the innovation process and identifies the need for senior members who are well connected and highly respected within the organization, who use their influence to remove organization hurdles that stand in the way of radical innovation projects. In the three cases he analyzes through biographical research, he points out that the success of the projects was closely linked to the actions of a senior executive.

While the positive role senior leaders play in innovation projects has been established, the contrary has also been shown through studies that point to senior managers' cognitive biases, which make them favor existing business over new ones (Levinthal and March 1993; Leonard-Barton 1992). As Tripsas and Gavetti (2000) show, it was the cognitive bias of the top management team at Polaroid that created barriers towards adopting the new business model that came with the shift toward digital photography. Thus, senior leadership plays an important role in steering the organization and allocating resources between existing businesses and new opportunities and exploring this role in light of disruptive innovations is crucial.

Within disruptive innovation theory, Christensen takes note of the importance of leadership support in successfully responding to a disruptive innovation in his case study of the disk drive industry. The one exceptional case of an incumbent that succeeded in developing the newer technology of disk drives from within the mainstream organization was one where the CEO heavily pushed the disruptive technology through (Christensen and Bower 1996). Christensen et al. attribute this to the "managerial force" of the CEO (Christensen and Bower 1996, p. 213). However, the case study remains silent on exactly what the leader did as the study focused on the recommendation of spinning out disruptive technology from the company.

7.2.2 Leadership and Ambidexterity

Top leadership is considered to be an important source and locus of ambidexterity (Tushman and Anderson 1986) and is recommended to hold the tension between the core businesses and new opportunities (Tushman et al. 2011); however, little is known about how leaders can act ambidextrously (Raisch et al. 2009).

While most current literature on ambidexterity focuses on company or business unit level of analysis, conceptual and empirical understanding about ambidexterity at an individual level is still being formed (Raisch et al. 2009; Gupta et al. 2006). This is why scholars in the area of ambidexterity are calling for more research on ambidexterity at the individual level of analysis (Raisch et al. 2009).

Few insights into characteristics of ambidextrous managers are available, for instance, it is known that behavioral integration among top management team members facilitates ambidexterity (Lubatkin et al. 2006). At an individual level, the manager's decision making ability, connectedness to other organization members and participation in cross-functional mechanisms have shown to positively affect a manager's ambidexterity (Mom et al. 2009).

Leaders must have both short term and long term thinking and manage the strategic contradictions that arise from balancing existing businesses and exploring new markets and lead ambidextrously (Tushman et al. 2011). To balance these contradictions, individuals would need to move away from either/or thinking towards paradoxical thinking (Gibson and Birkenshaw 2004). Thus, Smith and Tushman (2005) posit that paradoxical cognition, the ability to recognize and embrace contradictions, and the ability to differentiate and integrate between strategies for the multiple innovations streams is crucial for top-management.

Differentiating involves making distinctions between the existing products and innovation in their strategies and architecture. Integrating involves identifying synergies between strategies and organizational architectures of the multiple innovation streams. While differentiating and integrating are opposing, they are also complementary and enable each other (Smith and Tushman 2005).

7.3 Research Question and Methodology

7.3.1 Research Question

As noted in previous chapters, it is difficult for established companies to overcome their structures, processes and inertia in order to successfully commercialize disruptive innovations (Christensen and Bower 1996). Studying established firms that have successfully commercialized disruptive innovations from within can help further our understanding of how companies can ambidextrously pursue both disruptive and sustaining innovations (Danneels 2006). The Tata Group provides one such example. Tata developed the Tata Swach for the BOP markets from within its boundaries. In exploring how this was done, it became apparent that the Tata Swach project was enabled by the championing effort of a senior leader at the Tata Group.

As alluded to in Chap. 3, scholars have pointed to internal ventures as an organizational form for established firms to successfully respond to discontinuous technologies (Danneels 2006; Macher and Richman 2004). Moreover, Christensen has acknowledged the role of leadership in developing disruptive innovations from within (Christensen and Bower 1996). However, the concrete roles of the senior leader have not been dealt with thus far. Hence, this case study aims to shine light on how large companies can successfully create disruptive innovations through leadership support.

7.3.2   Methodology

Similar to the other studies, an exploratory case study methodology has been adopted for this study, as explained in detail in Chap. 4. This section provides a brief description of the methodology that is unique to this study.

This is a single case study of the Tata Group, focusing on the Tata Swach project. The Tata Group is well known in India for its philanthropic efforts (Haugh and Talwar 2010; Crabtree 2012). As a contribution to the health of the nation, Tata launched a low cost water filter, Tata Swach in 2009. This case was chosen, as it provided a unique setting to study under what conditions established firms can develop and commercialize disruptive innovations from within. Consistent to inductive research methodology, the detailed research question addressed in this study, developed as the case progressed.

Secondary data, including company press releases, annual reports, and primary data in the form of interviews as well as internal company documentation have been analyzed. In total nine interviews were conducted with management at the Tata Group involved in the Tata Swach project and other similar BOP projects, including senior executives. The semi-structured interviews lasted between 30 and 90 minutes. Most interviews were conducted in person and some interviews were conducted over the telephone because the interviewee was located in another city or because it was a follow-up interview. All interviews were recorded and transcribed, except two that were conducted over phone, where the facility was not available (these were transcribed immediately on the basis of notes taken). All other processes for coding and data analysis are described in Chap. 4. See appendix E for the list of all interviews and the interview numbers.

Finally, the insights arising from the case study were played back to the main interview partner (the senior director of Tata in charge of the Tata Swach project) in form of a written manuscript as well as verbally. The interview partner was in complete agreement with the findings and implications drawn.

7.4 Empirical Context

7.4.1 About Tata Group and Tata Chemicals

The Tata Group is an Indian business conglomerate founded in 1868 by Jamsetji Tata. The group consists of over 100 different companies ranging from steel and automotive to software and hospitality. The Tata Group had revenues of $100 Billion in the financial year 2013–2014. The group employs approximately 580,000 people in over 80 different countries.[3]

The Tata Group has a very unique governance structure. Two thirds of the Tata Group is held by a philanthropic foundation, the Tata Trust (Rowe and Guerrero 2012). The Tata Trust has supported several causes including healthcare, education and livelihood for many decades. This structure plays an important role in the company's value system, which emphasizes the value to "returning to society". This sentiment is mirrored in one its founder, Jamsetji N. Tata's statement:

> In a free enterprise, the community is not just another stakeholder in business, but is in fact the very purpose of its existence.
> (Graham 2010)

The Tata Group, with its long legacy, continues to remain strong in India, where it consistently makes it to the top national brand list (ET-Bureau 2013). Tata's strength is also growing abroad, where international acquisitions have enabled it to develop several markets outside India (Khanna et al. 2008).

Tata Chemicals is an associate company of Tata Sons, the holding company of the Tata Group, and is the world's second largest producer of soda ash.[4] Tata Chemicals is an important industrial player in the Tata Group as it accounted for an annual turnover of $ 2.2 billion in the financial year 2011–2012. TCL is organized under three verticals: [1] Living Essentials, which consists of consumer products, like Tata Salt [2] Industry, entailing bulk and specialty chemicals and [3] Farm Essentials that entails fertilizers and biofuels. It owns factories in UK, USA and Kenya.[5]

TCL is becoming increasingly active in the consumer segment. TCL entered into the salt business in the 1980s and was the first to start selling packaged iodized salt to counter iodine deficiency, a rather widespread problem in India. Tata Salt has

---

[3] http://www.tata.com/htm/Group_Investor_GroupFinancials.htm; *Accessed on 15.08.2014.*

[4] http://www.tata.com/pdf/Tata_fastfacts_final.pdf; *Accessed on 15.08.2014.*

[5] www.tatachemicals.com/

recently launched India's first packaged salt fortified with both iodine and iron. With Tata Salt, TCL went on to build one of the strongest brands, voted one of the 'Most Trusted Food Brand' in India (Group 2008). TCL has built up a vast network of distributors because of Tata Salt.

7.4.2   Tata Swach Project

7.4.2.1   Background

Disease spread stemming from the unavailability of safe drinking water is a major public health issue in India. It is estimated that preventable water borne diseases are the leading cause of death, responsible for taking nearly half a million lives annually in India. It is also a leading killer among children below the age of 5, where every fifth child's life is claimed by infant diarrhea. The main reason for this is the lack of sanitation and lack of access to clean drinking water (Boschi-Pinto et al. 2008).

Compounding the problem is the severe contamination of groundwater by toxins such as fluoride and arsenic in several places in India. In recent years, fluorosis, a crippling bone disease, has emerged as a major health issue in rural India (Srikanth 2009). High levels of arsenic in drinking water cause serious health problems such as nervous dysfunction and cancers of skin and kidney damage. In India, about 66 million people are estimated to be exposed to fluoride contamination in ground water and about 14 million people to arsenic contamination respectively. Other issues include varying iron levels and presence of nitrates and heavy metals (Pant 2002).

Purification of drinking water has to take place straight at the household since the largest source of drinking water in India is ground water (Shiferaw et al. 2008). However, water purification systems in India have a very low penetration level, both in urban as well as rural settings. In 2005, it was estimated that water purifier penetration was about 4 % in urban India and below 1 % rural India (IIPS 2007). Moreover, a majority of households in India would use the same water for drinking, bathing, washing clothes, etc. (IIPS 2007).

Until Swach came along, most purifiers in the market worked on Ultra-Violet or Reverse Osmosis technologies. Both these technologies require running water and electricity. Unilever's Pureit was the only branded water filter in the market priced at INR 2,000, which did not require either electricity or running water. Filters using Ultra-Violet or Reverse Osmosis technology typically started at a price of $100 and were, hence, out of reach for most Indians.

7.4.2.2 History of the Swach

The predecessor of Swach was Sujal, a rudimentary prototype created by Prof. Kapoor at TRDDC in Pune. Prof. Kapoor's aim was to exploit the adsorption properties of Rice Husk Ash (RHA), a commonly available waste product in India. RHA is a by-product when rice is removed from paddy and is available in large quantities in India, but typically has no commercial use except for generating heat. Prof. Kapoor saw potential in using RHA because of two important properties: RHA is mesoporous, i.e., for a certain volume it has a relatively high surface area and RHA has a high amount of activated silica (about 85–90 %) that can adsorb bacteria. By virtue of these two properties, RHA is ideal for applications in water purification.

The rudimentary prototype was made of RHA, pebbles and cements, and weighed about three kilograms. The initial idea was to build a water purifier where the purification material could be sourced and assembled locally as RHA was widely available everywhere. Sujal was capable of destroying about 85 % of germs and bacteria.

Sujal was relegated to the CSR department of Tata, which distributed over 250,000 pieces through NGOs, including 50,000 during the devastating tsunami and earthquake of 2004. For 4–5 years, development on Sujal had stalled since its purification performance did not meet world standards and also because the fabrication process was complex and commercially unviable. The TRDDC team had de-prioritized the project.

This changed when the then vice chairman of Tata Chemicals, Mr. R Gopalakrishnan, also known as RG, visited TRDDC in the beginning of 2006. While being introduced to the projects at TRDDC, the employees showed him a prototype of Sujal. As the project leader of Swach recalled,

> Even though they didn't say it in as many words, it made an impression that they were showing an item in a museum.
> (Interview 3A)

RG is also an Executive Director at Tata Sons, the holding company of the Tata Group and has held several executive positions at different Tata companies. He was very excited about Sujal and saw its potential in becoming a consumer product. Having spent about 30 years in FMCG companies, he brought a different perspective to the otherwise industrial company.

He soon realized that the initial product concept had to be changed. A consumer product had to be light weight and portable to be accepted in the mass market and thus, he moved away from the existing concept. Therefore he started, in his words, "scavenging for resources" within the organization. It did not fit naturally in the organization at first because it was a low cost consumer product, whereas Tata Chemicals was mostly a chemicals company, well known to be the second largest global producer of soda ash.

While describing his role in the project he said:

> My role is a sort of a rice nursery. You nurture it here, keep it away from the weeds and at a suitable time you transplant it into the ground. And from then on it's got to be robust

enough to survive that because it could face a new set of challenges. So that is exactly what we did, except unlike rice where it takes seven weeks we needed several months if not years.
(Interview 3D)

He, thus, became a sponsor of this innovative project. The chairman of the Tata Group, Mr. Tata, was also in favor of the company leading the way in creating affordable products and encouraged the Swach project. They shared a common philosophy.

RG made his executive assistant (EA) take the lead on the project. Initially this involved researching the business opportunity for a low-cost water filter on a part time basis. The project leader took about 8 months to put together a business plan. He also involved external consultants in putting together a story that reflected the need for such a product in India. RG described this role as being similar to an entrepreneur within a large company.

He also inspired some of the team members of the Sujal team to join in the project on a temporary basis in order to revisit the project and improve the filtering performance of RHA. However, the team soon realized that there was limit at around 92 % adsorption when using only RHA. The main task of the newly created team was to focus on improving the filtering capabilities and bringing it up to a world-class standard. The EA started to study the different standards of water purification and certification mechanisms globally. After this, the team decided to aim for clearing the US Environment Protection Agency standard, one of the highest water quality standards globally.

At the end of 2006, RG roped in the newly created Innovation Center of Tata Chemicals that was building expertise around nanotechnology. He called the Head of the Innovation Center, to ask him to come up with a solution to the problem of increasing the filtering performance of RHA, while keeping costs low. As the director of the Innovation Center recalled,

It all began when RG called me to ask me to work on this project. He explained the problem to me and asked me to look for a solution. About two weeks later he called again to check on the status of the project. That is when I knew he was serious... Tata Innovation Center was mandated to integrate nanotechnology in a way that did not bring up the cost but improve water purification standards that were world class.
(Interview 3C)

Following few months of research and testing, the R&D team developed a proof of concept that showed how nano-particles could improve the microbial-destroying properties while keeping the product affordable. The next challenge was to use the right amount of silver because if water was exposed to silver for too long, it could lead to silver leeching. Finding a low cost solution for this was also a demanding problem. In addition to that, the team had to work on finding a method to indicate when the cartridge, which contains the RHA and nano silver, had lost its efficacy. The team pushed to find a solution where simplicity was the main driver. As one of the senior managers responsible for the Tata Swach product development said:

Anything electronic, there is battery. So I kept pushing them to find a simpler solution. Simple solutions generally cost very less. . . so one of the drivers here has been high level of simplicity

(Interview 3F)

The team came up with a cartridge that had a labyrinth inside to ensure that the right amount of surface area of water was exposed to the RHA and silver nano particle mixture. It also developed a mechanical indicator that would automatically switch off the cartridge once its adsorption ability had elapsed.

Right from the beginning, the strategic intent of the key stakeholders involved in the project was to create an affordable product for the BOP. Since other filters before the launch of the product were targeted at high-end consumers, the aim was to create a new market for affordable water purifiers, which is why the product was priced at half of the closest competition, at INR 999.

Also the cartridge that is able to purify 3,000 liters of water was priced at INR 300. For a typical Indian household (family of five) it would last about 6 months. This was at a level that made drinking water cost only INR 0.1 per person per day.

At several stages during the product development process, different senior leaders of Tata, including the chairman himself, were involved in the project. They would get regular updates about the progress of the product and would also give their input on design and pricing.

Once the product prototype was ready, the team set up a product testing pilot at the Tata Management Training Center, which also reported to RG. The next stage was to industrialize production. For this, RG brought together engineers, plastic technicians and chemists from different companies of the Tata Group to work on this challenge. Titan, a company at Tata that makes watches, lent an engineering team to build a rotary machine for producing the outer shell of the cartridge. This also helped the team save capital expenditure required to setup the production process.

It was decided that the pilot plant would be setup in Haldia, a city in West Bengal, at an existing TCL factory that had vacant space available. This move was motivated by the potential cost savings as well as access to experienced personnel. The Board gave their approval for the plant without much resistance. RG mentioned how he used an "emotional play" to convince the Board of the viability of the business, to convince those on the Board who "thought it was just CSR".

As RG put it:

He [the project leader] put it all together. . .and it made a story. The story captured their emotion [of the Board members].

(Interview 3D)

Tata Swach was launched in December 2009, to be sold initially in three states before a country-wide release. At the launch, Mr. Ratan Tata, the chairman of the group, fortified the company's commitment to the social cause:

Safe drinking water is the most basic of human needs. The social cost of water contamination is already enormous and increases every year. Although today's announcement is

about giving millions more people affordable access to safe water, it is an important step in
the long-term strategy to find a solution to provide affordable access to safe water for all.
(TCL 2009)

The marketing team at Tata Swach is partnering with NGOs to spread awareness
for the need to use water purifiers. This is a necessary step in creating a market
(Prahalad 2004). It has been running awareness drives at large congregations across
the country (TCL 2013; Bureau 2013b). The research team is also working on new
models of the filter that can remove chemicals such as arsenic to sell in areas with
high levels of contamination in ground water.

7.4.2.3   Beyond Swach

As mentioned above, the Tata Swach project was operationally led by one of RG's
EAs. The EA took an idea and created a detailed concept, drafted the business case,
helped build proof of concept and prototype. Also, once the product and business
processes were established and integrated into one of Tata's companies, he led the
business unit.

RG started similar initiatives with succeeding EAs. While these projects were
not disruptive, they were inclusive innovations (George et al. 2012). These projects
were also briefly analyzed to explore the role RG played in these projects as they
followed a similar pattern to Tata Swach. In the following sections, these projects
will be briefly described.

The next project was the so called "MoPu" project that stands for More Pulses.
The idea behind MoPu emerged from looking for ways Tata could ensure India's
food security. India, primarily a vegetarian country, relies heavily on pulses for its
protein supply. However, there is a wide demand-supply gap primarily driven by
the stagnating production of pulses grown in India. This has led to high inflation in
pulse prices and a surge in imports of pulses. Consequently, this has pushed up
prices of pulses, which has made them too expensive for poor households (Reddy
2004).

The root cause of this issue is the low productivity of pulses in India compared to
benchmark countries like Canada, which exports pulses to India. In India, the yields
of lentils and pulses have also not increased significantly in the last 50 years in
comparison to the yield of wheat, which has increased about 3.5 times, as seen in
Fig. 7.1.

At Tata, this issue was viewed as an issue of national food security and RG
created a task force led by his EA to explore solutions for this crisis. An initial
exploratory proposal document was setup that put forward an idea for Tata's
agribusinesses like Rallis, an agro-chemicals company, to get involved in helping
farmers in pulse production to improve their yield.

On the supplier side, the MoPu initiative created strong relationships between
Tata and pulse farmers to ensure farmers receive right kind of information,
resources like good quality seeds and access to financing. The team also arranged

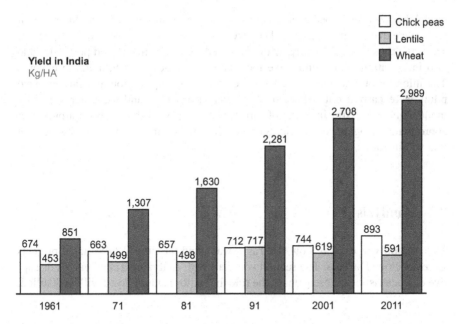

Fig. 7.1 Yield development of different crops in India from 1961 to 2011. *Source:* ICRISAT

buy-back agreements with these farmers through which they introduced a new product line at Tata, the iShakti Pulses. This branded offering of pulses was first of its kind in India and also introduced the unique selling point of unpolished and unadulterated pulses in the market. Since Tata's introduction, several other players have entered the branded market for pulses (Sally 2012). The business unit is now integrated into Tata Chemical Consumer business unit.

What started off as an idea arising from a social need, turned into a business unit within the Tata Group of companies and a new way to market pulses in the Indian retail landscape.

The other project RG embarked on was Samrudh Krishi ('Samrudh' means progress and 'Krishi' means farming in Hindi). The idea behind this project arose from the basic issue that Indian farmers lacked vital information on several aspects of agriculture such as market prices, crop nutrition, etc. This lack of knowledge was also reflected in the low yield for several crops compared to other developing countries. These insights led to an idea to develop IT-enabled advisory services to farmers as a way to fulfill a largely unaddressed need in the market.

The initial idea was conceptualized by RG and was in the form of a letter. This was taken up by RG's EA and elaborated into a concept presentation, which was then shared with business heads at Tata's agriculture-focused companies. This presentation was used to get buy-in from these companies to develop the idea further and create a pilot. Another EA was in charge of developing the concept along with Rallis, the agro-chemicals company as part of the Tata Group and rolling-out a pilot. At that point, RG was also the chairman of Rallis. The business model that was developed was an advisory service for farmers who could opt-in for the service over an entire season. The service entailed advisory on several aspects of growing crops in the best way, with optimized use of fertilizers and pesticides and also information about innovative tools and techniques from agriculture experts. The information was customized for the particular crop, region and farmer. Two pilots were carried out, where one was very successful and the other was only moderately successful in terms of farmers who renewed their subscription. After appropriate changes were made, Samrudh Krishi was integrated as a new service line within Rallis.

7.5   Analysis

This section will explore how the Tata Swach and the other BOP-related projects were developed at Tata. The section will start with analyzing Tata Swach's disruptive characteristics. Subsequently, the role the senior leader played will be distilled.

7.5.1   Disruptive Potential of Tata Swach

Table 7.2 shows the characteristics of Tata Swach along the aforementioned dimensions of disruptive innovations.

For water purifiers, the main performance attribute is water purification capability. The predecessor, Sujal, and Tata Swach have lower performance compared to existing technology such as Reverse Osmosis. Reverse Osmosis technology is able to remove chemicals, dissolved salts as well as bacteria. This is not the case with the Swach. However, Tata Swach has advantages for the customer segments it targets. It is able to function without electricity or running water, infrastructure that is often missing for the BOP segment. At launch, it was priced 50% of the nearest competitor. This price made it attractive for a large population in India that did not previously purchase a water filter since it either lacked the means or the infrastructure.

Tata Swach was targeted at non-consumers and the team's initial market research showed that 80 % of the households that purchased a Tata Swach, previously did not own a water purification system. The product was attractive mainly for first-time purchasers of water purifiers. At the high-end there was no need for a product that did not run on electricity since middle and high income families do not face these challenges.

Tata Swach has been steadily improving in quality. Not only does the Swach now meet US Environmental Protection Agency standards for pathogen removal, but the next improvements of Swach will be able to remove other particles as well. Some Tata Swach filters are also being used by households who own a purification

Table 7.2 Disruptive characteristics of Tata Swach

No.	Characteristic	Applicability	Tata Swach
1	The disruptive innovation initially underperforms on the performance attribute valued by mainstream customers	All	Yes, if performance criteria is purification ability
2	The disruptive innovation, however, has features that are valued by fringe or new customers and introduces a new performance criteria	All	Yes, lower cost as well as ability to function without electricity and running water
2a	A disruptive innovation can create new markets, as it attracts people who previously lacked the resources or skills to use it	New-market	Yes, product targeted non-consumers of water purifiers
2b	A disruptive innovation is typically simpler and lower cost	New market, Low-end	Yes
2c	A disruptive innovation can involve radical technology and attract high-end customers	High-end	No, not-applicable
3	Generally mainstream customers do not initially value these additional features and thus the disruptive innovation is commercialized in emerging markets	All	Yes, initially sold in rural markets through NGOs
4	The disruptive innovation is financially unattractive for leading incumbents to pursue	All	Yes, Tata Swach sold at lower cost and lower margin compared to high end filters
5	The disruptive innovation steadily improves in performance and attracts mainstream customers to it; either it improves along the main performance attribute or market preferences shift towards the newly introduced performance attribute	All	Yes, Tata Swach is now gaining a customer base in urban centers
6	The disruptive innovation takes significant share of the mainstream market	All	Process is ongoing

system as a second purifier or a container, which is initial evidence of "trickling up" in the market.

Whether this technology will displace existing technologies is yet to be seen. As the Head of the Tata Swach business unit put it:

> Has Swach made a discontinuous impact, substantial impact to the adoption curve? It is too early to predict anything. But what we have data of is the fact that around 80 % of Swach buyers are people who do not have any purification system previously. So that is another way of looking at it. . . 220 million households in India and we have sold only half a million units.
>
> (Interview 3A)

Nevertheless, there is evidence that storage or offline filters, like Tata Swach, which operate without electricity and running water, are becoming a dominant segment in the water filter market in India. In 2012, according to industry experts, 70 % of growth in water filters was driven by low-cost storage filter. Several new Indian players have entered this market in the past 2 years. HUL's Pureit and Tata Swach continue to dominate this segment (Bureau 2013a; Market-Pulse 2013).

Tata Swach shows all characteristics of a new-market disruptive innovation, including early evidence of moving up market and becoming dominant and shaping the overall filter market in India.

7.5.2   Role of Senior Leadership

This section deals with analyzing the main research question of this study, namely how established firms can successfully commercialize disruptive innovations from within.

Tata Swach is an example of a disruptive innovation introduced successfully into the market by an established company. In exploring how Tata succeeded in this, the path taken by other similar projects were also analyzed, namely Samrudh Krishi and More Pulses. Samrudh Krishi and More Pulse are not disruptive innovations, but can be termed inclusive innovations (George et al. 2012) for the BOP. Research has also pointed towards organizational challenges companies face in commercializing inclusive innovations (Halme et al. 2012; Olsen and Boxenbaum 2009). The approach taken by these three projects are similar and are thus, analyzed together. However, the Tata Swach project remains in the forefront of this study.

As empirical data of this study highlights, the role of the senior leader was crucial in enabling the Tata Swach project. In this section, the different forms of support RG gave the projects will be distilled, after which this role will be compared with the broader theory on innovator roles.

As mentioned earlier, RG is an executive director of Tata Sons, the holding company of the Tata Group. He also holds other titles within Tata, such as vice chairman of Tata Chemicals and Rallis and director at Tata Technologies and Tata Power and chairman at Tata AutoComp Systems. He was also previously on the Board of Tata Motors, Tata Teleservices. By virtue of his long history within Tata, he is well networked within the Tata Group.

The first form of support he lent to the project was resource allocation: financial resources as well as team members were assigned in the initial stage of the project by RG. This is critical as disruptive innovations often fail because resource allocation processes in established firms favor sustaining innovations (Christensen and Bower 1996). In fact, prior to RG's involvement, the Sujal project stalled because resources for R&D were not assigned to improve its filtering performance. RG was responsible for reviving the project and allotting resources, including a project leader and also involving the Innovation Center at TCL to explore nanotechnology applications for improving Swach's filtering performance. As RG put it:

At that time I was the vice chairman of Tata Chemicals, I scavenged resources for it [the
Tata Swach project]. . .and that scavenging went on for about three, four years
(Interview 3D)

Further, he leveraged his roles across different Tata companies and roped in key
people for the development of Swach. His unique position enabled him to do so as
this quote by a senior executive at TCL underlines:

RG had the ability to link what was happening in TCS, TRDDC and in the Poona lab and
say there could be an idea by which we could work here.
(Interview 3F)

Also in the other two projects, RG's EAs were in the lead and were responsible
for the detailed conceptualization of the project and the pilot. Resource allocation is
a key role the senior leadership plays in enabling disruptive innovation projects. As
seen in the case of Swach, the project would not have gained traction on its own
without the assistance and support of the senior leader.

The second key role that the leader played is that of **lending vision to the
project**. This is especially of relevance for disruptive innovations. New market
disruptive innovations address non-consumers and its successful commercialization
requires market creation (Christensen and Raynor 2003). Because of this, it is
difficult to estimate the market potential of disruptive innovations, compared to
launching innovative products for existing markets and critics often dismiss these
projects because they might consider the market size to be negligible (Christensen
and Raynor 2003; Govindarajan and Kopalle 2006).

This is where a senior leader, who can build credibility and vision for the
disruptive innovation, can enable it. In case of Tata Swach, the initial idea behind
the product was markedly different from its current profile. It was initially
envisioned to be operated in sites affected by natural disasters, when access to
safe drinking water gets cut off. This is why the initial prototype looked very
different from its current form.

It was the senior leader's vision to see this built into a consumer product for the
BOP market. It was under his direction that the concept for Tata Swach was set—to
develop an affordable, yet aspirational product for the non-consumers of water
filters. RG saw the challenges as well as the potential in creating this market. This
quote by RG shows how the vision of the product was shaped by him:

I come from a consumer background; much of Tata is an industrial background. Maybe, the
lens through which I was looking was different. . .And I therefore started to visualize this as
a consumer product and not as a CSR. I mean that was the first major shift. The moment you
visualize it [the product], parameters fit into place. It had to be affordable, it had to be
portable, it had to be light, it had to be replicable, it should not depend on electricity, should
not depend on running water and everyone should be able to use it.
(Interview 3D)

The third important role the senior leader plays is that of **legitimizing and
winning internal sponsorship** for the project.

As mentioned earlier, BOP initiatives, like Tata Swach require market creation,
where uncertainty is higher than launching a product for an existing market. This is

why, even though the project had to prove commercial viability, it had a larger "window of tolerance for generating returns", as noted by the operational project leader. This "window" had to be legitimized by the executive champion.

The three projects at Tata were undertaken not for tactical reasons, but for fulfilling a larger strategic goal of having social impact. In case of Tata Swach, the social goal was to "make a dent in whatever small way to the problem of water-borne diseases", according to the project manager. The MoPu project was concerned with the issue of national food security and the Samrudh Krishi project aimed at bringing knowledge and information to Indian farmers. Thus, all three projects had a social cause.

Strategic intent is defined by Hamel and Prahalad (1999) in their book, "Competing for the future", as an ambitious and compelling vision, which provides energy and pathos for the company and defines the journey to the future. Strategic intent, as opposed to a tactical or generic vision, creates excitement among employees and gives the company a sense of discovery and direction. This can help the company build competitive advantage (Hamel and Prahalad 1989). This is especially relevant for BOP markets, where an "unflagging commitment to a strategic intent" is necessary for innovating for the BOP markets, in order to overcome the challenges that these markets pose (Prahalad 2006, p. 9).

The senior leader promoted the strategic intent within the company to legitimize these projects. These projects required legitimization as they diverged from the norm of the company (Dougherty 1994). The "emotional and intellectual energy" (Hamel and Prahalad 1999, p. 137) behind the strategic intent helped legitimize these projects among key stakeholders, like the Board.

The process of legitimization and winning internal support was important at a later stage when the projects required substantial investment, for instance, in the case of Tata Swach when the factory was to be built. Also, once conceptualized and piloted, the projects had to be integrated into one of the Tata companies. Tata Swach was eventually integrated into Tata Chemicals.

This is where RG's leadership position within several Tata Group companies, including the holding company and at Tata Chemicals helped. He was well networked within the company and highly respected. Early on in the project, while the team was building a business case, RG commissioned a study from an external consulting firm on the market opportunity and social impact of introducing a low cost water filter in the Indian market. The team used this study to spread the idea to key stakeholders within the company, in order to win their commitment and "capture their emotion". These quotes underscore how RG legitimized and won internal support for the Tata Swach project:

> The story captured their emotion. If we don't have the emotion, the project is not going to move forward. . .did you know. . . you don't require half the world's hospital beds if you can eliminate this [issue]. That's a lot. . .More people die of waterborne disease than AIDS and heart attack and the diabetes all put together
>
>   So what did it [convince the Board], I think, it was a bit of emotional play. Because we used that study and showed what could be the size of the market. It [the filtering market] was a non-existent market. So how do you define the market? So we had to get out from

saying so many homes have a water filter to saying how many homes don't have a water filter. . .India has a billion people, 200 million homes. The number of [homes with a] water filter or purified water is 2 million or 3 million. So there are 197 million homes waiting to adopt a water filter.
(Interview 3D)

Thus, three roles the senior leader played was to allocate resources, lend vision to the project and to legitimize and win internal support for the project. All these functions were especially relevant because of the disruptive nature of the project.

The role the senior leader played in the Tata Swach projects is similar to the role of the executive champion or power promoter as described in Sect. 7.2. To recap, the main role of the executive champion or power promoter is to provide guidance (Rhoades et al. 1978), exert hierarchical power to protect innovation against organizational opposition (Hauschildt and Kirchmann 2001), and channel resources towards the innovation (Maidique 1980).

Compared to the Tata Swach case, all these roles apply. However, there were additional roles that the executive champion played, which were especially relevant for disruptive innovations. Firstly, the executive champion did not merely provide guidance, but lent vision to the project by shaping the idea and the vision for the project. Next, the role involved more than merely protecting the innovation against opposition. The executive champion played an important role in legitimizing and establishing the project within the organization and winning internal support for it. Finally, to re-emphasize the role of resource allocations: The executive champion bootstrapped the project initially through resources available to him. He also exerted his hierarchy to pull in crucial resources from other parts of the company when they were necessary.

Proposition: Disruptive innovations with strong senior leadership support are more likely to survive within established firms. Senior leadership support is required in resource allocation, lending vision as well as legitimizing and winning internal support for the project.

7.5.3 Differentiating and Integrating: A Process View of Ambidexterity at Tata

This section will take a longitudinal view of the Tata Swach project and will explore how the mechanisms of differentiating and integrating the project with respect to the mainstream businesses unfolded over time.

In the Tata Swach project as well as the two other projects described, the initial phases were operational led by one of RG's Executive Assistants (EA). RG's office is always staffed with one or more EAs. EAs who apply to the office are aware that one of the projects they would be tasked with is to lead a sort of corporate entrepreneurship project or internal venture of introducing a new product or service.

In all three cases, the initiative that stemmed from RG was taken up by the EAs and elaborated into a concept in close consultation with RG and sometimes also involved other key leaders within the Tata Group of companies. As part of building the concept, the EA was in charge of developing a business case and leading the project team. Once the concept was established, a pilot was undertaken as proof of concept. Once the pilot was successful, it was integrated within one of Tata's group of companies.

In the first part of this process, there was an increased level of differentiation of the project from mainstream business. However, the process of integration into one of Tata's companies became increasingly dominant as the project progressed. To recall, structural differentiation is necessary to create pragmatic boundaries that separate experimentation in the exploring units and more routine activities in the exploiting units (Benner and Tushman 2003). However, as more recent literature points out, integration is fundamental in achieving ambidexterity, without which, there is risk of isolation and decreased possibility of leveraging existing knowledge and capabilities (Siggelkow and Rivkin 2006).

Similarly, Smith and Tushman (2005) identified the simultaneous cognitive differentiation and integration of strategies and architectures as a means to help top management manage multiple innovation streams. This process of differentiation and integration also occurred at Tata Swach and the other projects analyzed. RG was very proactive in creating distinctions from the mainstream business and later integrating the project into existing company structures. As he eloquently described it, he played the role of the rice nursery in first nurturing and then integrating the innovation (see Sect. 7.4.2.2).

The differentiation and integration occurred in two aspects of the project, namely people and structure. Table 7.3 gives instances of differentiation and integration process from the Tata Swach project.

In the initial exploratory phase of the project, as Tata Swach was being conceptualized, the autonomous structure of the core team headed by the EA, worked to its benefit. However, as the project progressed, RG roped in different resources from the company, to create a cross-functional team for the product development and scaling phase of Tata Swach. This cross functional team worked as an integrating force (Jansen et al. 2009).

Similarly, in terms of organizational structure, the Tata Swach project was autonomous and reported directly to RG until the first stage of the pilot for testing the product was completed. The first stage of pilot was conducted at the Tata Management Training Center and RG also emphasized the pilot's entrepreneurial and bootstrapped nature. However, after getting board approval to pilot mass production, the second stage of the pilot was conducted within TCL in its Haldia plant to leverage existing synergies in terms of costs and personnel. Finally, during the scale up phase, the business was integrated into TCL.

While the other two projects also went through a similar process of gradual integration, the level of differentiation and integration at each phase differed. This mostly depended on the perceived synergies with existing businesses. For instance, in case of the Samrudh Krishi project, senior leaders from the respective business were integrated during the ideation phase and the pilot for the project was also structured from within Rallis.

Table 7.3 Mechanisms of differentiation and integration in the Tata Swach project

	Differentiating	Integrating
Team	For the Tata Swach project, RG established a dedicated core team led by the EA. The team was young and very enthusiastic about the social mission of the project.	RG brought in people at different hierarchy levels to support the project from different Tata Group companies during the product development and scaling phase.
Team	*"The team was very, very young. There was no one in the team who had a past baggage of successes or past laurels in their cap, which is why it is fair to say that the team was very hungry for success."—Project leader of Swach* (Interview 3A)	*"Then I got in touch with Murali Sastry, who was a nanotechnology expert . . .and I said, can you use any of these ideas to do this [water filtering]. . . he said I will think about it".—RG* (Interview 3D) *"We have another company that I am a Chairman. And they were taking around the factory and showing me various things and I saw their rotary machines. . .They said nobody makes this kind of machine, only Titan can do it. . .and I said why don't we go to Titan and ask them [to help us with the production of Tata Swach]."—RG* (Interview 3D)
Structure	Until the pilot phase, the Swach team was reporting to RG. Also the first pilot that involved testing the product was conducted independent of any other Tata company, at the Tata Management Training Center in Pune	During the scale up, the team integrated into TCL. The second pilot to test and optimize mass manufacturing of the product, was conducted in an existing TCL plant, in order to leverage synergies
Structure	*"[When] they started developing the prototypes . . . in the Tata Management Training Center at Pune, which also happens to report to me, a corner was created literally like a garage, you know, a little place under a tree where things were rigged up. . .This is the equivalent of a pilot now. All of this happening offline from the company, while the company is manufacturing millions of tons of soda ash and fertilizers"—RG* (Interview 3D)	*"For a consumer goods company you don't want to spend money on physical assets, you want to spend it on persuading people to buy a product. So do it low cost, treat like another pilot plant. Pilot plant stage two. So we put the two machines in Haldia where there is lot of paddy. . .And we started it. . .we took a shed within that existing chemical factory."—RG* (Interview 3D)

Figure 7.2 depicts the process of initial differentiation and progressive integration. The processes of the three projects can be broken down into four phases, detailed concept formation, business case, then pilot and finally the scale up. The initial phases were held autonomous from the mainstream businesses. It involved mostly RG and his EA leading a core team. In the case of Swach, although the initial prototype existed, the product concept was dramatically changed from the initial idea by RG. The development of the detailed product concept and business case was operationally led by the EA. During this phase, the EA had a small team

Fig. 7.2 Evolution of the
Tata Swach project

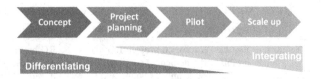

and reported to RG directly regarding the progress of the project. Thus, the team and the structure were differentiated from the mainstream business initially. As the project progressed, people and assets from existing business units were gradually involved and eventually after the pilot was successful, the team was integrated into the existing business. As a side note, one other idea was pursued by an EA at the office but failed to gain traction and was finally terminated and not integrated into any business unit.

This process played an important role in ambidexterity, the ability of the company to concentrate on its mainstream businesses, while simultaneously exploring disruptive innovations. Thus, in addition to the roles elaborated in Sect. 7.5.2, which primarily revolved around protecting disruptive innovation within the firm, this role revolved around enabling ambidexterity. His unique position within the Tata Group also enabled him to rope in the necessary people and resources at the right point of time. Moreover, he was able to initiate the disruptive innovation project, monitor it and progressively integrate the project into the company.

The role played by the senior leader in this case was to actively differentiate and integrate the disruptive innovation within the company. This protected the disruptive innovation from the companies' mainstream activities, while simultaneously leveraging synergies, such as key resources and capabilities, from the company. At the same time, the project progressed without interruptions to the companies' existing activities.

Thus, this process view of ambidexterity highlights an additional critical role played by senior leaders in pursuing differentiation and integration activities while developing disruptive innovations from within the company. This is very much in line with the cognitive model proposed by Smith and Tushman (2005) applied only on the evolution of the explorative project within the mainstream business. While the cognitive model is for the management of strategic cognitions that arise due to competing demands in a broad sense, in this case it only involves the project setup, in terms of structure and team, for explorative disruptive projects within an established firm.

Proposition Senior leaders can enable disruptive innovations within an established firm if they proactively differentiate it from the mainstream businesses initially and integrate it into the organization progressively.

7.6 Discussion

The first aspect this case study highlights is the role played by a senior leader in enabling disruptive innovations. From the Tata Swach case study we learn how critical a role the senior leader plays in promoting a disruptive innovation project within the company. Without the backing of the senior leader, the project would not have taken shape because disruptive innovations are inherently unfavorable for established firms (Christensen and Bower 1996; Christensen and Raynor 2003).

The study embeds the findings of the case into classical management literature on individual roles in the innovation process (Witte 1973; Rhoades et al. 1978; Schon 1963; Maidique 1980). The case study shows that the role the senior leader plays in promoting disruptive innovations is an extension of the power promoter (Witte 1973) or the executive champion (Maidique 1980). Beyond resource allocation, legitimizing the disruptive innovation project and lending vision to it are critical in order to overcome the inertia organizations face when trying to commercialize disruptive innovations.

The second aspect this study sheds light on is the process of ambidexterity. Literature on organizational ambidexterity has mostly had a static view, but the need to adopt a dynamic view has been noted by several organization theoriests (Raisch et al. 2009). A longitudinal view of the project was taken to explore how the mechanisms of ambidexterity unfolded over time. The Tata Swach project was highly differentiated from the mainstream business initially but its success came from the progressive integration into an existing company. This study draws from the cognitive model developed by Smith and Tushman (2005), using their insights in showing the benefits of actively differentiating and integrating architectures in order to develop disruptive innovations within the company boundaries. Thus, this study adds to current understanding of leadership-driven ambidexterity.

References

Benner, M. J., & Tushman, M. L. (2003). Exploitation, exploration, and process management: The productivity dilemma revisited. *Academy of Management Review, 28*(2), 238–256.

Boschi-Pinto, C., Velebit, L., & ShibuyaIII, K. (2008). Estimating child mortality due to diarrhoea in developing countries. *Bulletin of the World Health Organization, 86*(9), 710–717.

Brockhoff, K., Chakrabarti, A. K., & Hauschildt, J. (1999). *The dynamics of innovation: Strategic and managerial implications.* Berlin: Springer.

Bureau. (2013a). India's water purifier market likely to grow 229 % by 2017, says report. *Food and Beverage News.*

Bureau. (2013b). Tata Swach serves 5 lakh litres of water to devotees at Mahakumbh. *The Hindu.*

Chakrabarti, A. K. (1974). The role of champion in product innovation. *California Management Review, XVII*(2), 58–62.

Chakrabarti, A. K., & Hauschildt, J. (1989). The division of labour in innovation management. *R&D Management, 19*(2), 161–171.

Christensen, C. M. (1997). *The innovator's dilemma: When new technologies cause great firms to fail.* Boston: Harvard Business School Press.

Christensen, C. M., & Bower, J. L. (1996). Customer power, strategic investment, and the failure of leading firms. *Strategic Management Journal, 17*(3), 197–218.

Christensen, C. M., & Raynor, M. (2003). *The innovator's solution: Creating and sustaining successful growth.* Boston, MA: Harvard Business Press.

Cooper, R. G., & Kleinschmidt, E. J. (1995). Benchmarking the firm's critical success factors in new product development. *Journal of Product Innovation Management, 12*(5), 374–391.

Cooper, R. G., & Kleinschmidt, E. J. (2007). Winning businesses in product development: The critical success factors. *Research-Technology Management, 50*(3), 52–66.

Crabtree, J. (2012, March 30). Blighted benevolence. *Financial Times.*

Danneels, E. (2006). Dialogue on the effects of disruptive technology on firms and industries. *Journal of Product Innovation Management, 23*(1), 2–4.

Dougherty, D. (1994). The illegitimacy of successful product innovation in established firms. *Organization Science, 5*(2), 200–218.

Ernst, H. (2002). Success factors of new product development: A review of the empirical literature. *International Journal of Management Reviews, 4*(1), 1–40.

ET-Bureau. (2013, Jul 31). Best Indian Brands 2013: List of top 30. *The Economic Times.*

George, G., McGahan, A. M., & Prabhu, J. (2012). Innovation for inclusive growth: Towards a theoretical framework and a research agenda. *Journal of Management Studies, 49*(4), 661–683.

Gibson, C., & Birkenshaw, J. (2004). The antecedents, consequences and mediating role of organizational ambidexterity. *Academy of Management Journal, 47*(2), 209–226.

Govindarajan, V., & Kopalle, P. K. (2006). Disruptiveness of innovations: Measurement and an assessment of reliability and validity. *Strategic Management Journal, 27*(2), 189–199.

Graham, A. (2010). Too good to fail. Strategy and Business (58).

Group, T. (2008, June 24). *Tata Salt ranked No 3 most trusted brand by Brand Equity ET Survey 2008 f.* Tata Group Media Releases.

Gupta, A. K., Smith, K. G., & Shalley, C. E. (2006). The interplay between exploration and exploitation. *Academy of Management Journal, 49*(4), 693–706.

Halme, M., Lindeman, S., & Linna, P. (2012). Innovation for inclusive business: Intrapreneurial Bricolage in multinational corporations. *Journal of Management Studies, 49*(4), 743–784.

Hamel, G., & Prahalad, C. K. (1989, May–June). Strategic intent. *Harvard Business Review*, 63–76.

Hamel, G., & Prahalad, C. K. (1999). *Competing for the future: Breakthrough strategies for seizing control of your industry and creating the markets of tomorrow.* Boston, MA: Harvard Business School Press.

Hart, S., & Christensen, C. (2002, Fall). The great leap. *MIT Sloan Managment Review.*

Haugh, H. M., & Talwar, A. (2010). How do corporations embed sustainability across the organization? *Academy of Management Learning & Education, 9*(3), 384–396.

Hauschildt, J., & Chakrabarti, A. (1989). Division of labour in innovation management. *R&D Management, 19,* 161–171.

Hauschildt, J., & Kirchmann, E. (2001). Teamwork for innovation—The 'troika' of promotors. *R&D Management, 31*(1), 41–49.

Howell, J. M., Shea, C. M., & Higgins, C. A. (2005). Champions of product innovations: defining, developing, and validating a measure of champion behavior. *Journal of Business Venturing, 20* (5), 641–661.

IIPS. (2007). *National Family Health Survey (NFHS-3)* (Vol 2). International Institute for Population Sciences.

Jansen, J. J. P., Tempelaar, M. P., Van den Bosch, F. A. J., & Volberda, H. W. (2009). Structural differentiation and ambidexterity: The mediating role of integration mechanisms. *Organization Science, 20*(4), 797–811.

Johne, A., & Snelson, P. (1988). Auditing product innovation activities in manufacturing firms. *R&D Management, 18*(3), 227–233.

Khanna, T., Palepu, K. G., & Bullock, R. J. (2008). House of Tata: Acquiring a global footprint. Harvard Business School Case Study.

Leifer, R. (2000). *Radical innovation: How mature companies can outsmart upstarts*. Boston, MA: Harvard Business Press.

Leonard-Barton, D. (1992). Core capabilities and core rigidities: A paradox in managing new product development. *Strategic Management Journal, 13*(S1), 111–125.

Levinthal, D. A., & March, J. G. (1993). The myopia of learning. *Strategic Management Journal, 14*(2), 95–112.

Lubatkin, M. H., Simsek, Z., Ling, Y., & Veiga, J. F. (2006). Ambidexterity and performance in small-to medium-sized firms: The pivotal role of top management team behavioral integration. *Journal of Management, 32*(5), 646–672.

Macher, J. T., & Richman, B. D. (2004). Organisational responses to discontinuous innovation: A case study approach. *International Journal of Innovation Management, 8*(01), 87–114.

Maidique, M. (1980). Entrepreneurs, champions, and technological innovation. *Sloan Management Review, 21*(2), 59–76.

Market-Pulse. (2013). Trends and opportunities in the water purifier market. *Market Pulse.*

Mom, T. J. M., Van Den Bosch, F. A. J., & Volberda, H. W. (2009). Understanding variation in managers' ambidexterity: Investigating direct and interaction effects of formal structural and personal coordination mechanisms. *Organization Science, 20*(4), 812–828.

O'Reilly, C. A., & Tushman, M. L. (2008). Ambidexterity as a dynamic capability: Resolving the innovator's dilemma. *Research in Organizational Behavior, 28*, 185–206.

Olsen, M., & Boxenbaum, E. (2009). Bottom-of-the-Pyramid: Organizational barriers to implementation. *California Management Review, 51*(4), 100–125.

Pant, K. (2002). *India assessment: Water Supply and Sanitation.*

Prahalad, C. K. (2004). *The fortune at the bottom of the pyramid: Eradicating poverty through profits*. Upper Saddle River, NJ: Wharton School Publishing.

Prahalad, C. K. (2006). The innovation Sandbox. *Strategy & Business, 44*, 1–10.

Raisch, S., Birkinshaw, J., Probst, G., & Tushman, M. L. (2009). Organizational ambidexterity: Balancing exploitation and exploration for sustained performance. *Organization Science, 20*(4), 685–695.

Reddy, A. A. (2004). Consumption pattern, trade and production potential of pulses. *Economic and Political Weekly, 39*(44), 4854–4860.

Rhoades, R. G., Roberts, E. B., & Fusfeld, A. R. (1978). A correlation of R&D laboratory performance with critical functions analysis. *R&D Management, 9*(1), 13–18.

Roberts, E. B., & Fusfeld, A. R. (1980). Critical functions: Needed roles in the innovation process. Working Paper.

Rogers, E. (2003). *Diffusion of innovations*. New York: Free Press.

Rost, K., Hölzle, K., & Gemünden, H. G. (2007). Promotors or champions? Pros and Cons of role specialisation for economic process. *Schmalenbach Business Review, 59*, 340–363.

Rothwell, R., Freeman, C., Horlsey, A., Jervis, V. T. P., Robertson, A. B., & Townsend, J. (1974). SAPPHO updated-project SAPPHO phase II. *Research Policy, 3*(3), 258–291.

Rowe, W. G., & Guerrero, L. (2012). *Cases in leadership*. Thousand Oaks, CA: Sage.

Sally, M. (2012, January 25). Branded pulses being launched by Adani Wilmar, Lakshmi Energy Foods. *The Economic Times.*

Schon, D. A. (1963). Champions for radical new inventions. *Harvard Business Review, 41*(2), 77–86.

Shiferaw, B., Reddy, V. R., & Wani, S. P. (2008). Watershed externalities, shifting cropping patterns and groundwater depletion in Indian semi-arid villages: The effect of alternative water pricing policies. *Ecological Economics, 67*(2), 327–340.

Siggelkow, N., & Rivkin, J. W. (2006). When exploration backfires: Unintended consequences of multilevel organizational search. *Academy of Management Journal, 49*(4), 779–795.

Smith, D. J. (2007). The politics of innovation: Why innovations need a godfather. *Technovation, 27*(3), 95–104.

Smith, W. K., & Tushman, M. L. (2005). Managing strategic contradictions: A top management model for managing innovation streams. *Organization Science, 16*(5), 522–536.

Srikanth, R. (2009). Challenges of sustainable water quality management in rural India. *Current Science, 97*(3), 317–325.

TCL. (2009). Tata Chemicals launches 'Tata Swach. Tata Chemicals Media Center.

TCL. (2013). Tata Swach to connect with people on safe drinking water at Pandharpur Varkari Mela. Tata Chemicals Media Center.

Tripsas, M., & Gavetti, G. (2000). Capabilities, cognition, and inertia: Evidence from digital imaging. *Strategic Management Journal, 21*(10–11), 1147–1161.

Tushman, M. L., & Anderson, P. (1986). Technological discontinuities and organizational environments. *Administrative Science Quarterly, 31*(3), 439–465.

Tushman, M. L., Smith, W. K., & Binns, A. (2011). The ambidextrous CEO. *Harvard Buisness Review, 89*(6), 74.

Van de Ven, A. H. (1986). Central problems in the management of innovation. *Management Science, 32*(5), 590–607.

Westerman, G., McFarlan, F. W., & Iansiti, M. (2006). Organization design and effectiveness over the innovation life cycle. *Organization Science, 17*(2), 230–238.

Witte, E. (1973). *Organisation für Innovationsentscheidungen—Das Promotorenmodell.* Göttingen: Schwart.

Chapter 8
Addendum: Linking Paradox Resolution and Disruptive Innovations for the Bottom of the Pyramid markets

8.1 Introduction

Disruptive innovations for the Bottom of the Pyramid (BOP) markets can enable access to products and services, for millions of people, which were previously beyond their reach (Hart and Christensen 2002; Christensen et al. 2006). At the same time, disruptive innovations are "powerful means for broadening and developing new markets and providing new functionality" (Govindarajan and Kopalle 2006, p. 190). As evidenced in the case studies of GE Healthcare and Tata, companies pursuing BOP markets were doing so in order to seek new revenue streams. These projects also had strong pro-social motives. The same applies to Narayana Hrudayalaya and Aravind Eye Care. While their mission, to provide quality healthcare at affordable rates, is deeply rooted in the social cause, they are also enterprises that aim to be financially sustainable. Thus, enterprises addressing BOP markets, especially in sectors like healthcare have dual profit and social goals.

This duality became salient in the course of this research. As mentioned in Chap. 4, the research was inductive and exploratory in nature and continuously iterated between theory and empirical data from the field. When revisiting theory after the first rounds of interviews, it became apparent that there was interesting overlap between the empirical data collected and discourse on paradoxes emerging in various aspects of management literature, such as, leadership, innovation management and institutional thoery (Smith and Lewis 2011; Chen and Miller 2010; Pache and Santos 2010; Andriopoulos and Lewis 2010). Paradox theory has been establishing itself as a lens to explore tensions in organizations in scholarly research in the past decade (Lewis 2000; Smith and Lewis 2011).

To contribute to this discourse, this study explores the paradoxes evidenced during the development of Tata Swach. As mentioned earlier, due to the inductive nature of the research, this research question emerged post-hoc. This study is thus placed as an addendum within the research results.

© Springer International Publishing Switzerland 2015
A. Ramdorai, C. Herstatt, *Frugal Innovation in Healthcare*, India Studies in Business and Economics, DOI 10.1007/978-3-319-16336-9_8

The data from the field pointed to interesting paradoxes and tensions created by pursuing the dual goals of social mission and commercial profits with the Tata Swach project. Hence, the objective of this study is to show how embracing these paradoxes enabled the development of disruptive innovation in the BOP context. While other cases also pursued the dual mission to different extents, the tensions in the Tata case were most apparent as this case was the most recent of all and all key actors, including the senior leadership responsible for this project were accessible for interviews.

Scholars of paradox theory are calling to adopt the paradox lens in management research to explore the nature and management of the tensions and dualities in organizations. This study heeds this call by providing empirical insights on how embracing paradoxes enables the development of disruptive innovations in the BOP context.

8.2   Theoretical Foundations: Theory of Paradox

8.2.1   What is a Paradox?

A paradox denotes "contradictory yet interrelated elements that exist simultaneously and persist over time" (Smith and Lewis 2011, p. 382). The two key characteristics of paradoxes, namely the inconsistency of the elements and the dynamics over time, are well represented by the Taoist symbol of yin and yang. While independent, these two elements may seem logical and coherent, but taken together they may seem irrational yet complementary (Lewis 2000).

Organizations are inherently paradoxical (Jarzabkowski et al. 2013). Different types of paradoxes can be found in organizations, such as, the need for being efficient while staying flexible (Adler et al. 1999) and building relationships with competitors that forces companies to collaborate and compete simultaneously (Chen 2008). Studies have also shown the inherent tensions of balancing exploitation and exploration that leads to nested tensions in new product development processes (Andriopoulos and Lewis 2009). These tensions become increasingly salient in organizations as they globalize and function in resource-constrained and increasingly fast paced settings (Lewis 2000). Paradox literature offers different ways of dealing with contradictions that arise. While defensive strategies try to split or suppress contradictions, active responses find ways to resolve paradoxes. Another way to describe defensive vs. active responses is by comparing them to either/or vs. both/and strategies (Lewis 2000).

Active responses constitute acceptance of paradoxes, temporal or spatial separation and transcending paradoxes. While accepting that a paradox involves appreciating the differences between the two elements, transcending involves embracing paradoxes and seeking synergies between the seemingly opposite concepts (Lewis 2000; Poole and Van de Ven 1989).

Studies have shown varied benefits of paradoxical thinking. Paradoxical thinking can help organizations and individuals to break away from inconsistencies or choose between opposing demands and move towards finding synergies between these demands (Smith and Lewis 2011). Managing paradoxes can help companies become effective and sustainable (Cameron 1986). At an organizational level, paradoxical thinking can help organizations in sensemaking and develop innovative practices through the synthesis of paradoxical logics (Jay 2013). Lüscher and Lewis (2008) also show how adopting a paradoxical lens helped managers at Lego grapple with tensions and contradictory demands during a company transformation and also helped them and their subordinates find "workable certainties", thus facilitating the company to move forward.

At an individual level, juxtaposing paradoxes has the ability to generate novel and creative ideas (Rothenburg 1979). Eisenhardt and Westcott (1988, p. 170) substantiate this claim within organizations by stating that "the contribution of paradox to management thinking is the recognition of its power to generate creative insight and change." Lab studies have also shown how paradoxical cognition increases individual and team creativity (Miron-Spektor and Argote 2008).

Recent studies have theoretically and empirically pointed towards the benefit of paradoxical thinking on organizational ambidexterity and innovation (Smith and Tushman 2005; Andriopoulos and Lewis 2010). Smith and Tushman (2005) posit that "managerial frames and processes that recognize and embrace contradiction" influence whether top management is able to "embrace the tensions and benefit from them or are halted by the inconsistencies". Andriopoulos and Lewis (2010) deepen this claim that paradox may empower innovation. Their findings from successful product innovation companies emphasize the benefits of paradoxical thinking and processes by which managers embrace paradoxes.

While the study of paradoxes has a long tradition in Eastern philosophies, it is increasingly being applied in management research (Lewis 2000). In a dynamic and complex environment like today, paradoxical thinking becomes a critical theoretical lens to understand and to lead organizations that simultaneously attend to contradictory yet interwoven demands (Smith and Lewis 2011).

8.2.2 Pursuing Social and Financial Goals: A Performance Paradox

Balancing social and commercial goals represents a performing paradox that arises from having competing outcomes (Smith and Lewis 2011). This paradox is particularly salient in social enterprises that envision serving the society in the form of a commercial enterprise (Smith et al. 2012). However, traditional enterprises are also increasingly giving importance to the "double bottom line" and Corporate Social Responsibility (CSR) (Lindgreen and Swaen 2010).

In fact, the debate about businesses pursuing social missions has a long history in management scholarship (see Margolis and Walsh 2003). While Friedman's renowned statement "the social responsibility of business is to increase its profits", represents one extreme, companies today are feeling increasing pressure to act in a socially responsible way (Campbell 2007). With increased CSR efforts by companies, there has been a shift towards managerial aspects of CSR activities and towards the business justification and rationale for a company's CSR efforts (Lee 2008).

In the past, business justification of CSR mostly revolved around risk reduction, legitimacy, reputation building (Carroll and Shabana 2010) and corporate philanthropic efforts tended to be generic (Porter and Kramer 2006). However, in more recent times, the debate has shifted towards the convergence of economic and social goals (Carroll and Shabana 2010).

This view is favored by the proponents of the *shared value* concept, Porter and Kramer (2011). Their proposition looks beyond community expectations to opportunities to achieve social and economic benefits simultaneously (Carroll and Shabana 2010). It moves from "mitigating harm to finding ways to reinforce corporate strategy by advancing social conditions" (Porter and Kramer 2006, p. 85). Creating shared value represents expanding economic and social value rather than diminishing or choosing between either one (Porter and Kramer 2011). Thus, the concept of shared value views the two elements of social good and commercial value creation, not as contradictory, but as mutually reinforcing. This mode of thinking, particularly that of emphasizing the synergies rather than meeting trade-offs is a manifestation of paradoxical cognition (Smith et al. 2013; Smith and Lewis 2011).

The BOP approach presents an opportunity of creating shared value for companies (Porter and Kramer 2011). Serving the BOP market with affordable products and services could potentially give them access they previously did not have. As BOP markets are characterized by large unaddressed needs, the companies' offerings, especially in something as fundamental as healthcare can have significant social impact. At the same time, BOP markets represent largely untapped new growth segments for traditional companies that could be avenues for growth (Prahalad 2004), even if it can be challenging to tap their full potential (Karamchandani et al. 2011).

8.3   Empirical Context

This section analyzes the Tata Swach case study with a paradox lens. While it builds on the empirical data from Sect. 7.4, this study aims to highlight the nature and management of paradoxes that were salient in the process of development and commercialization of the Tata Swach project.

Large, unaddressed needs exist in the BOP market and many of them are fundamental, like access to sanitation, housing, energy (Hammond 2010).

Innovations for the BOP that address these basic issues, by definition have a social dimension. Access to clean drinking water is one such issue and the vision of Tata Swach was and still is to provide affordable drinking water to millions. As the operational project leader of the Tata Swach project recalled, "making a dent in in whatever small way to the problem of water-borne diseases" was the objective of the Tata Swach project. At the same time, companies like Tata pursue financial goals for their shareholders. Thus, the Tata Swach initiative pursued financial and social goals simultaneously.

Recalling the genesis of Swach, the idea and prototype emerged within TRDDC, the R&D center of TCS. Sujal, the predecessor of Tata Swach was part of a CSR initiative of TCS. About 50,000 Sujal water filters were distributed during the aftermath of the 2004 tsunami, which hit India and South East Asia. This initiative was emphasizing only one element of the equation, namely the social goal. The Sujal initiative hit a wall and work on it was discontinued for a number of years.

It was the intervention of the executive champion that helped take this project and turn it into a for-profit venture. This move also changed the concept of the product, from a 'do-it-yourself-type' water filter assembled at a disaster site to a consumer good—an affordable water filter that functions without the need for electricity and running water. Therefore, while the project took the shape of a for-profit venture with financial goals, it still retained the social goal of enabling access to drinking water to millions of households in India who previous did not have it. Thus, this new product concept reconciled the two goals by reframing it into a BOP-oriented, for-profit business.

As RG, the executive champion of the project recalled:

> I am sure it's not only the victims of the tsunami who are thinking about drinking water. And it's got to be something that one can easily transport and install. And it's got to take out 100 % of the bacteria. And I therefore started to visualize this as a consumer product and not as a CSR. I mean that was the first major shift.
> (Interview 3D)

This quote by the head of Tata Chemicals justifies the need for the dual goals of Tata Swach:

> We did not want this to be a through and through CSR without a profit motive because there are no successes in terms of volume purely on CSR. We need the money to be ploughed back into the business and into newer products so we wanted it to have a commercial motive.
> (Interview 3F)

The tensions between pursuing social and financial goals manifested at different levels and with different individuals attached to the project. Over the course of the study, three different manifestations of the social-economic tension within the organization became salient. The first tension was pricing. The aim of the project was to create an affordable water filter and consequently, the price had to as low as possible. At the same time, for the project to make money a certain minimum price above cost had to be met. Thus, the pricing strategy of the project had to meet both demands that were competing with each other.

Another aspect was the question of competition. The launch of Tata Swach resulted in other players also entering the offline water filter market (Jain 2012). Competition was perceived to be positive as well as negative by the Tata Swach team. While competition would hurt Tata's market share, it would help in building the market as awareness levels would increase. This quote from an external interview with the project leader and the head of the water purifier business unit underlines this paradox:

> The more intense the competition, the merrier. The biggest challenge we face is awareness generation. And no single player can generate awareness single-handedly. When reputed players are around for the long haul, it helps in market development... Unlike in other categories, in this space, we (companies) should look at each other as allies and not competitors. Because it has a strong social motive, it places a lot of responsibility on players.
> (Sharma and Anand 2012)

And finally there was a paradox in the integration of sophisticated technology for a low-cost innovation. While these might seem contradictory, the Tata Swach managed to combine state-of-the-art nanotechnology to make the innovation cost-effective. Again, these two seemingly contradictory elements were reconciled with ease. As the head of the Innovation Center recalled:

> I feel with the Swach we showed that high end technology can be integrated in products to make the product affordable and for the mass market. It is, of course, also a product with immense social impact.
> (Interview 3C)

8.4 Analysis

The data from the field pointed to the fundamental performing paradox between achieving the social mission and the business purpose of the project. This manifested in different aspects of the project—pricing the product for profit while at the same time keeping it affordable, welcoming competition for promoting market awareness even though competition could hurt market share, and finally creating a low-cost product with state-of-the-art technology.

Interestingly, in each case, the paradoxes were expressed by the interviewees unsolicited. Moreover, these paradoxes were not expressed as a trade-off or a conflict, but with a sense of seemingly contradictory elements having been resolved. This shows how the entire project team had assimilated the paradoxes salient in the project.

As noted in the previous chapter, the Tata Swach project was driven by RG as he was responsible for marshaling resources, winning legitimacy and internal support for the project. The leader's role in embracing the paradox of pursuing social and business goals simultaneously also fueled the innovation, by lending the new vision to the project.

So how did the paradox resolution take place in the mind of the executive champion? While there was no structured approach, the first point that was identified with each of these innovations was whether there was a clear social and customer benefit. And once this was answered and the concept took shape, the business proposition was worked out. This quote underscores the thinking:

> The fact that it has a social good is actually a spur to me to look for the commercial possibilities out of it rather than the other way around
>
> We started to build a business case, for Swach quite late. We just worked on the basis that if it does a lot of good to the consumer, there must be a way to build a business case, that's how we went about it. So in the initial stage of the project we worked on what is consumer benefit and strengthening it. The next stage of the project was, now let's put some numbers and shape to it and see if it is worthwhile. So I didn't see a conflict between the two.
>   (Interview 3F)

When the executive champion was first introduced to the prototype and decided, together with the chairman of the Tata Group, to champion the project, the social goal of the project was clear. Right from the beginning, it was clear that the output would be a product that addresses the need for affordable drinking water for the mass market. This way, the social goal was to decrease the incidence of water borne diseases. A business case and the commercial motivation to serve this vision came later, with the change in the conceptualization of the product. Similarly, the MoPu project began as an idea to address the nation's food security issue, in particular protein security. Only after long deliberation and trial and error, did the idea and business case take shape. As RG described the process of the development of Tata Swach:

> We just worked on the basis that if it does a lot of good to the consumer, there must be a way to build a business case.
>   (Interview 3G)

8.5   Discussion

This addendum was part of the Tata Swach case study and arose because field data pointed to interesting aspects of paradoxes and disruptive innovations at the BOP. Academics in organization research and other areas of management are increasingly adopting a paradox lens to explore underlying tensions in organizations (Smith and Lewis 2011). To contribute to this debate, this study deepens current thinking on how paradoxical cognition can fuel innovation (Smith and Tushman 2005; Andriopoulos and Lewis 2010).

The initial concept behind Tata Swach was created as part of a CSR initiative within a Tata company. The progress on this effort, however, stalled until RG, along with the chairman of Tata, decided to push the project forward. The key enabler was the alteration in the product concept by envisioning it as a consumer product—an affordable water filter for the BOP. Moreover, this was structured to be housed within a Tata company as a for-profit initiative. This recognition and balance of the social and financial goal enabled the project to take its current shape.

The case study with Tata Swach gives us a deeper insight into how this paradox was recognized and managed. As the quotes and interviews showed, the executive champion responsible for the project did not perceive the goals as being conflicting. While there were contradictions, the emphasis was laid on the synergies.

The study uncovered other inherent paradoxes nested within the paradox of social good vs. profit motivation. The study also tried to explore how the leader managed these paradoxes while establishing new projects to pursue. The first step in his cognitive process was to address the social need and the customer benefit that the innovation brings. Once this was established and a clear potential was discerned, the leader sought a business case for the venture. The attitude taken was that a business case can be made possible if a clear social need is identified that Tata was well positioned to address.

A previous study has shown how a trade-off mindset, i.e., perceiving sustainability and financial performance as mutually exclusive and a trade-off, within the organization were a significant barrier to the progress of BOP projects (Olsen and Boxenbaum 2009). Complementary to this, the empirical evidence from this study points to how a paradoxical mindset enables disruptive innovations for the BOP.

Paradoxical cognition has been recognized to be of importance for senior leadership to manage tensions arising from simultaneously exploring and exploiting. While this has been theoretically established, scholars in the area of paradox theory, call for deeper insights through case studies and empirical data (Smith and Lewis 2011). This case study heeds this call and provides empirical insights to deepen our understanding of the benefit of paradoxical cognition in fueling innovations in the BOP context.

References

Adler, P. S., Goldoftas, B., & Levine, D. I. (1999). Flexibility versus efficiency? A case study of model changeovers in the Toyota production system. *Organization Science, 10*(1), 43–68.

Andriopoulos, C., & Lewis, M. W. (2009). Exploitation-exploration tensions and organizational ambidexterity: Managing paradoxes of innovation. *Organization Science, 20*(4), 696–717.

Andriopoulos, C., & Lewis, M. W. (2010). Managing innovation paradoxes: Ambidexterity lessons from leading product design companies. *Long Range Planning, 43*(1), 104–122.

Cameron, K. S. (1986). Effectiveness as Paradox: Consensus and conflict in conceptions of organizational effectiveness. *Management Science, 32*(5), 539–553.

Campbell, J. L. (2007). Why would corporations behave in socially responsible ways? An institutional theory of corporate social responsibility. *Academy of Management Review, 32* (3), 946–967.

Carroll, A. B., & Shabana, K. M. (2010). The business case for corporate social responsibility: A review of concepts, research and practice. *International Journal of Management Reviews, 12* (1), 85–105.

Chen, M.-J. (2008). Reconceptualizing the competition—cooperation relationship a transparadox perspective. *Journal of Management Inquiry, 17*(4), 288–304.

Chen, M.-J., & Miller, D. (2010). West meets East: Toward an ambicultural approach to management. *The Academy of Management Perspectives, 24*(4), 17–24.

Christensen, C. M., Baumann, H., Ruggles, R., & Sadtler, T. M. (2006). Disruptive innovation for social change. *Harvard Business Review, 84*(12), 94.

Eisenhardt, K. M., & Westcott, B. J. (Eds.). (1988). *Paradoxical demands and the creation of excellence: The case of just-in-time manufacturing* (Paradox and transformation: Towards a theory of change in organization and management). Cambridge, MA: Ballinger.

Govindarajan, V., & Kopalle, P. K. (2006). The usefulness of measuring disruptiveness of innovations ex post in making ex ante prediction. *Journal of Product Innovation Management, 23*(1), 12–18.

Hammond, A. (2010). *The next 4 billion: Market size and business strategy at the base of the pyramid.* Washington, DC: World Resource Institute.

Hart, S., & Christensen, C. (2002, Fall). The great leap. *MIT Sloan Managment Review.*

Jain, D. (2012, July 4). Competition hots up in water purifier business. *The Times of India.*

Jarzabkowski, P., Lê, J., & Van de Ven, A. H. (2013). Responding to competing strategic demands: How organizing, belonging, and performing paradoxes coevolve. *Strategic Organization, 11*, 245–280.

Jay, J. (2013). Navigating paradox as a mechanism of change and innovation in hybrid organizations. *Academy of Management Journal, 56*(1), 137–159.

Karamchandani, A., Kubzansky, M., & Lalwani, N. (2011). Is the bottom of the pyramid really for you? *Harvard Business Review, 89*(3), 107–111.

Lee, M. D. P. (2008). A review of the theories of corporate social responsibility: Its evolutionary path and the road ahead. *International Journal of Management Reviews, 10*(1), 53–73.

Lewis, M. W. (2000). Exploring paradox: Toward a more comprehensive guide. *Academy of Management Review, 25*(4), 760–776.

Lindgreen, A., & Swaen, V. (2010). Corporate social responsibility. *International Journal of Management Reviews, 12*(1), 1–7.

Lüscher, L. S., & Lewis, M. W. (2008). Organizational change and managerial sensemaking: Working through paradox. *Academy of Management Journal, 51*(2), 221–240.

Margolis, J. D., & Walsh, J. P. (2003). Misery loves companies: Rethinking social initiatives by business. *Administrative Science Quarterly, 48*(2), 268–305.

Miron-Spektor, E., & Argote, L. (2008). The effect of paradoxical cognition on individual and team innovation. In: Academy of Management, 2008. *Academy of Management Proceedings,* (pp. 1–6).

Olsen, M., & Boxenbaum, E. (2009). Bottom-of-the-Pyramid: Organizational barriers to implementation. *California Management Review, 51*(4), 100–125.

Pache, A.-C., & Santos, F. (2010). When worlds collide: The internal dynamics of organizational responses to conflicting institutional demands. *Academy of Management Review, 35*(3), 455–476.

Poole, M. S., & Van de Ven, A. H. (1989). Using paradox to build management and organization theories. *Academy of Management Review, 20*(3), 562–578.

Porter, M. E., & Kramer, M. R. (2006). Strategy and society. *Harvard Business Review, 84*(12), 78–92.

Porter, M. E., & Kramer, M. R. (2011). The Big Idea: Creating shared value. How to reinvent capitalism and unleash a wave of innovation and growth. *Harvard Business Review 89*(1–2).

Prahalad, C. K. (2004). *The fortune at the bottom of the pyramid: Eradicating poverty through profits.* Upper Saddle River, NJ: Wharton School Publishing.

Rothenburg, A. (1979). *The emerging goddess.* Chicago: University of Chicago Press.

Sharma, S., & Anand, N. (2012). We are looking at other low-cost offerings under Tata Swach. DNA

Smith, W., Besharov, M., Wessels, A., & Chertok, M. (2012). A paradoxical leadership model for social entrepreneurs: Challenges, leadership skills, and pedagogical tools for managing social and commercial demands. *Academy of Management Learning & Education, 11*(3), 463–478.

Smith, W. K., Gonin, M., & Besharov, M. L. (2013). Managing social-business tensions: A review and research agenda for social enterprises. *Business Ethics Quarterly, 23*, 407–442.

Smith, W. K., & Lewis, M. W. (2011). Toward a theory of paradox: A dynamic equilibrium model of organizing. *Academy of Management Review, 36*(2), 381–403.

Smith, W. K., & Tushman, M. L. (2005). Managing strategic contradictions: A top management model for managing innovation streams. *Organization Science, 16*(5), 522–536.

Chapter 9
Discussion of Findings and Conclusion

9.1 Integration of Findings

9.1.1 Overview

This research explores the phenomenon of disruptive innovations addressing the Bottom of the Pyramid (BOP) markets, in the context of affordable healthcare innovations from India. Inductive qualitative research was chosen as the methodology to probe into this emerging and vital phenomenon. Innovations from four companies were examined in detail to obtain a deeper understanding of the nature and origins of these innovations.

Empirical insights from the four companies informed three studies. The first study aimed at setting the scene and analyzed previous research to build theoretical links between the BOP concept and disruptive innovation theory. It also examined the case studies of two low-cost hospital chains from India, namely the Aravind Eye Care System and Narayana Hrudayalaya hospitals. The analysis of the innovation drivers of these companies revealed that the BOP market is a very fitting and favorable context for disruptive innovations. Subsequently, the disruptive innovation theory was used as a framework to explore the phenomenon of BOP innovations. In turn, aspects of this phenomenon were analyzed to enrich disruptive innovation theory.

The case studies of Tata and GE Healthcare provided empirical evidence to analyze under what conditions established firms are able to successfully commercialize disruptive innovations in the BOP context. The following section will discuss and compare findings from these case studies, which were, until now, treated separately in this work. This chapter provides a good opportunity to contrast and integrate findings from the GE and Tata cases. After this, the theoretical contributions of this research will be discussed. In the following section, pertinent managerial implications will be derived. Finally, limitations of this research and

© Springer International Publishing Switzerland 2015
A. Ramdorai, C. Herstatt, *Frugal Innovation in Healthcare*, India Studies in
Business and Economics, DOI 10.1007/978-3-319-16336-9_9

future research agenda will be discussed and conclusions to this research will be drawn.

9.1.2 Organizational Conditions at Established Firms for Pursuing Disruptive Innovations

9.1.2.1 Comparing GE Healthcare and Tata Projects

As alluded to earlier, the phenomenon of frugal innovations from the BOP helped enrich disruptive innovation theory, namely the question how established firms can successfully commercialize disruptive innovations from within the organization (Danneels 2006). The two case studies of GE Healthcare and Tata show two, in some respects, diverging organizational approaches and were thus far treated distinctly from each other. A cross-case comparison is therefore appropriate at this junction.

Several distinctions can be identified when doing a cross-case comparison between GE Healthcare and Tata. As evidenced in Chap. 6, GE Healthcare leveraged structural ambidexterity to create distinct organizational entities of premium and value segments to deal with sustaining and disruptive innovations respectively. Every relevant product group within GE Healthcare (like Maternal and Infant Care, Computed Tomography Ultrasound, Patient Monitoring) has distinct value and premium segments. The entities have distinct resources and capabilities. Moreover, the overall vision of the company was reconfigured with the aim to pursue both quality and affordability. This reflected pursuit of sustaining attribute (quality) as well as disruptive attribute (cost, access) in their innovation endeavors.

In contrast, Tata's was a leadership-driven approach to ambidexterity. Tata Swach was championed by a senior director at Tata. As shown in Chap. 7 other BOP-related projects also followed a similar pattern. The leader played a distinct and vital role in initially differentiating the project from the mainstream business and finally integrating it into the company. Thus, the key driver was not structural; it was leadership-based ambidexterity, which is also considered an important antecedent (Raisch and Birkinshaw 2008).

Table 9.1 systematically compares GE Healthcare and Tata's approaches along the framework discussed in Sect. 6.5.1.

As it is apparent from Table 9.1, the enablers at GE Healthcare were led by corporate initiatives, while at Tata they were personality-driven. Corporate structures and processes like the GE India P&L, ICFC program and the organization structure of value segment enable BOP innovations at GE Healthcare. At Tata, the Tata Swach project and other BOP initiatives were championed by a senior leader who created a dedicated team, bootstrapped resources and managed the project in the initial stages before scaling up and integrating the product into an existing Tata company. Further, the corporate values at GE Healthcare that enable the

Table 9.1 Cross-case comparison between Tata and GE Healthcare

	GE Healthcare	Tata
Company Type	Global multinational, with headquarters in USA	Emerging market multinational with headquarters in India
Disruptive Products	Frugal medical devices	Low-cost water filter
Antecedent of ambidexterity	Structural	Leadership-based
Resources	Dedicated resources set aside through corporate initiatives	Bootstrapped in the initial stages by executive champion
Processes	Dedicated processes for enabling disruptive projects, set up at country level (India P&L) as well as corporate level (Global Growth Organization and In Country For Country initiative)	Projects initiated and managed by executive champion, operationally led by his executive assistant
Values	Corporate initiative and vision set values that accommodated disruptive innovations	Based on leaders values to enable change in society
Capabilities	Built relevant market-related capabilities locally	Leveraged existing capabilities

development of affordable products were driven by healthymagination, a corporate initiative. At Tata, it was not part of a specific corporate initiative.

Another key difference is that while GE Healthcare had to build local capabilities, especially in upstream product development in Bangalore, Tata, with its deep and wide presence in India, could leverage its existing expertise. In fact, as the senior director at Tata mentioned, all the projects he championed leveraged existing capabilities across multiple Tata companies and combined them to create new opportunities. Despite these two distinct approaches, several similarities do exist between the two cases. These similarities exist when comparing the Tata Swach project to the early frugal innovation projects at GE, like the ECG MAC 400 and MAC i and the low-cost portable ultrasound project from China, mentioned briefly in Sect. 6.4.1.2.

The ECG MAC 400 and MAC i projects were initiated in India around 2002, before any of the structural enablers described above were put in place. In fact, as suggested by Immelt and Govindrajan (2009), initiators of projects for emerging markets faced an uphill task around that time. At that stage the MAC 400 project succeeded because of leadership support from the head of the business unit. He was responsible for setting up the development team in Bangalore and also bringing in know-how and technology transfer from Germany. Also the ultrasound project in China was directly reporting to Omar Ishrak, the then CEO of GE Healthcare who championed the project (Immelt and Govindrajan 2009).

The MAC 400 project gained visibility within GE, which helped in building legitimacy for the project. To build legitimacy within GE, these projects were showcased in the annual report and as part of other global initiatives. This brought

Table 9.2 Comparison between early GE Healthcare projects and Tata Swach

	GE Healthcare	Tata
Leadership support	The MAC 400 project received leadership backing from the head of the business unit, after several years of the Indian team calling for a low-cost ECG project. The leader allocated resources and shielded the investment	The Tata Swach project was revived because of championing from a senior executive director, who allocated resources, lent vision to the project and built legitimacy to win internal support for the project
Legitimacy building efforts	Showcasing of MAC 400 in the annual report as well as in a global commercial, put this disruptive project on the map. It helped draw attention to the new market creation opportunities at the BOP and capabilities in Bangalore. This success paved the path for further disruptive projects like the MAC i	Tata Swach's management leveraged the external report on opportunities in water filtration that emphasized the vast unmet needs as well as the social good in offering affordable alternatives to the poor to convince the Board and other employees to support the project
Project assessment criteria	GE's leadership accepted that the MAC 400 and MAC i projects were strategic investments for the long term and wouldn't break even fast enough compared to developed market project launches.	The management was willing to be more tolerant in terms of longer pay back period since this project was "unchartered territory".

recognition to the MAC 400 project and also helped the succeeding project, the MAC i. This is very much in line with the findings at Tata, where a crucial role played by the executive champion was in building legitimacy for the project.

Finally, while standard decision criteria were applied to the product development process, at both GE Healthcare and Tata, the decision makers accounted for the higher uncertainty in creating markets while addressing the BOP. More concretely, at Tata, when the conventional return on investment calculations were undertaken, the key decision makers accounted for the higher uncertainty and increased the tolerance threshold for the time it would take the business to break even. Similarly at GE Healthcare, the initial projects like the MAC 400 and MAC i are viewed as strategic investments for the long term (see Sect. 6.4.1.2. for more details). Also today, while GE Healthcare decision makers are aggressive about value segment or BOP-related products returning a profit to the business, they take a more long term approach to it and account for the longer time period to achieve returns because of market uncertainties. This admissible laxity in decision making criteria helped these disruptive projects, in that they were not compared with the same yardstick as other competing projects (Table 9.2).

9.1.2.2 Discussion

The two cases, GE Healthcare and Tata were explored to understand the conditions under which established firms can successfully commercialize disruptive innovations in the BOP context. As shown above, GE Healthcare and Tata adopted different approaches in doing so. However, before GE Healthcare adopted these structural enablers, there were similarities between the two approaches.

Analyzing the similarities, in how the initial projects at GE Healthcare, like the MAC 400 project and the Tata Swach project were enabled within the firms, a few points become salient. In both cases leadership backing was critical, without which the projects would not have progressed within the firms. Also legitimacy building efforts in both cases immensely influenced the initial success and acceptance of these projects within the company. Further, both companies accepted the uncertainties involved in these projects and were committed to these projects for the long-term.

This also highlights an evolution within GE Healthcare. Initially GE Healthcare's senior leadership backed individual projects. Only after initial product development successes, did it move towards a structural approach to ambidexterity, with organizational structures and processes that enabled these disruptive innovations for the BOP and emerging markets at large. Thus, two approaches can be distilled by comparing these two case studies. Further, this comparison shows that the leadership-driven approach may be a precursor to the structural approach.

The leadership-driven approach is similar to an internal venture championed by a senior leader, who is very high up in the hierarchy of the company and enjoys respect and legitimacy within the company. The role this senior leader plays in enabling the disruptive innovation has been shown in the Tata study. Allocation of a team and financial resources for the disruptive innovation project are the first steps and crucial in countering the resource allocation processes within established firms that do not favor disruptive innovations. A further crucial role played by the senior leader is to build legitimacy and internal support for the project. Finally, the leader's seniority and experience also must be leveraged to lend vision for the project as the potential for disruptive innovations is often underestimated. In order to manage this venture within the mainstream business, differentiating and integrating mechanisms may be adopted by the leader.

The second approach is establishing an ambidextrous organization through a structural approach. This entails setting up two separate entities focusing on sustaining and disruptive innovations projects, which are integrated at the business unit level. It also includes an overarching vision for sustaining as well as disruptive innovations, which enables the company to pursue both simultaneously. Further, dedicated resources, processes, reconfigured values and emerging-market focused marketing competencies, are also necessary to overcome the innovator's dilemma that established firms would otherwise face.

As the evolution of GE Healthcare shows, the leadership-driven approach may precede the structural-approach as companies take first steps in trying to develop innovations for a new market segment and taste initial success before transforming their organizational structure and overall vision.

9.2   Theoretical Contributions

This research examined different facets of the BOP phenomenon. It started with embedding innovations from the BOP in innovation management literature, namely disruptive innovation theory. Subsequently, innovations from BOP were explored to enrich disruptive innovation theory. This section will discuss the theoretical contributions of this research in four areas.

9.2.1   BOP as a Context for Disruptive Innovations

The first part of this research involved embedding the phenomenon of BOP innovations into disruptive innovation theory. The study explored why BOP markets are a favorable context for disruptive innovations. Empirical data from low-cost, specialty hospitals provided useful insights to answer this, particularly because they innovated inside and outside their realm in order to propagate their vision of affordable healthcare for the poor.

The BOP markets are unique and drive companies addressing these markets to develop disruptive innovations for two reasons. Firstly, the resource constraint of these markets incentivizes companies to develop extremely affordable products. Secondly, the vast unmet needs that exist in these markets offer companies immense opportunity to develop new market disruptive innovations that fight non-consumption (Christensen and Raynor 2003).

To re-iterate the proposition derived from the first study:

Resource constraints and the large unmet needs of the BOP drive players addressing the BOP market to develop 'good enough' solutions through disruptive innovations.

9.2.2   Organizational Ambidexterity and Disruptive Innovation Theory

Disruptive innovation theory's explanation for how an established firm's decision making processes ignore simpler, cheaper, 'good-enough' products that do not cater to their mainstream customers has resonated among practitioners and academics (Danneels 2004; Henderson 2006). Since its inception, several academics built on the existing theory (Adner 2002; Govindarajan and Kopalle 2006; Christensen and Raynor 2003), and also highlighted several unresolved issues (Danneels 2002, 2004).

One of these issues is dealt with in this research, namely, how established firms can commercialize disruptive innovations from within their boundaries (Danneels 2004). Christensen and colleagues have proposed that established firms spin-off the entity pursuing disruptive projects to disassociate these projects from the mainstream business' routines and processes (Christensen and Bower 1996). On the contrary organizational theorists posit that companies can be ambidextrous, and pursue multiple innovation streams simultaneously (Tushman et al. 2010).

This work, through the GE Healthcare case study, shows that companies can leverage structural ambidexterity (Raisch and Birkinshaw 2008) to simultaneously pursue disruptive innovations and sustaining innovations. An ambidextrous organizational structure (Tushman and O'Reilly 1996; O'Reilly and Tushman 2004), along with strategic intent and an overarching vision (O'Reilly and Tushman 2008) was shown to enable the dual pursuit. The organization design creates differentiation by creating a dedicated team with distinct capabilities from the mainstream business, yet has necessary integration mechanisms at the top to leverage existing capabilities in product development (Jansen et al. 2009). This separation also gives the necessary empowerment to the teams pursuing products addressing BOP markets. At the same time these teams can leverage existing knowledge from the mainstream product platforms because of exchange facilitated by integration mechanisms at the top. The overarching vision strongly articulates the need for the company to pursue emerging markets like BOP markets, while being relevant in existing markets. These cornerstones of structural ambidexterity enabled the pursuit of the dual innovation streams.

Restating the proposition that was derived from the empirical insights of the case:

Established firms can ambidextrously manage disruptive and sustaining innovations through structural differentiation and integration as well as an overarching vision and strategic intent that reconciles both innovation streams.

However, disruptive innovations require special attention to overcome their inherently unfavorable characteristics. This is why established firms that have dedicated resources and dedicated processes catering to these innovations are more likely to be successful in commercializing them from within. Further, this research shows that companies may need to reconfigure their values, particularly those that govern the product development process. Finally, it was shown that companies need to build competencies related to the emerging market segment the disruptive innovations aim to address. Thus, beyond structural ambidexterity, these protective measures are necessary to enable disruptive innovations from within an established firm.

This research explores an incumbent pursuing disruptive innovation for BOP markets to fill gaps in disruptive innovation theory. In particular this work contributes to existing literature by elucidating underlying mechanisms that facilitate established firms to pursue disruptive innovations from within their boundaries in a systematic and sustainable way.

9.2.3   Leadership and Disruptive Innovation Theory

The Tata case study revealed a very different approach to managing disruptive innovations within an established firm. In the Tata Swach case, the development process was championed by a senior leader at Tata and once the project was successfully piloted, it was integrated into the company.

Christensen's prominent case study on the historical evolution of the rigid disk-drive industries, points to the exceptional case of an incumbent that successfully responded to the next wave of smaller disk drive technology by developing the product within the company (Christensen and Bower 1996). The main success factor in this transition was attributed to "managerial force" (Christensen and Bower 1996, p. 213). However, the paper failed to examine details of how and why the CEO achieved it.

To contribute to understanding what roles senior leaders in established firms play in building disruptive innovations from within, the Tata Swach project and two other BOP market initiatives that followed a similar development process to Tata Swach were examined. The analysis shows that the role the leadership played was crucial, without which the project would have arguably been stuck within the organization without progress. There are three key roles the senior leader can play to overcome the mechanisms that deprioritize disruptive innovations within established firms.

Allocation of a team and financial resources, building legitimacy for the disruptive innovation and lending vision to the project were identified as crucial roles played by a senior leader in enabling the disruptive innovation project. These roles and actions enable disruptive innovation projects to overcome the inherent deprioritization based on a firm's resource allocation processes (Christensen and Bower 1996; Christensen 1997) and underestimation of the innovation's market potential (Christensen 2006).

Existing literature on leadership roles in innovation processes (Rhoades et al. 1978; Hauschildt and Chakrabarti 1989; Witte 1973) support these insights. The role identified in the study is similar to the power promoter role or executive champion. However, there are additional roles essential for championing disruptive innovations, as described above, like lending vision to the project as well as legitimacy building within the organization.

The case study also contributed to the current understanding of leadership-based antecedents of ambidexterity. Literature on ambidexterity acknowledges the key role played by senior leadership and top management teams, there is, however, a significant gap in the detailed understanding of how leadership-based ambidexterity works in practice. Taking a longitudinal view of the Tata Swach project, elucidated the critical role senior leadership can play of proactively differentiating and integrating disruptive innovation projects with respect to the mainstream business. This was informed by the cognitive model for managing strategic contradictions developed by Smith and Tushman (2005).

The propositions derived from the study are:

Disruptive innovations with strong senior leadership support are more likely to survive within established firms. Senior leadership support is required in resource allocation, lending vision as well as legitimizing and winning internal support for the project.

Senior leaders can enable disruptive innovations within an established firm if they proactively differentiate it from the mainstream businesses initially and integrate it into the organization progressively.

Thus, this work took a dynamic perspective in studying ambidexterity at an individual level to contribute to deeper understanding of how ambidexterity works in practice.

9.2.4 Paradox Theory

Paradox theory is emerging as a useful lens to explore questions about organizations (Smith and Lewis 2011). The addendum to the Tata case study explores how paradoxical thinking enables disruptive innovations in the BOP context. It showed how disruptive innovations for the BOP context inherently carry a paradox, namely pursuing social and commercial goals simultaneously. While companies pursue financial targets, their disruptive innovations addressing the BOP also aim at creating a market and improving access to vast populations.

The case study showed how recognizing this paradox, and managing this tension by seeking synergies between these aims rather than highlighting conflicts was conducive for engaging in disruptive innovations in the BOP context. It should be added, that this is not particular to established firms, but perhaps leaders in established firms find this tension more challenging than social entrepreneurs.

The addendum to the Tata case study answered the call by paradoxical theorists for future empirical research through actively "searching for and surfacing those tensions to enhance creativity and performance" (Smith and Lewis 2011, p. 397). This addendum, albeit brief, offers empirical evidence for how paradoxical thinking can facilitate disruptive innovations in the BOP context.

9.3 Implications

The primary managerial implication that can be drawn from this research is for managers who aim to address BOP markets with disruptive innovations. This guideline could help these managers in steering their organization towards this goal. Another set of implications that emerges from this study is for global healthcare policy. This section will discuss both these aspects.

9.3.1 *Managing Disruptive Innovations Within Established Firms*

This research learns from the ventures of two large companies: a global multinational and an emerging-market multinational. The first learning from examining the projects of these companies is that creating a market at the BOP with disruptive innovations is not trivial, and fraught with several challenges. Therefore, to begin with, an implication drawn from this research would echo the recommendation of Karamchandani et. al. that the BOP market "isn't for every company" (Karamchandani et al. 2011, p. 2) and strong commitment and strategic intent is required to enter these markets.

Having said this, there is a lot that managers interested in addressing BOP markets can learn from these cases. Once the decision is taken to address the BOP market, a strong leadership-driven model would facilitate these disruptive projects initially, like in the Tata case and the initial projects at GE Healthcare. Strong leadership backing involves a leader at least at the head of a business unit, with blessing from the CEO. This research distills the role of the senior leader backing disruptive innovations into three areas. Firstly, the leader allocates the resources necessary for the project, both financial and personnel. In some cases, arguing for allocating a team can be more challenging as it may involve pulling them out of projects for conventional markets.

The second area is the necessity of lending vision to the project and seeing the potential of the business. And finally, it is very essential to build legitimacy for the project within the organization and winning internal support for it. One manifestation of this leadership backing is having a long-range mindset for these projects. This entails accepting a longer period for return from projects addressing the BOP because of their low-margins and the additional effort required in creating markets.

Testing the waters can also help. Often, development budget required for projects developed in emerging markets is not very high. Thus, companies would be advised to take baby steps and see how first projects pan out without investing large budgets into BOP projects.

Once there have been initial successes, mangers could consider the evolution towards structural changes that are more likely to sustain the systematic development of disruptive innovations for the BOP. This would entail structural organizational changes as well as reconfiguring the vision of the company to integrate both mainstream businesses as well as BOP market opportunities. A corporate vision that accommodates disruptive innovations addressing BOP markets would involve integrating the value of "affordability" or "accessibility" for poor, i.e., integrating a social value.

Thus, this research offers concrete actions for senior managers trying to initiate and sustain disruptive innovations in the BOP context within their established organizations.

9.3.2   Policy Implications for Healthcare Sector

The healthcare system in every nation is in crisis. Healthcare costs are soaring in developed countries (in the USA healthcare costs have grown 1.5 times faster than GDP (Reinhardt et al. 2004)). These steep healthcare expenses are in part attributed to the fact that the healthcare industry in developed markets has been built through sustaining innovations—helping doctors solve ever-more complex problems and, hence, not focused on increasing affordability (Hwang and Christensen 2008).

Also in developing countries, bringing quality healthcare to the millions who lack access to it is a severe challenge. Disruptive innovations, some featured in this research, have the potential to address both these issues. As recent studies show, experts believe that the US healthcare industry can learn from their Indian counter parts (Govindarajan and Ramamurti 2013).

This research shows why and how the BOP can be a hotbed for disruptive innovation. The vast unmet needs and resource constraints of the market drive companies addressing the BOP to develop disruptive solutions. In particular to the healthcare industry, limited regulatory frameworks prevalent in emerging markets can also facilitate the development of disruptive innovations (Curtis and Schulman 2006).

Recent research into evaluating BOP markets as lead markets for frugal innovations also draws similar conclusions (Tiwari and Herstatt 2012). Emerging countries like India have a strong potential to be lead markets for frugal innovations that can diffuse overseas. The research into lead markets recommends companies to leverage large emerging markets like India as a test bed for frugal innovations (Tiwari and Herstatt 2012).

This research shows that India's lead market potential could be especially relevant for the healthcare industry. In order to leverage this lead market, companies can setup local R&D to pursue disruptive innovations or look to acquire or cooperate with local companies to develop disruptive innovations. Universities and publicly funded R&D institutions can setup cross-border research to pursue research for affordable healthcare.

This process has already begun, with companies like GE Healthcare as well as universities like Stanford University, which has setup a biodesign center in India[1] aiming to foster research into medical technologies for resource-poor settings. Also the USA and India have setup a joint forum to cooperate in science and technology research. They have recently established a Grand Challenge initiative to setup a joint cooperation between the two countries to develop affordable blood pressure measurement technologies.[2] Such initiatives can foster frugal innovation capabilities in India and offer exchange and learning opportunities between India and other countries. Such models of exchange should be encouraged and replicated. For Indian settings, enacting policies that incentivize creating low-cost healthcare

---

[1] http://biodesign.stanford.edu/

[2] http://www.indousstf.org/

technologies will also be very beneficial. The private sector should also create funds that invest into startups and companies pursuing low-cost healthcare technologies and delivery services.

Coming back to global healthcare policy, consensus exists that healthcare models in different parts of the world, especially in developed countries require rethinking (Reinhardt et al. 2004). This research shows that insights for this change can be sought in BOP markets.

9.4   Limitations of the Research

As in the case of any research, the results presented must be considered within the context of its limitations. All studies in this book are based on in-depth dual or single case studies. This research is also based in a certain market for a certain industry. Thus, the question of generalizability becomes relevant.

It is difficult to establish that the findings in this research are generalizable to all companies. Also, there could be several idiosyncrasies particular to these two companies that may not make the results transferrable to other companies. More-over, the healthcare industry has some peculiarities. Firstly, making healthcare affordable to the poor or improving the health of the poor can be considered a social cause. Secondly, healthcare challenges exist all across the world and there is immense potential through disruptive innovations in this industry. These two factors may make several results relevant particularly for this industry. As an example, from the GE Healthcare case study, take the proposition positing that reconfiguring values that accommodates the values of disruptive innovations facil-itates the development of these within the company. GE Healthcare specifically did this through stating that affordability will be a key driver of their future innovation. While making healthcare more affordable can be considered a worthwhile vision to pursue, it might not be the case for other industries. Having such a vision in another industry, like say cosmetics, may not be considered positive, in fact critics of the BOP proposition have vehemently opposed this (Karnani 2007).

The empirical evidence for this research was based on interviews. While all the interviewees for this research were chosen because they had the best insights into the projects that were of interest for this work and could be considered experts in their field, the interviews were based on their opinion and perspective, hence, there is always a risk of bias. Much effort has gone into triangulating the results through different projects (e.g., two projects are GE Healthcare and three projects at Tata were analyzed) and by interviewing multiple people, to keep this risk at minimum.

9.5 Future Research Agenda

The future of BOP research is bright. This work has spawned several interesting avenues for future research. One interesting avenue of research could be to explore which capabilities are required by companies to develop disruptive innovations for the BOP market. While this work explores organizational conditions, it did not pay much attention to individual competencies. Therefore, future research could look into competencies at an individual level required for developing low-cost disruptive innovations.

The BOP research community is still debating whether MNCs are best fit to develop innovations for the BOP. This research looks into Indian medium-sized enterprises, a large Indian conglomerate, as well as a global MNC. It would be interesting to compare how the capabilities for developing disruptive innovations for the BOP differ among these three segments. Under what conditions would one be more successful than the other?

Further, this work alluded to the benefits of paradoxical thinking for facilitating disruptive innovations in the BOP context. A deeper look at the tensions at different levels of analysis and how they are managed by different individuals would be another interesting avenue of research.

There remains a question on the applicability of these results to disruptive innovations outside the BOP context. It would be interesting to analyze successful and systematic commercialization of disruptive innovations within established firms outside the BOP context to uncover similarities and differences between contexts and organizational conditions within firms.

And finally, there are several fascinating research avenues with respect to the phenomenon of reverse innovations. It would be interesting to study the transferability and diffusion of disruptive innovations from BOP contexts to developed countries. Some questions are: how can this diffusion take place? Who is best positioned to initiate and propagate this diffusion and why?

Thus, several engaging and relevant research questions remain in exploring the BOP phenomenon and also within theoretical frameworks such as disruptive innovation theory and reverse innovation.

9.6 Conclusion

The aim of this work was to gain a more in-depth understanding of innovations emerging from the BOP market and to embed this phenomenon into contemporary management literature. This work did so by linking the BOP concept with disruptive innovation theory. The first study showed how resource constraints of the BOP markets along with the large unmet needs of the market are drivers of disruptive innovations by firms addressing the BOP.

The next part of the book drew from the BOP phenomenon to enrich disruptive innovation theory. By exploring the GE Healthcare and Tata case study, the research contributed to enriching our understanding of disruptive innovation theory and organizational ambidexterity.

The research shows how structural ambidexterity and dedicated processes, resources, values and competences can enable disruptive innovations within established firms. Further, the research also discusses the role of leadership in promoting disruptive innovations and enabling ambidexterity. Another aspect this work empirically highlighted was the salience of paradoxical thinking for disruptive innovations in the BOP context. Thus, this work drew from two rich case studies to shine light on different aspects of how companies can enable disruptive innovations in the BOP context.

Disruptive innovations in healthcare addressing BOP markets have the potential to enable access to quality services to millions who previously lacked it by bringing to the forefront virtues of simplicity and frugality. Organizations seeking to develop disruptive innovations for these markets can have immense social impact. As the famous quote by E. F. Schumacher, presented in the beginning of this book, advocated, these organizations would have to learn to retain or recapture simplicity. However, the journey in pursuing this simplicity may be challenging for established firms. Insights from this research can guide companies along this journey.

References

Adner, R. (2002). When are technologies disruptive: A demand-based view of the emergence of competition. *Strategic Management Journal, 23*, 667–688.

Christensen, C. M. (1997). *The innovator's dilemma: When new technologies cause great firms to fail.* Boston: Harvard Business School Press.

Christensen, C. M. (2006). The ongoing process of building a theory of disruption. *Journal of Product Innovation Management, 23*(1), 39–55.

Christensen, C. M., & Bower, J. L. (1996). Customer power, strategic investment, and the failure of leading firms. *Strategic Management Journal, 17*(3), 197–218.

Christensen, C. M., & Raynor, M. (2003). *The innovator's solution: Creating and sustaining successful growth.* Boston, MA: Harvard Business Press.

Curtis, L. H., & Schulman, K. A. (2006). Overregulation of health care: Musings on disruptive innovation theory. *Law and Contemporary Problems, 69*(4), 195–206.

Danneels, E. (2002). The dynamics of product innovation and firm competences. *Strategic Management Journal, 23*(12), 1095–1121.

Danneels, E. (2004). Disruptive technology reconsidered: A critique and research agenda. *Journal of Product Innovation Management, 21*, 246–258.

Danneels, E. (2006). Dialogue on the effects of disruptive technology on firms and industries. *Journal of Product Innovation Management, 23*(1), 2–4.

Govindarajan, V., & Kopalle, P. K. (2006). Disruptiveness of innovations: Measurement and an assessment of reliability and validity. *Strategic Management Journal, 27*(2), 189–199.

Govindarajan, V., & Ramamurti, R. (2013). Delivering world class healthcare, affordably: Innovative hospitals in India are pointing the way. *Harvard Business Review, 91*(11), 1–7.

Hauschildt, J., & Chakrabarti, A. (1989). Division of labour in innovation management. *R&D Management, 19*, 161–171.

Henderson, R. (2006). The innovator's dilemma as a problem of organizational competence. *Journal of Product Innovation Management, 23*(1), 5–11.

Hwang, J., & Christensen, C. M. (2008). Disruptive innovation in health care delivery: A framework for business-model innovation. *Health Affairs, 27*(5), 1329–1335.

Immelt, J., & Govindrajan, V. (2009). How GE is disrupting itself. *Harvard Buisness Review, 87* (10), 56–65.

Jansen, J. J. P., Tempelaar, M. P., Van den Bosch, F. A. J., & Volberda, H. W. (2009). Structural differentiation and ambidexterity: The mediating role of integration mechanisms. *Organization Science, 20*(4), 797–811.

Karamchandani, A., Kubzansky, M., & Lalwani, N. (2011). Is the bottom of the pyramid really for you? *Harvard Business Review, 89*(3), 107–111.

Karnani, A. (2007). Doing well by doing good—case study: 'Fair & Lovely' whitening cream. *Strategic Management Journal, 28*(13), 1351–1357.

O'Reilly, C., & Tushman, M. (2004). The ambidextrous organization. *Harvard Business Review, 82*(4), 74–81.

O'Reilly, C. A., & Tushman, M. L. (2008). Ambidexterity as a dynamic capability: Resolving the innovator's dilemma. *Research in Organizational Behavior, 28*, 185–206.

Raisch, S., & Birkinshaw, J. (2008). Organizational ambidexterity: Antecedents, outcomes, and moderators. *Journal of Management, 34*(3), 375–409.

Reinhardt, U. E., Hussey, P. S., & Anderson, G. F. (2004). US health care spending in an international context. *Health Affairs, 23*(3), 10–25.

Rhoades, R. G., Roberts, E. B., & Fusfeld, A. R. (1978). A correlation of R&D laboratory performance with critical functions analysis. *R&D Management, 9*(1), 13–18.

Smith, W. K., & Lewis, M. W. (2011). Toward a theory of paradox: A dynamic equilibrium model of organizing. *Academy of Management Review, 36*(2), 381–403.

Smith, W. K., & Tushman, M. L. (2005). Managing strategic contradictions: A top management model for managing innovation streams. *Organization Science, 16*(5), 522–536.

Tiwari, R., & Herstatt, C. (2012). Assessing India's lead market potential for cost-effective innovations. *Journal of Indian Business Research, 4*(2), 97–115.

Tushman, M. L., & O'Reilly, C. A. (1996). Ambidextrous organizations. *California Management Review, 38*(4), 8–30.

Tushman, M., Smith, W. K., Wood, R. C., Westerman, G., & O'Reilly, C. (2010). Organizational designs and innovation streams. *Industrial and Corporate Change, 19*(5), 1331–1366.

Witte, E. (1973). *Organisation für Innovationsentscheidungen—Das Promotorenmodell.* Göttingen: Schwart.

Appendix A. Bottom of the Pyramid Innovations from India Mentioned in Studies by C.K. Prahalad

Company/innovation	Description	Company type	Industry	Source
Jaipur rugs	Non-profit that connects artisans from different states in India to the global market	Non-profit	Consumer goods	a
Unilever	Fast moving consumer goods MNC that sells variety of products to rural markets in India	MNC	Consumer goods	a
ICICI	Indian bank that works on rural banking initiatives	Indian Corporation	Banking	a
Jaipur Foot	Manufactures and fits low-cost prosthetic leg	Not for profit	Healthcare	a, b
Aravind Eye Care	Hospital network that performs low cost cataract surgeries for millions	Not for profit	Healthcare	a, b
ITC	Indian agriculture-focused conglomerate that runs initiative to link directly to farmers via internet	Indian Corporation	Agriculture	a
Narayana Hrudayalaya	Hospital that performs low-cost cardiac surgeries, and has expanded to other health services	Indian SME	Healthcare	b
Bharti Telecom	Mobile telephony provider that offers low cost mobile services	Indian Corporation	Telecom	c
Tata Nano	Tata's cheapest car in the world	Indian MNC	Automotive	c
EMRI	Low cost emergency services	Non-profit	Healthcare	c
Lupin	Lost cost drug for psoriasis	Indian SME	Healthcare	c

Sources: This list is taken from C.K. Prahalad's book and two papers, which have compiled a database of BOP innovations as case studies.

[a]Prahalad, C. K. (2004). The Fortune at the Bottom of the Pyramid: Eradicating Poverty Through Profits. Wharton School Publishing

[b]Prahalad, C. K. (2006). "The Innovation Sandbox." Strategy and Business (44): 1–10.

[c]Prahalad, C. K., & R. Mashelkar (2010). "Innovation's Holy Grail." Harvard Business Review (July–August 2010): 132–142.

© Springer International Publishing Switzerland 2015
A. Ramdorai, C. Herstatt, *Frugal Innovation in Healthcare*, India Studies in Business and Economics, DOI 10.1007/978-3-319-16336-9

Appendix B. Interview List Study I

Interviewee	Duration	Date, place	Interview
Chairman and CEO, NH Hospitals	30 min	3rd Aug 2011, Bangalore	1A
Managing Director, AECS	45 min	10th August 2011, Madurai	1B
CEO Aurolab	45 min, 60 min	9th August 2011, Madurai, 7th May 2013, phone interview	1C, ID
Product Manager, Aurolab	20 min	9th August 2011, Madurai	1E
CEO, Forus Health	60 min	16th August 2011, Bangalore	1F
Vice President, NH Hospitals, responsible for Trimedx JV	20 min	20th August 2011, phone interview	1G
Vice President, NH Hospitals, responsible for Mysore Hospital project	45 min	18th May 2013, phone interview	1H
Vice President, NH Hospitals, responsible for Cayman Islands project	45 min	29th May 2013, phone interview	1I
Several employees of Aurolab, AECS, NH during company visits and field observation	3–4 h observation	9th–11th August 2011	1J

© Springer International Publishing Switzerland 2015
A. Ramdorai, C. Herstatt, *Frugal Innovation in Healthcare*, India Studies in
Business and Economics, DOI 10.1007/978-3-319-16336-9

Appendix C. Interview List Study II

Interviewee	Duration	Date, place	Interview
Sales Leader, MAC i, MAC 400	60 min	1st Aug 2011, Bangalore	2A
Program leader, MAC 400 and MAC i	90 min, 60 min	26th Sept 2011, Dec 16th 2011 Bangalore	2B, 2C
Mechanical engineer, MAC 400, MAC i	30 min	26th Sept 2011, Bangalore	2D
Senior Vice President, Diagnostic Cardiology	60 min	18th November 2011, Dusseldorf	2E
CTO, GE Healthcare India	30 min, 60 min	24th Jan 2012, Bangalore, Feb 16th 2012, phone interview	2F, 2G
Program Manager, ICFC Programs	35 min, 45 min, 30 min	29th Feb 2012, phone interview, 17th December 2012, Bangalore, 6th March 2014	2H, 2I, 2J
Leader, MIC Value Segment	60 min	3rd Jan 2013, Bangalore	2K
Marketing Executive, MIC Value Segment	45 min	22nd Aug 2012, Bangalore	2L
Engineering Lead, MIC Value Segment	45 min	3rd Jan 2013, Bangalore	2M

© Springer International Publishing Switzerland 2015
A. Ramdorai, C. Herstatt, *Frugal Innovation in Healthcare*, India Studies in Business and Economics, DOI 10.1007/978-3-319-16336-9

Appendix D. Interview List Study III and Addendum

Interviewee	Duration	Date, Place	Interview
Project Leader, Tata Swach	60 min	16th Aug 2011, Mumbai	3A
Marketing Manager, Tata Swach	30 min	16th Aug 2011, Mumbai	3B
Head of Tata Innovation Center	30 min	18th Dec 2011, phone interview	3C
Tata & Sons, Executive Director	60 min, 45 min	13th Dec 2011, Mumbai, 28th June 2013, phone interview	3D, 3E
Managing Director, Tata Chemicals	60 min	13th Dec 2011, Mumbai	3F
Vice President, Tata Quality Management Services, Head of Tata Group Innovation Forum	30 min	6th Jan 2011, phone	3G
Project Leader, Samrudh Krishi project	60 min	7th Jan 2013, Mumbai	3H
Project Leader, MoPu project	60 min	8th Jan 2013, Mumbai	3I

© Springer International Publishing Switzerland 2015
A. Ramdorai, C. Herstatt, *Frugal Innovation in Healthcare*, India Studies in Business and Economics, DOI 10.1007/978-3-319-16336-9

Appendix E. Interview Guidelines

Study I

Aravind Eye Care System

How would you describe the Aravind model?

Please describe some of the process innovations at Aravind and how do they happen?

What are the partnerships that Aravind has built?

What are the expansion plans at Aravind?

What innovations have been transferred to other hospitals? How has this been done?

Aurolab

Who are Aurolab's current customers and what are your expansion plans?

How does Aurolab achieve its cost effectiveness?

How do you prioritize new areas to enter?

How do Aravind and Aurolab work together?

What are instances of innovations that have come out of this cooperation?

What are future plans for product development at Aurolab?

Forus

What is special about the diagnostic equipment developed by Forus?

How did this idea come about?

How did the cooperation with Aravind help during your product development?

How were the doctors helping during the product development process?

Narayana Hrudayalaya

What is the vision of NH?

What are the innovations at NH that have allowed it to follow its volume strategy and target the poor?

© Springer International Publishing Switzerland 2015
A. Ramdorai, C. Herstatt, *Frugal Innovation in Healthcare*, India Studies in Business and Economics, DOI 10.1007/978-3-319-16336-9

What are other benefits NH faces from playing the volume strategy?

What are partnerships NH has developed with companies? How have these partnerships come about?

Please tell me more about your plans for medical tourism and the hospital in Cayman Islands?

What is special about the NH Mysore project?

What are the other areas in which NH is innovating?

Study II

GE MAC 400 and MAC i projects

What is the history of the MAC 400 project?

What makes the product cost-effective and how is it different from the traditional models?

What was the product development process for the MAC 400 and MAC i like? How was it different from the developed market products, e.g., with respect to target costing, upstream marketing?

Did the MAC 400 and MAC i team face any opposition? How did senior management react to this project?

How are the successors of the MAC 400 being received in the traditional markets?

How did you think about cannibalization of sales from existing high-end products, especially in the traditional markets?

What would say were the critical factors that led to the development and commercialization of the product? What challenges are you facing in the commercialization of the MAC i?

GE Maternal and Infant Care Products

Please give me an overview of the Maternal and Infant Care (MIC) products developed in India for the emerging markets. How are they different from premium segment products? What specific features do they have? Where are they being sold?

What are the challenges you are facing in the market?

What products are currently under development?

How do you work together with the global product development teams? How are you integrated? What are the processes in which you engage with them?

How do you ensure autonomy for the local team?

What processes in product development for BOP markets are different from conventional product development?

How does the MIC India team fit into the organization? How do you leverage GE India and the global product teams?

How has the Healthymagination initiative helped you?

What kind of partnerships has the MIC team in India entered into?

How have you created visibility within GE for your products?

How do you perceive the social impact that these MIC products for the BOP segment have?

Healthymagination

What is the Healthymagination initiative?

How do the Healthymagination initiative and its pillars play into the product development process?

How has it affected the development of the low-cost products for India?

What are other Healthymagination products in the pipeline?

Organization

What is the history of this R&D center in Bangalore?

What are the organizational processes in place that have empowered GE India to develop such disruptive products for the local BOP market?

What is the organizational structure in place at GE currently and how has that changed?

What is the In Country For Country (ICFC) program and what are specific roles that are part of it? When was this started and why?

How are the teams in India autonomous and how do they stay integrated with the premium segment teams in traditional markets?

How is the product development process different for these disruptive products, e.g., with regard to project evaluation?

Study III and Addendum

Tata Swach Project

Please give me background history of the Tata Swach project.

What was Tata Swach's aspiration initially?

Who are the customers of the Tata Swach?

How do you plan to develop the product further?

How important was the social cause as a driving force of the project?

What are the formal innovation management systems at Tata?

How has the Tata Swach business developed so far?

What roles did you/the executive director play in the project?

Did you face any resistance from the board or others in the company?

What is the Tata Innovation Center and what role did it play?

How was Tata Swach different from other conventional projects at Tata? How do such projects fit through the innovation management process like stage gate?

Samrudh Krishi Project

Please give me a description of the project.

How did the idea of the project come about?

What role did the executive director play in the project? What role did you play in the project?

How was it integrated into a Tata company?

More Pulses Project

Please give me a description of the project

How did the idea of the project come about?

What role did the executive director play in the project? What role did you play in the project?

How was it integrated into a Tata company?

Paradoxical Thinking

How do you see the interrelationship between financial goals and social goals, how does this affect these projects and how does your thinking behind this affect the company on the whole?

How do you integrate, the social commitment of a project and the financial goals of a project? Do you perceive them as being synergistic and reinforcing or contradictory?

How much is this thinking driven by Tata's value system?

Your executive assistants operationally led these projects. What are you looking for in your executive assistants?

Printed in the United States
By Bookmasters